# UNACCOMPANIED MINOR

# UNACCOMPANIED MINOR

### a memoir

## ALEXANDER NEWLEY

QUARTET BOOKS

First published in 2017 by Quartet Books Limited
A member of the Namara Group
27 Goodge Street, London, W1T 2LD

A catalogue record for this book is available from the British Library

ISBN 9780704374461

Text design and typesetting by Tetragon, London
Printed and bound in Great Britain by TJ International Ltd, Padstow, Cornwall

*Some names have been changed.*

# CONTENTS

# DRAMATIS PERSONAE

ANTHONY NEWLEY: Holey Father. Artful Reality Dodger. Cockney Colossus of Stage and Screen. Unflagging Lover of Women. Unsurpassable Source of Paternal Warmth (when he was there).

JOAN COLLINS: UnVirginal Mother. Stargazer/Starlet/Star. Dynastic Diva. Conspicuous Absence. Tense Presence.

SUE DELONG: Nanny. One Tough Mother-Surrogate (when she was there, and when *wasn't* she?). Butch Bully. Unstable Giantess. Destined to Die by Her Own Hand in an Ice Cream Van.

TARA NEWLEY: Sister. Punkster. Fellow Traveller and Fellow Sufferer in Beverly Hills, Mayfair and the South of France.

RON KASS: Eminently Forgettable Stepfather. Appetizing Starter to the Maternal Palate and Unsavoury Finisher. Fritterer Away of Funds. Master of...

THE MASERATI: Dragon Car and Star Vehicle that carried UnVirginal Mother away.

DAWN: Schoolteacher. Child Whisperer. Muse.

MRS BENET: The Good Shrink. The Snake Charmer.

CATHY PRICE: Succulent Stew. Girl Next Door Who Homed In. (Eventual) Stepford Stepmother.

DANA PEPP: First Crush. So Nearly Touched.

ALVY SHAPIRO: The Bad Influence. Fluent in Pussy and Pot.

THAXTED: Cut-throat Pet Snake. Uncharmable.

PIRATE: Dalmatian. The Only and the One. Puppy of Puppies.

TEDDY: Unloved. Stabbed to Death.

CLAY DINOSAUR: Shaped and gripped by the all-engendering hands of...

ALEXANDER NEWLEY: Aka Sacha, Sachie, Sarch, Sasquach... Yours Truly. Yours Very Truly. Yours *Brutally* Truly.

*Self-Portrait with Myself as a Child*

# PROLOGUE

*The little boy is scared stiff. He's not sure he wants to come to the lip of the stage that is all the world. I gently urge him on, take his tender hand in mine and try to lead him to the next level of difficulty. I tell him, 'Everything's going to be all right. I'm right here beside you.' He hangs on to my shorts and takes a baby step forward. And then another...*

*He can complete those steps only through the brave and benevolent agency of this book. I am not his father; but, in a way, I am. I walk in his shoes. I am prey to his anxieties and I suffer his withholdings of joy. He was never taught to trust; but now, with my help, he is beginning to. It's a painful process. Sometimes he will not even talk to me. Other times he whispers and I have to bend down low to hear. He never had the words to say what he felt. Well, he has them now.*

WHEN I LOOK BACK AT THE BROKEN STORYLINE OF MY CHILD-hood, I see that the chief culprit was an ogre called Show Business. It yanked my helpless father, Anthony Newley – of blessed memory – and my mother, Joan Collins – of amazing fortitude – back and forth between England and America: Broadway, Hollywood and the West End. My parents were both enslaved by the monster's demands. It gave them no security, no safe haven of self, but kept them in the precarious state of wanting and needing the phone call from the agent with the next big gig – the only thing between them and oblivion.

As a child I could feel their insecurity, and knew their focus was elsewhere, not on me. There would have been no point in acting out. The fact was, they were mired in childhood themselves; a useful state for artists, who need to keep alive their belief in dragons and princes and princesses, so that they might pursue the make-believe of making themselves whole through art. But faced with the second coming of these energies in their children, there was instant and ongoing competition, and no clear winner.

Ever since, I've been doing my damndest to impose a retroactive order on the crazy quilt pattern of my past. Through various means – poetry, New Age questing, old fangled analysis... But until I found painting in my early twenties – or painting found me – nothing worked. I needed the confines of a canvas, within which everything must be resolved – composition, colour, texture, subject matter – in order to catch up all the threads of my unravelled self.

I began by buying myself some cardboard sheets and acrylic paints. Although I had dabbed, dabbled and daubed as a child, this was my first self-conscious foray into the world of art. I propped a sheet against the wall and sat down cross-legged with the palette beside me. I loaded the brush and began. My arm moved confidently, in fluid strokes, as if obeying some inner necessity. I squeezed more paint from the tubes. In a matter of minutes, I had created a large 'head' portrait, rendered in thick, expressionistic brushstrokes.

I sat back and stared at the painting, which stared right back, equally astonished. We had created each other. My first ever completed creative effort had been accomplished in under fifteen minutes. I called the painting *Zeus*, grandiloquently. It went right up on the wall, as did the several other paintings that followed in quick succession. I was on a roll.

Eventually I found my way to painting people from life, which saved me from my self-obsession, and gave me a trade to boot – portraiture.

But I happened to be working directly from my imagination again when a friend visited my studio in 2006. *Mother and Child* was up on the easel: my contemporary version of Mary giving suck to the Christ Child.

*Zeus*

As I discoursed on the holy presence of the mother in all Western painting, my friend shook her head. 'That's not what *I* see here,' she said. 'She's not even looking at the child. She's like some self-involved Prada model, gazing into the distance. The child senses this and reaches up to tug at the mother's heart. To me, it's a shocking image of disassociation.'

I was amazed.

My friend smiled. 'You should be happy – you've painted the truth.'

I looked at the painting again, this time with a grudging admiration for my incorrigible subconscious. While I thought I had been composing a paean to the ideal of motherhood, I wound up portraying the essence of my relationship with most of the women in my life, starting, naturally, with my formidable mother.

I could feel my old obsession for making sense of things stir.

*Mother and Child*

# 1106 Summit Drive

IF YOU TURN OFF SUNSET BOULEVARD BY THE BEVERLY HILLS Hotel and continue up Benedict Canyon, you'll soon come to the shaded and embowered beginnings of Summit Drive. A tight, meandering road will take you up and over a canyon ridge dotted with pine, elm and cypress to an open shelf of land where our old house still sits pretty.

Whenever I'm back in Los Angeles, I make the pilgrimage up there. The plantation-style facade has fewer columns than it boasted in the embellished haze of memory, and the windows seem less tall, less stately. Sammy Davis Jr bought the house when we were forced to leave and it went on to enjoy a renaissance as the court of his fabulous excesses – a Castle Perilous of sexual antics and voracious drug taking. When he died, deep in debt, the place fell under the auctioneer's hammer, never quite recovering its dignity.

I always turn away from the place with a sense of loss and sickly, titillated yearning. What could I possibly still want from poor old 1106 Summit? As a preamble, all the holy books speak of a paradisal garden that predates the world and perseveres beyond it.

Well, I, Alexander Newley, lately lived there.

From 1965 to 1969, I tasted the sacred fruit and saw the golden light. I was present at the birth of wonder and collected the speckled eggs of immortal birds. Summit was my Edenic beginning and the source of all my subsequent wanderlust. I was exiled from there for a crime I did not commit and wouldn't have understood had it been explained to me.

Summer, 1967. I am all of age two in a photo taken in the garden at Summit: my sister Tara and I are in matching outfits astride my father's back; he's on his hands and knees in white pants and a sailor jersey – our passionately handsome beast of burden. My mother, mouth-watering in a watermelon-pink housedress and beribboned beehive, attends us with a look of enchanted distress. It's a prehistoric moment before the world – the real world – began. A lie, but no less beautiful for that.

A year later, it would all be over. My father would be living in his office on Doheny Drive, having his tawdry affair with the automobile heiress, Charlotte Ford. My mother would be having hers with the record producer Ron Kass, and considering a move back to England.

But for this one moment, everything is perfect. Tony Newley, the cockney firebrand, has met his match and found completion in fiery Joan Collins, the alpha jezebel from RADA. He is domesticated and at peace. Their adorable children will grow up in the shade of the great house.

When I found this photo, forty years later, rummaging through an old box in my Manhattan studio, I felt an odd dissociation – not unlike that I'd portrayed and betrayed in *Mother and Child*. I was there, and not there – a little boy of two and a half, bookended by doting parents. In fact, I have no memories of them together as a loving man and wife, talking and touching. It's all just a bright blank. The only thing that penetrates and then pervades the dazzling vacuum is an argument.

I hear it loud and clear, coming at me courtesy of my bedroom intercom early one morning: an angry sea of static, crashing and booming. Tara enters and walks toward me, tying her robe, inclining her head to listen. We hold hands and stand there, like two children posed in a Renaissance portrait. The argument crests and plunges: Daddy is monster-loud, Mummy is weeping. Then the door slams in a thunder crack of electricity. A noise on the stairs. Tara and I turn in unison. Somebody is pounding up… we tighten with fear: is it all our fault? The door bursts open and it's Daddy in his blue terrycloth robe, hair uncombed and wild. He gathers us up into his arms, breath musty with sleep, and whispers, 'I love you.'

He loves us – so it wasn't our fault, after all. In many ways, it wasn't theirs. They married blind, and by the time their eyes opened, Tara and I were already there.

Looking at the 'happy' family photo in my studio, I felt the inevitable wave of sorrow. What would I say, I wondered, if I could somehow travel back in time and speak to these innocents? How would I spare them the fate that awaited them? Dream on, Sacha! But perhaps, as an artist, I was not so powerless. Maybe I could paint my way back into the scene using the canvas as my time machine. But once there, what would I do? How would I compose myself within that frame? Would I return to them all smothering and loving, draping my arms around them like some long-lost uncle? Or would I withdraw to an ironic distance and look on, solipsistically aware of the final curtain about to fall?

The finished painting invites the viewer to look across the ancient river of time divide and embrace the quietly contemplating witness in the background. The beautiful dream in the foreground is about to end, but he must never stop believing in it.

My parents arrived in Hollywood in the mid-sixties. My father was fresh from his Broadway mega-success, *The Roar of the Greasepaint – The Smell of the Crowd*, a show he'd not only starred in but co-written with his collaborator and close friend, Leslie Bricusse. It had run for 232 performances and garnered six Tony nominations. At thirty-five, he was painfully aware, in the hit-and-miss world of show business where a single misstep can spell the end, that he had to make audacious choices to keep his career moving. The grind of rewriting the problematic book of *Greasepaint* by day and perform-ing it by night had sapped him and led to a fatal decision: no more

*Self-Portrait with Happy Family*

Broadway, no more musical theatre – from now on it would be the movies, because that's where the real action was.

Hollywood was to be the default setting for his new life. And there he brought us, me aged six months and Tara two. And my mother, then in her ravishing early thirties. This was her second foray into Tinsel Town. Her first, in the fifties, had been all happy abandon amid the lotus leaves. It was a jungle and the casting couch was king; but she outfoxed the predatory Zanucks and Starks and captured the hearts of the golden boys: Marlon Brando, Harry Belafonte and Warren Beatty, by whom she became pregnant.

This time around she was joined to the man of the hour, Tony Newley. She was a wife and mother – roles for which she wasn't exactly typecast but which she worked hard at nonetheless.

Her husband was as impossible as he was fabulous. Everyone wanted a piece of *that* action. And there was plenty to go round. Acting was only one of his talents. He could toss off song standards like old lapel carnations and pluck up new inspirations just as effortlessly. He was both a lord of language and a liege to the music of the spheres, and the lyrics he co-wrote with Bricusse were borne aloft by a melodic sense that ensured their imperishability.

> Who can I turn to
> When nobody needs me?
> My heart wants to know
> And so I must go where destiny leads me…

and:

> What kind of fool am I
> Who never fell in love?
> It seems that I'm the only one that I've been thinking of…

The music he arranged around these words voluptuously clung to them. And if that wasn't enough, he could sing his creations in a voice whose authority and radiance seemed to come from some hallowed fountainhead. He had never been taught, he had never studied anything – he had been conceived in poverty and born on a wooden pallet in a workhouse – but his voice belonged in those ultimate choirs with Johnny Mathis's, Sammy Davis Jr's, and Frank Sinatra's.

Did I mention dancing? Bravura clowning? A gift for mime and visual storytelling that would be the envy of Marcel Marceau? Did I mention a sense of humour so virile and instinctive that the reigning Jewish comics of the day – Milton Berle, Red Buttons, George Jessel – embraced him as their own? If you were in a room with Tony Newley you weren't listening to or looking at anybody but him: you were thrilled by his mannerisms and ad-libbed one-liners, you were unmanned or unwomaned by a gaze so searching that it seemed to undress you. He was a fire-starter, a Promethean gift to the already sublime sixties. And he wanted me, his adoring son, to grow up to live and carouse as he did – a sentiment forcibly expressed in his song, 'Gonna Build A Mountain':

> With a fine young son… to take my place…
> I'll leave a son in my heaven on earth
> With the good Lord's grace!

Like everyone else, my mother was madly in love with him. But, unlike everyone else, she had to live with him day in and day out. He was withdrawn. He was prickly. He was a hypochondriac. OK, she could live with all that. But worst of all, he was flagrantly unfaithful. Nowadays he'd be tidily labelled a sex addict. He depended on the promise of an after-show tryst with a starlet or groupie to get him through the grind of a performance. He lived to screw, to dissolve in orgasm before the in-gathering of himself back to loneliness and self-exile.

He had been honest with my mother about his appetite for young girls, but she, through some mixture of denial, biological ticking, and uncontrollable excitement that the great man was within her grasp, married him anyway. And they became the Brangelina of the day. Only Burton and Taylor outpeered them.

They first met in London, backstage after a performance of *Stop the World – I Want to Get Off* – my father's first trailblazing musical written with Bricusse. My mother was on Robert Wagner's arm that night, and RJ's heart must have sunk as he quickly realized that Newley had designs on his date. But truly, who wouldn't have? She was the total package: sexy, beautiful, and bright, with an underlying shyness to her charisma.

As my father was hell-bent on seducing any and every beautiful woman he happened across, he immediately suggested to RJ that they all go to dinner. At Alvaro's, the hip, post-show watering hole for West End stars and their hangers-on, he launched into a full-scale charm offensive, squeezing RJ's arm in a gesture of brotherly companionship even as his eyes burrowed deep into the sacrificial maiden. Humour was the weapon he used to soften all resistance so that the work of seduction could begin in earnest. I'm sure RJ enjoyed himself, laughing all the way to irrelevancy.

My mother knew, as she kissed my father lightly goodnight, that something irrevocable had happened.

In his 1969 autobiographical film *Can Heironymus Merkin Ever Forget Mercy Humppe and Find True Happiness?* – a balls-out confession in which he rakes over his entire life, recasting it as a grail quest for the perfect piece of ass – my father re-imagines this first encounter as a cosmic 'meet cute' orchestrated by the spheres. My mother, aka Polyester Poontang, is first sighted on an astrological stage set, with dancers moving about a central dais in costumes designed to identify them as Crab, Ram, Lion and so on. In wanders the unsuspecting Heironymus (played by my father) butt-naked, following a mummified double of himself, The Mask, who has no face, just his wavy dark hair and long sideburns. Polyester steps out from behind the Gemini twins (her actual sign), fatally gorgeous in a white, floor-length silk dress and star-spangled tiara, and proceeds to ensnare our hero with caustic one-liners. Heironymus, explains the narrator, is smitten:

> NARRATOR: He adored her reckless candour, her inconstant
>     moods, her funny ways...
> MASK: You must forgive me, I'm not myself these days.
> POLYESTER: Oh really? Who do you suppose you are?
> MASK: Someone who admires you enormously.
> POLYESTER: Phuff... You Show People... Next thing I know
>     you'll be putting your hand on my knee...

So Heironymus pushes the Mask aside and manages to press his puppy love upon her directly, at which point she sings the ambivalent love ballad, 'Chalk and Cheese':

> How did you get into my horoscope
> You funny irascible loveable dope?
> Chalk and Cheese
> We're as different as Chalk and Cheese...

But just as Heironymus succeeds in bedding her, she admits:

> I'm a fool maybe
> But I don't mind chalk with my cheese...

In reality, they'd been married in a dingy, overly air-conditioned county courtroom in upstate New York in the summer of 1963. Their sole witness and best man was the actor Mike Lipton, a full-time friend and foil who was not-so-secretly in love with them both, doing his best not to giggle because the court official's fly was open – a most inappropriate omen of marital infidelity. My father was smirking. My mother tried focusing on the bowed head of the official as he droned on, a lone bead of sweat trickling down his bald pate betraying his nervousness at marrying a megastar.

The megastar in question was on a weekend break from *Stop the World*, and after a wedding picnic in a nearby meadow, they all drove back to town where the whirligig world was just winding up anew.

Tara was born during the run of *Stop the World* and I during that of *Greasepaint*. My father's motility seems to have been galvanized by Broadway. I was conceived, he once confided to me, on another weekend break from the stage – in Montauk, at the top of Long Island, with the waves crashing melodramatically close. He said he'd had an extravagant vision just before he inseminated my mother: a wild-headed youth in a flaming chariot crossing the sky in an arc of flame, his whip poised for release as his horses pounded the air. In this fantasy, I was Helios, god of the sun, and of course he was Zeus, father of the universe and creator of all things. Bit of a stretch? Or a fantasy befitting an East End kid who had risen out of abject poverty to take Broadway by storm.

Outside Mount Sinai Hospital, on upper Fifth Avenue, my parents posed with newborn me in front of the assembled press corps. My father, gaunt from overwork – the very picture of a Kafkaesque émigré complete with pencil-thin tie – knelt down into shot with a high-wattage smile as my mother, lovelier than ever in her post-natal ampleness, showed me off to the insatiable cameras: answered prayers.

In *Heironymus Merkin*, the narrator exclaims, 'A son! A son! A son to carry the legend into all the years ahead.' But this much-vaunted little boy will forbear to take centre stage; he will spend years listening in the wings for his cue and never quite hearing it. In time he will come to understand that there *is* no cue – that he will just have to barge onstage and *make it happen*.

9

In photos and home movies I am quite a little cherub, perfectly shameless in Eden, all blonde ringlets and bulb belly, my miniature member trembling as I toddle about the great lawn at 1106 Summit. Flowers are head-high to me. Butterflies wing by in slow sweeps of fairy dust. Redbrick pathways lead through the heat to new scenes of enchantment: a furry black caterpillar squirming in my hands; a yellow lizard, prone on a rock, its neck pulsing. The hissing sprinklers fling their diamonds and the lawn rolls down to the emerald pool where I am taught to swim by my Irish nurse, Una, her breasts bulging toward me in the star-spangled chlorine. My dogs are everywhere at once. I pet Matthew, my black-and-white Collie, as his sister Twiggie knocks me over with one ferocious lick. She's an explosion of honeyed fur I lose my face in.

I smile for my father's camera. His shadow falls across me like an oil derrick. With legs firmly planted he films me and I shade my eyes to take him in. I'm older now and have expressions. My mother dresses me like Little Lord Fauntleroy: white sailor caps, red bandanas tied rakishly around my neck, white patent leather shoes, pantaloons of every colour and fabric... I have my own little garage on the patio stocked with pedal cars and tricycles. In my bedroom, I have a framed Union Jack over my bed, fleets of toy cars, and snowdrifts of furry animals.

Alice, my Portuguese nanny, wears a starched white uniform. When she picks me up and kisses me I can smell the sweet oil of her skin and the floral freshness of her uniform. The warm timbre of her voice vibrates in my head as she presses against me saying, 'My Dahling... My Dahling...' in her passionate Portuguese accent. Her dark eyes and wave-crest of a smile open me even now. Her husband, Umberto, is all jesting servitude; while their twelve-year-old son, Bino, is the easygoing playmate who never tires of me, even as I tire of myself.

My paternal grandmother, Grace, has come to live with us, along with her new husband, Ron Gardner – or Pops as we call him – who habitually scratches a cheek with his pipe stem and turns self-consciously from the camera. He helps prop up our lifestyle of metastasizing luxury by becoming the estate handyman and driver. He's a crusty old Englishman whose communications with Grandma are confined to the parade-ground bark: 'Grace! Tea!' But Little Me loves him. Watching him work in the garden – weeding and watering and hunting for stray growth – is my first apprenticeship in the cut-and-snip of portrait-making: trimming the bulge of a cheek, lifting an eyebrow just so, toning an eye socket until the likeness is truer than truth.

Daily we trawl the flowerbeds together, Pops and I – me in my enormous sun hat, dragging the garden shears, he in his baggy work-pants and string vest. We dawdle by a bed of roses, nodding from the weight of bees, and I look to Pops for direction. His shoulders are abubble with sweat. Sunlight sparks off the hot lenses enlarging his eyes. I follow his gaze to a rose that has impertinently strayed beyond its border. He scratches his cheek and says, 'That one can go, I reckon.' I love the way he says, 'I reckon,' end-stamping his sentences with this manly expression that crackles with pipe phlegm.

He gives me the heavy flower cutters and cups his hands over mine, which feel sure inside the cave of his. We slide the stem between the spread edges, down into the violent pocket of their crossing. I feel his hands squeeze, and mine squeeze as well. The blades crunch-snap together and the flower falls soundlessly past me, lying on the grass as long as it was tall. I pick it up by the middle and it swoons. Pop starts up the hill – a striding giant. The severed rose flexes and pricks my little finger.

Accidents will happen, even in Paradise. Digging in my sandpit, I discover what appears to be a chunk of sandy chocolate and take a bite. It's bitter, and I can't get the taste out of my mouth, no matter how hard I spit. I run crying to Alice, who swills out my mouth with antiseptic and takes my temperature. While the dogs who are identified as the likely defilers of my pit pace around and bark protectively, my fever rises to an alarming 105. The ambulance is called and my mother sweats out three days in intensive care, sleeping by my bed on the hard floor, while I hover near death from gastric poisoning.

I recuperate at home. Daddy buys me a new toy: a wood-burning kit with a hot stylus for making designs. Mummy watches from the doorway as he plugs it in and tests it with his finger, taking a piece of wood and slowly incising a wavy line of burn. 'Be careful, Sachie,' he says, as he hands me the instrument. Mummy moves inside as I steady the wood panel on my knee. The sweet smoke affirms my pleasure as the nib creeps across the grain, making its charcoal line. Daddy's voice is deep and reassuring at my ear as I flaunt my new skill. I try to curl the line around to make a spiral but the stylus slips and bites my hand. I scream and Mummy is on me in a storm of kisses, cursing and shooing him away, lifting my wound to reproach Daddy with: a yellow, pearling blister – my trophy and shame. 'Look at this!' she cries. 'I told you that fucking toy was dangerous!'

Una soothes and bounces me in the pool. The surrounding water curls and crashes against us, sprinkling the slit dough of her cleavage with pearls and diamonds. 'Whee, whee, whee...' she sings, her frilled cups rising and falling. I'm happy in the warm valley of her surrogate mothering. The sun is hot on my back. Over waving yellow trees it shines down and deliriously scribbles in the blue bowl of the pool.

One morning I wake early and pad over to the window, drawn by the light. The eucalyptus trees are already glowing. Birds sing encouragingly as the garden emerges from slumberous blue into warm islands of colour. The house throws a lavender shadow across the grass and the sun reddens as it climbs the trees in livid watercolour till the leaves dazzle in sharp relief. Now a breeze stirs the leaves lazily, as if underwater. My lungs fill and empty. I see my cars and trucks laid out in perfect, sparkling rows on the table beside me. Peace fills me to overflowing and I leave my body, lifting up and away to witness myself from behind: a small boy against the wall of light. This is rapture – my first experience of a beautiful, mysterious world that exists with me and apart from me at the same time.

As an artist, I am still standing there. The canvas is my window, through which I perennially strive to reach through to that other, numinous dimension. I never succeed, and I never stop trying.

When I came to paint the memory, I had the boy lift his hands to touch the glass, beyond which his reflection looms. He is that beckoning otherness; that far-flung horizon tugging at his heart.

My father's desire to move from theatre to film was swiftly consummated by the script of *Doctor Dolittle* arriving on his desk. The protean Bricusse had written the words, music and screenplay. The producer, Arthur Jacobs, was desperate for my father to play the doctor's Irish sidekick, Matthew Mugg. With Ian Fraser, the brilliant musical director of *Stop the World* and *Greasepaint* attached, the project was a dream vehicle for my father, even though, as Bricusse had observed, he made 'the most unlikely Irishman.'

He was all abuzz the summer before shooting began. He pored over his script like it was the Torah: notating, questioning. And he delighted in thinking up extra bits of business, polishing his cameo to a point where he would outshine Rex Harrison, who was to play the gentle doctor. Ah, Rex. He was, my father would gainsay, the finest light comedian England had ever produced. He was also a son-of-a-bitch who routinely referred to my father as 'that cockney Jew bastard.' During filming, Dr Dolittle's animal friends – monkeys, llamas, parrots – bit and pissed on Rex with pointed regularity, which only pushed the Great Complainer to greater heights of tantric fury. My father gave him a wide berth, spending most of his time with

*Boy at a Window*

his lovely co-star, Samantha Eggar – or mugging for laughs with the monkeys, who of course loved him. He was also busy on set picking up tips for his own, dreamed-of debut as a director.

With its huge budget and far-flung locations, *Dolittle* took over a year to shoot. My father virtually disappeared on us, reappearing as a visiting genie at cherished intervals. In the golden light of Summit, he suddenly and supernaturally materialized over the garden rise, a cockney zest in his step, the sun sparking off his sunglasses as he called out: 'Hey Kids! How about Shelley's!'

'Daddeee…!' we scream, as we run toward him, and he gathers us into his arms like sheaves of wheat.

He drives us down to the toy store in his new chocolate-brown Cadillac. I'm entranced by the way he plies the shiny ribbed wheel, rotating the power steering with one open palm as we pull into the parking lot. A short walk down Rodeo and we are pushing through glass doors. Shelley, the old Irish owner, is always there, with his alcohol-scorched face and wall-eye. He seems to be in a permanent sweat, his oily hair glued to his skull. He's all smiles when Tony Newley walks in; the store is all ours. Tara and I run down the closely stacked aisles; she makes a beeline for the dolls, I gravitate toward the guns and cars. I hear Shelley telling jokes and Daddy laughing his broad laugh as I scan the top shelves for the bigger boxes, the ones that contain toys built of many parts, complete with instruction manuals and stickers.

At home we open the toys Daddy's bought us and study the instructions. He takes the directions from us and dramatically throws them away, then starts building intuitively, making the thing through trial and error, which is far more thrilling for us. This is the way of Art, which I inherited from him: the way I endeavour to do everything in life. Without signposts – my way – for good and for ill.

Those visits to the toy store were as much for Daddy as for us. The child in him was so alive – an angry, marvellous child that was at once his creative salvation and his emotional ruin. He showered us with gifts to fill the void in himself. But that void could never be filled. Little Tony was just too empty to fill, too broken to fix. He was born illegitimate, and his abandonment by an unknown father was the darkness at the core of him. But it was a darkness that nourished many of the finest songs he wrote with Bricusse:

> With no star to guide me
> And no one beside me
> I'll go on my way
> And after the day
> The darkness will hide me.

I feel I spent my childhood in competition with Little Tony. How could he not have resented me? Here I was, the apple of our mutual father's eye, living in a manor house with servants and dogs, while *he* hadn't even known his father from a face in the crowd. This continued to eat at him until, in his early forties, he had the man tracked down by a detective.

Although it's now considered something of a classic, *Doctor Dolittle* was a flop on first release. It was too long, for one thing; Rex and the songs were uneven; and not even the spectacle of it all could repay the exorbitant studio expense.

My father was crestfallen, to say the least, but the reviews for his performance were good enough that the Warners top brass gave him another shot: in 1968, he was offered the starring role opposite Sandy Dennis in *Sweet November*. It was the saccharine story of a free-spirited bohemian with a terminal illness, who's determined to make the most of her final year on Earth by taking a different lover for each month. My father plays her November. All too patly, he falls terminally in love with her and refuses to make way for Mr December.

Sandy Dennis was my father's worst nightmare: a woman who remained immune to his charms. His default setting when confronted with such an insult was to defensively retreat into himself. But he couldn't do that on-screen; the camera would know. So his performance amounted to a vortex of tics and mannerisms as he alternately hid from and desperately tried to overwhelm Dennis's bovine indifference. She was too sexless for the part and her halting, Method-style of acting totally mismatched his. Theatrical pro that he was, he gave his all on the first take. Dennis couldn't find herself until the fifteenth, by which point my father was struggling to keep it fresh with third-rate stagecraft. The result was a movie that showed him at his worst and her at her best.

My father was left to reflect uneasily on the difficulty of this new medium. He had longed to throw off the shackles of servitude to theatre, and embrace the sassy, high-flying ethos of the movies. Film acting appealed to him because he could hold back, reveal himself in concentrated increments, and not have to deal directly with that 'monster with a thousand eyes' – the audience. The problem was that he possessed a great vaudeville talent keyed and pitched to hit the back of the theatre. This translated disastrously to the screen, where he was forced to dial the volume way down and suggest rather than express-deliver. The camera, such a sensitive instrument, did the work of depth penetration, and the screen, of magnification. He must at one and the same time bare himself and endure the exposure of his blandness; only then could the audience project themselves on to him and supply his thoughts and feelings for themselves – a vital part of the movie-house covenant.

He just couldn't do it. His tendency to overact was deeply ingrained from childhood – a defence mechanism and ruse to get him the love and attention he needed. Fame did nothing to alleviate the problem. And, riddle me this, my father was born to perform but hated it. He was a pained introvert, whose manic outbursts propelled him to theatrical self-display. But it never stopped feeling like perversity to him.

With no movie work on tap, he marked time in Las Vegas doing cabaret. The mob ran Caesars Palace where he headlined and they knew how to take care of Tony Newley. Whenever Tara and I visited we would find our suite stuffed with toy animals courtesy of the management. After one mega successful engagement, the boys upstairs asked my father what he would like by way of a present, and he had offhandedly replied: 'A chocolate-brown E-Type Jaguar would be nice...' On closing night, as he bowed low to acknowledge the standing ovation that always greeted his climactic rendition of 'What Kind of Fool Am I?' at the end of the show, a louder roar drew his attention. Rolling on from stage left came a spanking-new E-Type Jag, chocolate as specified, tied with a big red ribbon, and complete with a besequinned tart waving from the driver's seat.

He alighted from his chariot one lurid sunrise at 1106 Summit, having driven all night through the desert from Vegas. I was three, and already car crazy. I ran my hand ecstatically over its flowing body as it ticked with heat. To my horror, he sold it a week later to Tony Curtis, complaining, 'The steering's too tight.' It was life itself that was too tight and coarse to fit him comfortably.

My mother failed to understand his helpless morbid sufferings. She was not a natural empath, and his extreme complexity made her feel even more lost and alone in the marriage. Like him, she possessed no middle setting, no common touch to heal over the chasms in understanding. They cohabited in the big house on Summit, but they rarely lived together. My father preferred to repair to his study over the garage where he could noodle with songs, dream his dreams, pop his pills, and smoke his dope. My mother had her gay friends who were always up for another long night at The Daisy while the Man of Inspirations was holed-up 'scribbling'.

She was rarely sick and rarely tired. He was a committed napper and hypochondriac; perennially in bed with some ague or other, the pillows pulled close over his face so that only the nose protruded. She was forever at the door trying to entice him to come out, but he would just shake his head and intone: 'You go, Flower... have a wonderful time. And remember, Flower... start a trend!'

She took him literally and started several: knee-high white boots, bangle earrings, rakish bob haircuts... She was a comet, a whirlwind, an It girl. He didn't really know or even dimly appreciate what he had in her. They argued all the time about her career, which she rightly felt she was sacrificing for him. Her best friends like Natalie Wood and Dyan Cannon – inarguably less magnetic and gorgeous than my mother – were sitting in make-up chairs at 20th Century Fox while she was sitting at home. She knew she had to get out there, but my father insisted that we kids needed a full-time mother. She for her part argued that he wanted her at home so *he* could stay away. Resentment reigned until they came to a silly compromise: she would find another outlet for her creative energies in interior decoration. It was something, he laughed, that she could do from home.

She got busy right away. Summit was subjected to a total make-over, as were several of her friends' places. She set up a crafts table and made beautiful Christmas decorations (ones that we use to this day), but tinsel and ribbons and swatches couldn't hold her for long, and soon she was funnelling her cyclonic energy into making life at Summit a dizzying round of parties and happenings. Saturnine Dad couldn't fail to be tempted out of his garage-bound self-reflections by the laughter and tinkling of drinks down by the pool. Eventually he would appear, to be adored and fawned over, and the party would kick into euphoric swing.

Wander if you will among those gorgeous bodies of work, the smashing white smiles, the flowing Pucci dresses. Here is Natalie Wood with her all-devouring brown eyes and melting smile; here is Peter Lawford throwing his suave head back in hilarity. On the sun lounger sit Paul Newman and Joanne Woodward deep in conversation with Sammy Davis Jr, while Pierre Salinger stands off to one side, looking a little awkward in blazer and bowtie, until Billy and Audrey Wilder arrive and he falls in with them. Through it all, weaves my mother, diaphanous in floating colours, taking the temperature of every huddled conversation, making sure the simmer is just right.

And there, if you part the crowd for a moment, you will see a small child face-down in the pool and sinking, his sodden clothes fanned out like a burial shroud. My mother screams and the party freezes. My father to the rescue! He jumps in and splashes out to save me. Back at poolside, I vomit water and start bawling. My mother collapses with a brandy into Paul Newman's arms, while Jimmy Webb croons over the poolside speakers: 'What goes up, must come down...'

Later, toddling about unsupervised, I discover James Caan, alone in the pool house, lining up a billiards shot. His attack-dog aura is terrifying, and I instinctively keep my distance; but he sees me, reverses his tweed cap, and challenges: 'You wanna play, kid?' I shake my head, but he draws me between his enormous thighs, straining in white bellbottoms, and we crouch together, sighting down the cue. His forearms are shocking with their red fur. I hear the mess of chewed gum at my ear, smell the liquor and tobacco on his breath as he coaches me in that wise guy voice: 'Yeah, that's it, a little to the left; now pinch your fingers and slide the cue. Yeah, that's it...' The shot goes wide... But a few years later all that troubled maleness will drop perfectly into the pocket of his breakout role as the hot-tempered meathead Sonny Corleone in *The Godfather*.

After dinner it's time for my father to lace up the 16mm projector so we can relive the glory of our days. The home movie runs a little fast, lending the action a comic urgency. I watch the screen raptly as Sammy Davis Jr and my father, both swim-suited, engage in a mock duel by the pool. They laugh, royally dismissive of each other, and put themselves en garde. Sammy lunges first and my father draws back, unsheathing his riposte. They go at it, scorpion-quick, vivisecting the air as they moonwalk back and forth beside the pool. The elan and precision are breathtaking. When they break down laughing and hug each other, it's like two ghetto boys who've stormed the highest ramparts and gotten away with it.

The action cuts to Christmas time. My father stages a home-movie nativity. My mother, draped in a white sheet, gazes down at the Christ Child (one of Tara's swaddled dolls) while Herod (in the person of my father's agent) gleefully twists his moustache and plots mass murder. Now the Three Wise Men appear (Bino, Leslie Bricusse's four-year-old son Adam, and I) covered in tinsel and improvised turbans from Hermes, leading my collies to the manger. We kneel and offer our gifts. My mother accepts them with a heavenly smile of gratitude. There is ample room on her fluttering eyelashes for the Dove of Peace to perch.

Another jump cut. It's Palm Springs and we're visiting Steve McQueen at his house by the golf course. He puts me on his motorbike and drives me slowly up and down the street. I pound the handlebars and don't ever want to get off. Steve smiles and gives me another turn...

Capri. The waves roll in. The self-proclaimed 'Famous Four' – my mother and father and Evie and Leslie Bricusse – are holidaying together. My father can never appear on camera without his trade-mark shtick: pointing with outsize fingers and pin eyes at Evie's cleavage, or upsetting his shades, twisting his sailor cap sideways and waddling like a duck. The two girls mug for the camera, too, collapsing in delirious laughter, while Leslie takes in the view – aloof and self-contained in his National Health specs – plotting, as ever, the day's events.

21

Pompeii. My father is behind the camera, where he's more comfortable. Leslie and Evie wander arm-in-arm through the ruins as my mother looks back at her increasingly remote husband: *when will he break shot and join her?* She gives up and joins the others, her canary-yellow beach pants jolting the primordial scene. Against a terracotta wall pocked with mosaics, the girls vogue for the camera, giving it maximum shoulder and butterfly eyes. There's enough siren beauty here to wreck a thousand ships (Evie had been professionally pursued by Fellini until Leslie put his foot down). Now our absent auteur reveals himself. A stone phallus by the road points the way to an ancient brothel, and he can't resist giving over the camera, and remarking the protuberance with raised eyebrows. He pats his pocket feeling for condoms, shrugs at their absence; and, in Chaplin fashion, waddles off into the ruined atrium as the film blanches out to nothing…

Late summer 1968. Suddenly I am three. The house is quiet as I explore slowly, wearing a yellow space helmet and mechanical pincer gloves. I pick up and examine the oddest things: a pink flip-flop decorated with daisies; a cigarette lighter shaped like a torso… I lift and turn an antique hourglass and observe the draining grains. What a place the moon is… A distant door, cracked open on a lunar light, arouses my curiosity. I whisper to NASA control that I'm going inside, and husband my oxygen for this furthest of all explorations. I push open the door and see a raised plateau of torrid sheets and, beyond it, a Martian bloom of lamplight. Nearby, wobbly electric bars slip up the TV screen as Andy Williams sings 'Moon River', his eyes infested with static. Movement on the bed… I freeze. Something is stirring there. I make out a foot, a leg – leading up to a dark halo of lamplight. An arm comes out with a finger, beckoning me. I come round the bed, entering the lamplight. A head comes forward and I see the crescent-moon of my mother's face. She taps my yellow dome with a red nail. I try to speak but she shushes me

*Self-Portrait as Spaceman*

and points to her throat. I understand: the wadded up tissues, the potions – she's lost her voice. She smiles and recoils into spiny light. I move away, glancing back – she's eating chocolates and watching Andy. My beautiful space mother.

'Don't go, Una, I'm scared,' I cry out to my nanny.

She hushes me and turns off the light. I turn it back on. She turns it back off. I turn it back on and stand on the bed. She picks me up, lifts the blankets and binds me under them tight. Darkness again. She goes to the door. I reach for the lamp – she sees it and returns, with splinters in her eyes.

'Please don't, Una!'

She grabs me, gathers me up and carries me to the cupboard. She throws me inside and turns the latch. Darkness swarms around me and makes an airless block. I bang against the cupboard door and finger a crack of light until it snaps out. I'm buried twice deep. I rock back and scream my head off. The walls, the ceiling, coming in at me. I hear a car leaving, gunning outside to take Una on her date. My voice can't reach her. I'm blind inside my head. I can't breathe…

In the kitchen, Alice hears my screams. She comes upstairs to my room and tries to locate the source. She can't find me at first. Then she rolls me out of the cupboard. I'm a ball of sweat and cling to her like a limpet.

This 'crime' is reported to my parents, but nothing is ever done about it. They have other things on their minds.

## 2

# Heironymus

My father's thirty-seventh birthday, that September. Flags fly and trumpets blare. Summit is the Castle Fabulous. The extremely sexy, truly great, near-great, and once-great all dutifully pull up outside its freshly painted portico. Inside there's a thrum of expectation. The King appears and works the room on full vibrate: kissing, squeezing, joking... And joy of joys, he even agrees to sing! Bobby Short tickles the ivories as the Man of the Hour – whose day this is – belts out 'What Kind of Fool Am I?'

Now Sammy takes the mic and croons: 'Jew can I turn to, when nobody needs me, my heart wants to know and so I must go where this... cockney Jew leads me...' Dad laughs the loudest, head slung back, lips peeled, slapping his thighs for emphasis.

Now it's Streisand's turn: 'Tony is very important to me...' she says, 'Let me tell you how much... Newleee... people who need Newleee... are the LUCK-i-est people in the world...'

My mother's antennae quiver; her eyes go to quick-zoom on her ogling husband. She will later dissect the moment in her memoir *Past Imperfect*: 'Something in the way Tony looked at her while she was singing this made my feminine intuition kick in with "He's been to bed with her – I'm sure he has."'

Surprise surprise! There was enough largesse to go round – the problem was that the bit of himself he meted out to my mother was getting smaller and smaller, dissolving like morning aspirin.

The need to share himself with all and tawdry, as he confessed to his children (and the world) in *Heironymus*, was born of boredom:

25

Your father thought he would go out of his mind in Tinsel Town. Your mummy is made of stronger stuff. She thrived on the incessant chatter of those technicolour parakeets. I was able to endure by leaning heavily on my trusty bottle. And then [holding up a vial of tablets] the Devil introduced me to my new mistress…

As Jim Morrison would later dreamily proclaim, 'The West is the best…' and sound the rallying cry of a sexual gold rush fuelled by drugs. Everyone wanted a part in those 'weird scenes inside the gold mine.' My father fell all too easily into lockstep with the New Children. My mother didn't need dope; she was on a maddening natural high *all* the time. She watched the carnival of sixties experimentation with a sort of nerdy detachment, snapping her fingers and waiting for a good tune she could dance to. Her favourite trip was a visit to The Factory, the ultra-hip club that had started in Hollywood because The Daisy, she complained, had lousy music and was overpriced. The Factory founders, who included my father, had roped in the likes of Paul Newman, Peter Lawford and Steve McQueen as co-directors to raise the profile of the venture. They soon found an abandoned munitions factory off the Sunset Strip to serve as a venue. With its exclusive door policy and VIP clientele, the place quickly became a huge draw. Jimmy Stewart, Bobby Kennedy, Marlon Brando and Frank Sinatra rubbed shoulders and other body parts upstairs in the elite Director's Rooms, to which the most beautiful girls were funnelled upon arrival. But the place got so excited that it prematurely ejaculated: the VIP door policy cracked under herd pressure and the stars began staying away.

Drugs had become key in my father's new mood of trippy optimism. He used them to console himself after the broken promises of *Dolittle* and *Sweet November* – and they magnified his conviction that the answer to his movie-career impasse was to go deeper and farther than ever before. In an interview at the time, he admitted:

'I'm beginning to feel more and more that the only things I really enjoy are things that emanate directly from inside my small cockney head.'

Only not small. Swelled was more like it. His great stage successes had all been very personal. Why not take all that self-revelation and candour and unleash it on-screen? If Fellini and Bergman could do it, why not he?

He decided to up and create his own 8½. He toiled on the script between cabaret dates and TV appearances, harnessing ideas and images, hammering together his nuclear device in the depths of his own unique story and pain. It would be a sort of *Stop the World* on celluloid, amplifying the winning autobiographical candour of *Stop the World* to breaking point. The title for this debut project of his introduced a new form, the tragic burlesque, into the film canon: *Can Heironymus Merkin Ever Forget Mercy Humppe and Find True Happiness?* (Or, put less egregiously, 'How am I ever going to stop lusting after underage girls and become a proper family man?') It was to be a testament to the unbridled sinfulness of his sex life, and it was a holy mess.

My father's star power in the late sixties was such that Universal Studios, then under Jay Kantor, gave him a million dollars and carte blanche to make the picture he wanted. It didn't matter that he was a first-time director, had never so much as framed a shot or laboured in a cutting room or sweated the final drafts of a screenplay – they had complete and utter faith in his vision (unthinkable in today's stultifying climate of corporate paranoia and second-guessing).

He had Billy Wilder to the house so he could pick his considerable brains on how to tackle the problem that sets up the failure or success of any given scene: where do I put the camera? Billy disappointed him with straightforward advice: 'If the audience is aware of the camera, you've failed.' But my father wanted to thrill the audience with the cocksmanship of the camera – a thing he'd picked up from the French New Wave. Billy only smiled – the seduction should all be in the script, he said; make that fail-safe and the camera will follow, knowing its place. (Had Wilder actually gotten a load of the script, his 'brain full of razor blades' would have gone into cutting overdrive.) My father brought in the writer of *Sweet November* to help shape the screenplay. His chief distinction was that, unlike Bricusse, he wouldn't question my father's wilder ideas.

*Heironymus* would dispense with linear narrative, à la Truffaut and Godard. It would be stylistically diverse: part dream sequence, part skin-flick, part Broadway musical. My father had gambolled about this schizophrenic terrain in *Gurney Slade*, the daringly offbeat TV show he had conceived and starred in back in fifties England. Now he would supplement that avant-garde surrealism with the full buffet of a Broadway score. It was an untried hybrid. He would just have to follow his bliss and let rip.

While the screenwriter scrutinized the star's stream-of-consciousness notes and jottings, attempting to graft joints and bone into the gelatinous maw of the script, my father rushed about fulfilling the obligations of his hyper-manic life: fifteen minutes with the kids here, augmented by toys from Shelley's; a talk show appearance there; a one-off cabaret performance in Atlantic City; a quickie with the latest ingénue…

When he turned to Bricusse for help with the score, he hit a wall. 'If you want my advice, Newberg,' his old friend and collaborator told him, 'you'll take this script and bury it under the nearest rock.' Instead, my father sought out the songwriter and journalist who'd had considerable success with the musical version of *The Admiral Crichton* and compositions for *That Was the Week That Was*.

He was primed to go wild. In went the full musical score; in went the nudity and the sex scenes and the funny camera angles and the film-within-a-film; in went the allegories and the cut-away commercials and the built-in critical commentary. The film bulged with ambition, arrogance, humour, and fat.

Every actress passed on the part of Polyester until the producer gamely suggested, 'Why not Joan?' So my mother dutifully read the script and, God bless her, was disgusted. (In Alexis Carrington guise, she would have cut my father's cock off and salved the wound with vinegar; but this was a full two decades before her invention of the uber-bitch who took no prisoners.) My father patiently explained to her in his warm, patronizing way, that a serious artist must be afforded a lot of latitude to tell his truth. 'Flower' nodded and batted her eyelashes, proud of her husband for being so brave and uncompromising. She was of course also getting a film role (albeit one in which she would be playing herself) after a long dry spell, *and* she would be getting a chance to sing. Better shut up and just do it.

In 1970, my father recalled the moment of marital detente for *Playboy* magazine:

> My wife wasn't the first one I'd thought of to play Polyester Poontang, but when it was pointed out to me that she would be ideal, I suddenly realized it was true. If one were to ask how my wife felt about playing in a picture so autobiographically erotic, I would answer that my wife is a highly sophisticated, intelligent and urbane lady who understands the human creature and has enormous compassion for him. She's not about to make my life miserable. She gladly accepted the role in the film and was deeply moved by the script…

By the winter of 1968, the Newley family, such as it was, was in London for pre-production. Tara and I were to play, guess who, ourselves: Thaxsted 3 and Thumbelina 5. The English character actress, Patricia Hayes, was cast as Grandma – since our real grandma, Grace, had shied away from the klieg lights and the part *did* require some acting.

My father installed us at 12 Park Street, Mayfair, and took a suite of rooms at the nearby Playboy Club to serve as his production offices. Morning ritual: wife kisses husband goodbye and wishes him: '...a good day at the Playboy Club, darling...' Nannies were hired so my mother could spend the requisite hours bustling about her beloved shops in Knightsbridge and the King's Road.

My father's first priority in his bunny warren was to cast his love interest. Location filming in Malta was scheduled to begin in under a month, and he still hadn't found his Mercy Humppe. The casting call went on and on, rivalling the search for Scarlett O'Hara in its dedication and intensity. Oh, the long hard days in open studio inspecting an endless cattle call of naked nincompoops. Would he *ever* find her?

Then one day as he rode up to his offices she stepped on to the elevator. Her name was Connie Kreski and she was the girlfriend of Victor Lownes, who ran Hugh Hefner's operation in London. Blonde and blue-eyed, with a waif-like innocence enveloping her ample curves, she was the embodiment of my father's 'perfect child lover.' Ian Fraser, the musical maestro who had gone from working with Bricusse/Newley to being similarly indispensable to Shirley Bassey and Julie Andrews, was then in London finishing a project for MGM and signed on to orchestrate the songs. With Kreski and Fraser firmly in place, my father was free to leave London and go off to scout locations.

By the time my mother arrived in Malta and saw for herself what was happening in real time, it was too late. She had in her mind accepted the lubricious nature of the enterprise, but now, seeing the word made flesh, she balked. A steady stream of adrenalized, bikini-clad girls scampered toward the beach like fresh recruits to the front. My father was the mad general pacing in the sand, framing shots and huddling with his minions – set designers, script girls, accountants – to discuss the grand execution of his battle plan. Tavernas around the island buzzed with gossip about the dark doings down at the shore.

The Catholic authorities got wind of things and convened an ugly inquisition. They had granted tax breaks for filming, only to discover too late that this was no ordinary movie – this was pornography! They succeeded in shutting down production for all of a week.

My father's eroticism was epic in scale. He'd arrived at last on the open plain of visionary concupiscence. The wide, sweeping curve of the beach was his timeless stage. On this living plateau he would contrive a puppet musical, a radical confession of the modern soul *in extremis*; a strict, Nordic meditation on death, silence and showbiz.

Unaccountably, for all its easy displays of female flesh, that Maltese summer has left no memory traces in me. I'm told I developed painfully sunburnt hands from beach play between set-ups, and that I blew out the soundman's ears when Grandma applied stinging moisturizer to my tender little mitts. I can be seen in production stills, aloof and grumpy-looking in my sailor suit, oblivious to the surrounding mayhem.

If I had been old enough to grasp what was happening, I might have asked my father what he thought he was doing, exposing his kids to all this filth. As it was, I was just a three-year-old witness for the prosecution, conveniently mute.

The script of *Heironymus* has our father's alter ego taking us down to the seashore for a night-time screening of his erotic autobiography. There we remain till dawn – aged mother, captive innocent son and daughter – sitting cluelessly in our beach chairs as he loads the rickety old projector and exhorts us to pay attention. We are witnessing something very important, he tells us: a full disclosure of Daddy's libidinous time here on earth.

Mummy doesn't appear until the second reel, when we see her in flashback, meeting Heironymus for the first time. Her voice, however, is heard from beginning to end, plaintively calling from a house on the cliff: 'Heironymusss…' as she desperately searches for her missing family. Tara's only line in the picture, 'Daddy, Daddy, Mummy's calling…' is oft repeated, but he can only glance up the beach, angered by the interruption. His show *must* go on, no matter the cost. He projects its scenes, or chapters, on to a pull-up screen, placed in the sand – with suitable pauses for thought during which he paces in front of us and offers up glib apologies for his real-life failings as a man – husband, son and father. We children look on blankly. His doting mother can only forgive (Grandma Grace's feeble habit in real life): 'It wasn't your fault, Son…'

This primary spectacle turns out to be a film within a film when the camera pulls back to show a second crew, actually filming Heironymus and his family. This 'shadow' unit includes the film's writers and a coven of on-site critics who vociferously dismiss the Felliniesque excesses of the piece out of hand. (Victor Spinetti is brilliant as a Ken Tynan clone, complete with oddly clasped cigarette and machine gun stutter.) By anticipating the critics, my father is hoping to disarm them while keeping the audience on his side. And all the while trying to salve his guilt by confessing it out loud.

There follows a time lapse sequence charting his rise as a show-biz god – and his equally unstoppable exploits as a Don Juan. He reprises *Piccadilly Lilly* from the movie's opening, which mutates into a Bobby Darin-like cruise vehicle for his steadily expanding voice range, until there he is high-kicking and sassy in his Vegas incarnation, the girls hanging off him like tacky jewellery.

At this point my father cuts the projector and looks thoughtful: 'Some of you may have noticed a tendency on your Daddy's part not to give a fig for other people's feelings… This gets worse as Daddy gets older.'

I suck my thumb and pick my nose. Grandma looks on adoringly: 'It's all right, son, you didn't know any better…' Enter Good Time Eddie Filth, played by the grand wizard of Jewish comedy, Milton Berle. He ascends from the underworld in a thermal updraught of sulphur fumes, his glasses and horns askew, wearing an ill-fitting pair of shaggy trousers with cloven-toed shoes. 'Oh boy, there's got to be a better way to get up here…' he coughs and complains, then spies Heironymus: 'Oh there you are, Kid, I've been watching your act… definitely hall of flame material.'

So they take up together. Good Time Eddie becomes the Kid's true agent, pushing him to realize his full potential as 'a lecher, rapist and all-round good guy.' Heironymus's sexcapades, thus turbo-charged, reach to the sky, literally: in what must be a high point of sexual hubris in cinema, the camera lifts to find a long line of bikini-clad women disappearing into the distance as our hero reclines on his tented bed of exertions in the foreground, calling out 'Next!' to another love patient who obligingly disappears behind the curtain.

Eddie looks on proudly, and remarks to Grandma, 'He's in my hands now, Madam. Your work is finished. Mine is just beginning...' But after blundering into an unwanted pregnancy, and beset by a feeling of alienation from his adoring fans, Heironymus is left to reflect that the Devil's done him wrong. In reaction, he climbs a mountain to address God Almighty:

HEIRONYMUS: Look – I've never shown a great interest in you but that doesn't mean I haven't thought about you. Come to think of it, you haven't exactly shown a great interest in me.

GOOD TIME EDDIE [echoing]: Hey, Felonius! I got a couple live ones down here!

HEIRONYMUS [ignoring Eddie]: Just between you and I, it's a joke, isn't it? We made you up because we wanted someone to be there, didn't we? Well, looks like you've had it down here. And if I were you – I wouldn't worry about it. [Music swells, he sings]:

> I'm all I need
> If I've got me
> I've got a sky full of bluebirds
> If I've got me, just you see
> How the world goes away...

The song is a shameless bid to salve his Oedipal wound and achieve something on the exalted level of 'What Kind of Fool Am I?' and 'Who Can I Turn To?' But whereas those songs allow us to feel the artist's desolation and even pity him, 'I'm All I Need' is a paean to egotism. It never became a standard because, despite a lush melody and all the right grace notes, the sentiment was screwy – 'My Way' on acid.

In the end, the only way for Heironymus to escape the judgement of his critics (both inner and outer) is to go numb. And so he falls asleep – and into a Midsummer Night's wet Dream of a movie. His seductively self-deprecating sense of humour remains on guard to convince us he's still in charge – of both himself and his meandering narrative – but the comedy can only patch so many holes.

The fascinating thing about the film is how honest it is, and how sublimely unconscious of itself. Bergman, Fellini, and Godard are not great masters for nothing – they can stay awake while they dream, orchestrating the primal scream into an aria. But in *Heironymus*, my father plunges into a self-reverential trance; he might as well be alone on that beach, adrift in a sea of solipsism. He has the trusting, infantile attitude to the audience that the patient has to the analyst. And we don't even get a happy ending. When Polyester finally finds her errant husband and sleeping children as the morning sun peaks over the cliffs, she makes good on a long-time threat:

You do this kind of thing… You do it all the time. You don't think and you don't care… all of us could die for all you care. Well, I've had enough… I'm taking the children, yes – I am… anywhere, away from you. And this time I mean it. I really do… [Polyester leaves, carrying Thaxsted and herding Thumbelina and Grandma as the policeman helps. They get into the patrol car and drive off.]

34

The camera moves in to contemplate our hero. He is playing with a small marionette that fell into the sea earlier in the film. 'He is very much alone.'

> NARRATOR: And that is the end of our first instalment. Will Heironymus Merkin discover The Secret Cavern of Resplendent Riptides? Will Polyester make real her threat to take the children and leave him? Can Heironymus Merkin ever forget Mercy Humppe and find true happiness? Don't miss our next episode…

Mercifully, there wasn't one. *Heironymus* hit theatres in 1969 as the first and last wide-release film ever to receive an X rating. My father had privately screened it beforehand for a number of friends and the response was encouraging – Roman Polanski, for one, ate it up. But the critics slaughtered it: Newley was no more than a self-indulgent poseur and con man. My father was devastated. He felt that he'd given everything.

We resumed life at Summit Drive, but it was never the same. My father withdrew more and more into himself. My mother fretted and despaired. The revelations of *Heironymus* had breached her defences. Her marriage, she now realized, was a sordid joke.

They would stay together 'for the sake of the children' – the rallying cry of so many lost causes – but it was all just a contractual show of guilt before the dirty deed of divorce. Neither one of them could ever change. What she could have become to him is unclear; his besotted mother perhaps, who looked the other way every time he strayed and was always there for him when he came slinking home. But she'd been a willing fool for love long enough, and it was time to wake up. She knew there was no future with Tony, and that she had better make her own.

In 2003, in Surrey, rummaging through an old box of papers after Grandma Grace's death, I find a hastily scrawled letter in my mother's hand, dated 13 February 1970. It is addressed to my father:

The cupboards are bare and the pain becomes more intense – a pain which has been for many months lurking in my subconscious – afraid to raise its head and announce itself – or I have been afraid to invite it in –

I'm desolate and destroyed – seeing the closets and shelves bare of your clothes I begin to realize, perhaps for the first time, that our marriage has ended.

You are gone, to another house and another life – if not now – yet in store for you – the rosebud cheeks and unfurrowed brows you yet have to explore –

And I – I – who wanted and wished for an end to our 8-year farce am unutterably miserable.

There is – or would be no chance for us anymore – right?? – am I right? – or can one regain the last threads of one's hopes and dreams of 8 years ago –

What the fuck happened to us?? –

Certainly I loved you terribly – and I'm not one to love lightly – I was always hoping for something more – always expecting that one day you would start enjoying me more and enjoying life more – You didn't –

It began to wither and die – gradually – I can see it in my photographs – The bitter expression that started permeating my face –

I guess it started about 1967 – just between *Dolittle* and *Heironymus* – I changed from a girl to a woman – I'll never change back –

I'm a shitty writer – I want you to know and have something of me – to realize that there was always something more than what you perceived – I did try – really really – but it was a losing battle –

It's like crying on someone's grave – it's gone gone gone gone – you and me – Tony and Joan – Finis.

It's such a waste and I'm so sad – You'll never know how sad, miserable, bereft I felt coming to the end of our marriage. You think I'm cold or don't care – I did – and I do – but it's too late isn't it – too many girls – too many lies – too many nights spent without each other – without the truth – without reaching out to find each other in each other's wilderness –

That we will always be friends I hope – we have never been truly lovers – one thing I know – I am not cold or frigid – I became that because I couldn't commit myself totally to a man who was unable to commit himself –

There was always a part of you looking on – like the Mask in *Heironymus* – You said often that I wasn't sensitive – you were wrong – so wrong – unfortunately I was too sensitive – too aware of where your mind was when we made love –

I think you love me now – in your own way – You won't find our sort of love easily – I still love you and I always will – Nothing can change it – I see and understand you more and I wish I could have helped you – and helped us – we are both so lost in the wilderness, and truth was so far away –

I hope you understand what I'm trying to say – God knows we've played enough games in the last year –

But Oh – those empty cupboards – how they hurt me – It's a symbol of our failure –

Are you happy in your new house? Are you happy with the 'Connies' and 'Debbies' and 'Sandys' and 'Sheryls'?? – Were they worth it?? – were they??? – Tony – Only you can know.

I'm not being recriminatory, just searching my soul – but my eyes are full of tears – 3AM Beverly Hills.

Underneath, there's a drawing… of a flower.

Fall, 1969. Not quite four, I stand alone in the driveway at 1106. Ferns and flowers brush me as I kneel down and push my toy car over the gravel, making an engine sound. It gets louder and louder and then I realize it isn't coming from me. I stand up and look down the driveway. Something's coming. It's spitting fire and cackling. A dragon? I take a step back as the monster finds our driveway and turns in, raging up the hill, coming for me… A steepening wave crests with a roar as the white nose tips up and over, seething toward me and grinning chrome. I seize on my back foot as the beast stops just short, venting its hot, swirling breath about my knees. There's a man inside, wearing dark glasses. He punches the horn, jangling my insides, and looks sideways to the house with a smile. Mummy appears, surprised and happy, and runs down to him. They kiss, framed by the windscreen, and then the man looks over his shoulder, tugs at the beast and pulls it away in reverse. There they go now… swerving back down the driveway. A loud roar takes them away… until only my own engine sounds are heard again, sobbing and climbing the gears of grief as Mummy leaves me.

The interloper's name was Ron Kass. He would be paying regular visits to 1106 now that my father was living full-time at his office. Whenever he came, I closed myself off in the little guest bathroom with the stained-glass window and all the soaps in the big shell tray. The sweet scents of juniper, strawberry, lemon, and clove – and the softly-coloured light – made a safe place. My father's absence was underscored daily in the accumulating Christmas presents that arrived from the office: *Daddy was not in those boxes. Daddy would not pop out of those boxes come Christmas Day.* So I hated them.

My father later confessed to me that on Christmas Eve he parked in the street outside 1106. He stole around the side of the house and jumped a locked gate into the garden. He went up to a window and peaked inside. There we were, dappled by the soft light of the tree, lifting and shaking our presents. My mother smiled wanly at our pleasure as my father watched through fogged glass. He would not be there tomorrow to see my face brighten as the latest toy car, or the cowboy outfit, or the rocket launcher, was revealed. Nor would Tara embrace him, dressed as a princess, her eyes full of tinsel.

He dropped his head and looked at the dark earth beneath his Gucci shoes. He wanted to press down into it and be nothing. Then a cry lifted him. My mother was laughing, prompted by something she'd just read on a card. She put it aside and he saw the wan look return. The children were in her lap now, rising and falling with her breath. I was happily engaged in sucking my thumb, gently massaging the bridge of my nose with a little finger – the blessed scene amounting to a stake in my father's heart. He turned and walked off through the glistening ferns, leaving a shrinking stain of breath on the window glass to symbolize his care.

> What kind of fool am I
> Who never fell in love?
> It seems that I'm the only one
> That I have been thinking of.
>
> What kind of man is this?
> An empty shell
> A lonely cell in which
> An empty heart must dwell.
>
> Why can't I fall in love
> Till I don't give a damn
> And maybe then I'll know
> What kind of fool I am?

His own words from 'What Kind of Fool Am I?' had become his marriage epitaph. 'Fool' was the great poem he'd etched on the door of discovery, but he never pushed through. He simply pushed on with his affairs and one-night stands.

My father's divorce from my mother marked the beginning of a long, slow descent in his career. He would buck the trend with the score for *Willy Wonka* and the one-off *Goldfinger* hit; but as stellar as these achievements might have been in the life of a lesser talent, in my father's they rank as mere consolation prizes. Twin peaks had been reached with *Stop the World* and *Greasepaint* and all subsequent highs were steps down to the valley of dissolution that awaited him in the late seventies and early eighties.

Today I am four. The air smells of eucalyptus and cake. My friends wear party hats at the long, low table, pulling party crackers and throwing streamers. I move among them like a little prince, handing out treats because it's my birthday. I like the feel of the elastic cord of the party hat, tight under my chin. When I burp, the orange soda tickles my nose. Now Mummy walks from the house with Alice, singing in unison and carrying my cake. It's in the shape of a tugboat (blue) with four funnels (red). Mummy alone puts it down in front of me and my breath gets bursting-big to blow out the candles.

Now Pops puts out more chairs because there's a clown coming. I sit on the patio looking into the dark house, waiting. Suddenly there's a whooping noise and a burst of colour and he's there. His shoes bounce and his shirt flies out of his jacket and he already can't stop laughing. He comes over to me, all painted eyes and hot-dog mouth and shows me a flower that squirts me. Everyone laughs. He falls back with jumping shoulders and then the laugh gets stuck in his throat and he starts hiccupping. He's trying to stop but he can't and he slaps his face and gulps soda. He smooths down his shirt front and a long, low burp comes out. I'm laughing too, now. Then a flower grows out of his hand. It droops and his smile does too. He tickles the stem and it perks up again. He presents it to me but it ups and dies in the space between us. I tickle the stem and it springs up again. He nods and smiles with all his teeth, then punches out a top hat. He taps the brim and pulls out an old boot, a plucked chicken, a rotten egg... But something appears to be amiss. He looks inside, taps the bottom, then pulls out a toy crocodile, hanging from his nose! We scream and climb the air. Now he tosses the croc over his shoulder, shuts his eyes, and makes big important sweeps over the hat. Searching inside, one eye squinched, he finds it. A big hammer pops out and bangs him on the head! He falls about and lands in Mummy's arms. All the parents laugh and their flash bulbs go haywire. He tips his hat to Mummy, squares his shoulders, and comes back over to me. He asks for a kiss. I give him one and he wants another and another. I toggle his nose and can see, underneath his big, greasy eyebrows, the real ones, powdered white. I recognize the fibres – the thick weave of them – and suddenly I know him. I lean over to Tara and whisper: 'It's Daddy...'

He hears me say it. So now it's OK to *be* Daddy. And he performs for me only, standing close with patched, baggy pants, bending a balloon. He can't manage to make a balloon dog, and the ladies laugh because the tube looks rude. He tries again but it pops and scares him half to death. He wags a finger at me for laughing, but I can't stop, and then he sweeps me up and runs away with me! Everybody screams and follows. He's running down to the pool, breathing hard and sweating make-up. He puts me down by the water and goes to the end of the diving board. Everyone stops to watch. He looks scared, like it's a cliff. We cheer as he starts working his arms around, gearing up for the big jump... then POP, he's up in space, stiff as a board, before falling with a splash. We scream and pile in after him. He comes up laughing and gasping; flashbulbs bleach his face which is now melting red and black paint. I climb on to him and pump his shoulders because he's my Daddy and I want everyone to know it. Then he swims to the side, heavy with children, and pulls himself out. We follow him back to the board as he keeps jumping with robot quirks, scissor legs, and flapping arms until he passes out cold on the concrete like a shipwrecked man. My friends walk up and kick him for more fun, but he's done.

I kneel down and feel his breath on my cheek.

'Did you like that, Sachie?' he says, with slitty eyes crusted with paint.

'*Yes*, Daddy.'

'Good,' he says. I can see that he's happy.

Then I help him towel off and we walk up to the house together. He goes inside and I don't see him again on my birthday.

He's back a few days later. I'm pushing my Tonka toy across the patio, liking the way the herringbone bricks make it tremble, when I hear him at the study door, calling me inside. His face looks sad and I don't really want to go, but he keeps calling me and getting angry when I still don't come. Then his hands are on me roughly and I struggle as he drags me inside.

It's dark and cold in his study. Mummy and Tara are already sitting there. Daddy plunks me down next to Tara and takes his seat next to Mummy and the two of them hold hands.

'Mummy and I have something to tell you that isn't easy. We've been thinking about this for a long time. We love you both more than anything in the world and what we are doing has nothing to do with you. The fact is... Mummy and Daddy don't know how to live together any more. We fight too much and we don't like to fight. We want you to know how much we love you both, but we just can't be together any more in the same house. Mummy and Daddy are getting a divorce, which means we'll live in different houses but we're still your Mummy and Daddy. And we always will be. D'you understand?'

Tara nods and tries not to cry.

I suck my thumb and say: 'Can I go back and play now?'

## 3

## 30 South Street

*Blue Boy*

THE BOY IN THE PAINTING IS LOST IN SWIRLS OF PAINT. HE'S
ensnared by serpentine shapes, held in the tension between over-
lapping layers. The depth of the canvas is an infuriating tangle of
intentions, a fine watch mechanism gone wrong. Time has stalled
and he's the spanner in the works. He feels the pressure of the
frustrated machine. His eyes open and see the world through a

blue scarf of paint. Even the sun is caught as a spinning pinwheel, driving the gears of his confusion. Will he ever escape? There's no help from his foetal arms and legs which have no strength to pry apart his prison cell. He must wait, hoping for some deliverance from his plight.

I don't remember transitioning from Los Angeles to London. I don't remember leaving Alice and Pops, saying goodbye to 1106 and my dogs. There's just a disorientating jump-cut from the sunny abundance of Beverly Hills to the greys and muddy greens of never-ending English winter. It's 1970. Callaghan's incompetent government has sunk the British economy and driven England into the Winter of Discontent. Strikes and anger dominate the public discourse. Uncollected garbage piles high in Berkeley Square and there are regular power cuts.

I, of course, take in very little of this, but the national mood happens to perfectly mirror my own. 1106 and all it stands for is on the cutting-room floor and I don't know why. Sundered from my father, I slowly deflate, drifting beyond the margins of living colour into a speculative world of semitones. The grief-stricken greys and greens of the miserable English winter *are* me.

My mother has found a flat in Queensway, off the northern end of Hyde Park – about the size of the maid's quarters at 1106. I attend a nearby church nursery school whose gothic interior is all shadows and dampness. At long, low tables I concentrate on forming letters and learning to count. At break time I haggle in vain for my turn on one of the rusty tricycles in the side alley, then sit it out, staring at the bone-white sky through a dark confusion of branches. *Where's Daddy? Where are Pops and Alice? What am I doing here where the sun never shines?* I don't ask these questions, I can't even form them to myself. I am a child. I have no choice but to trust what's happening.

Mummy is a gypsy. She says it's always a good move to move. It's 'lively'. We live in a 'flat'. It's called that because there are lots of ones just like it piled on top. Tramp is our new dog – a terrier. He's named after the club Mummy goes to every night with Auntie Jackie. She lives in London, too. Sometimes my friend Adam Bricusse comes over and we play Doctor Pee with Tara. We hide in the closet with flashlights and show Tara our privates and she shows us hers. Then we do an operation – Tara is usually the nurse, Adam's the doctor and I'm the patient.

I hate my new school. It really is more like a church. The ceiling is high and made of stone. The light that comes through the windows is always grey. But at least the moss on the outside has colour. And the spreading spots of lichen look like fireworks.

Mummy wears T-shirts and jeans at home. Her hair is long and black and shiny and she's beautiful. Her eyes are big and her eyelashes are bigger and longer than anybody else's mummy's. She makes me cucumber-and-tuna-fish sandwiches and jugs of orangeade. And she buys me Jaffa Cakes with marmalade filling and McVitie's chocolate digestive biscuits for dipping in tea. The chocolate in London tastes really good.

Mummy sees Ron Kass an awful lot. He's got shiny cheeks and a suntan and he's always smiling. His laugh is like a bumblebee got caught in his nose, making him bark like a dog. I guess I like Ron, but he's not Daddy – he doesn't show me things. The best thing about Ron is his Maserati. It's white, and blue inside, and goes fast, fast, fast. And his shoes – he has a whole closetful of them on tilted racks so you can pick and choose. He told me they are all made in Italy where only the very best shoes are made. Ron wears long beige pants with a sharp crease and smart ironed shirts, and his cheeks shine with Old Spice. He really likes taking Mummy to Tramp.

I watch her get ready. She sits at her make-up table, takes a deep breath, and pins her hair. Then she sponges her face with skin-colour paint and then powders it dry. She looks like death then. Time to put her eyes on. She uncaps a pencil and makes a black line along the bottom lid; her hands are so still and careful. Then she goes over the top lid doubling the lines so they're really, really black. Then she does the same on the other eye, just as careful. Her eyes are bigger now, whiter. With a little sponge she darkens the insides, making them peacock-blue or sparkly-green, or gold, which is my favourite. She blinks and smiles and I'm happy too. Her eyelashes are in a little box. She uses a gummy clamp to hold them in place till they stick. But they're still not thick enough, so she dips an oily stick in black and works it along the hairs until they're spidery and clumpy. Now I see why Daddy called her Flower, because her eyes are like flowers. She twists out a lipstick. My lips stretch, too, as I watch her put the redness on. She asks me about school in a strange voice that has no teeth or tongue, but I don't want to talk, I just want to watch her. Now she flutters the powder puff over her nose like a butterfly and presses her lips to save the gloss. Her wig sits on a Styrofoam head staring back at us. She fits it like a helmet and pulls it down at the back. Her head is bigger now, more important. She takes two squirts from her magic crystal and rubs her wrists together. Her perfume is called Jungle Gardenia and stings my nose. She kisses me and disappears into her closet. I can hear her singing and choosing her costume. She knows it's going to be a night to remember.

My father painted his face, too. I watched with equal fascination when he made himself up for his performances. I loved the crowded array of pencils and sponges on his make-up table, the powders and trays of aromatic toner. Now, when I prepare my palette for a day's work, I observe the tools of my trade with the same satisfaction and sense of mystery. All my toil is memorialized in those bent tubes and bursting bouquets of old brushes. Unlike my self-painting parents, I have applied my paint to the faces of others, but the reward is the same: the joy of transformation; especially when I paint my

*Painter's Table*

own face on canvas. At first, there's only a ghost that I must flesh out and remodel from the inside. The paint starts as thought, and soon becomes feeling, riding the features like a searching brail. Slowly, over time, it recovers what is hidden and makes it known, to oneself and others. Only when the viewer meets its gaze does the portrait come to life.

When my mother first met him in Los Angeles, Ron Kass was working for MGM Records. By the time we moved to London, he had a job at Apple Records producing The Beatles' final two albums. He was riding high. And he badly wanted to marry Joan Collins. My mother resisted, preferring not to impose another father on us so soon after the trauma of divorce, but she did consent to move in with him. His lavish Georgian townhouse in the heart of Mayfair

*Self-Portrait in Kangol Cap*

was a giant step up from our cramped Queensway flat. My mother soon helped him restyle it into a hip party pad, complete with a psychedelic basement lined with pleated fabric like a Maharaja's tent and filled with Beatles memorabilia.

*Yellow Submarine* had just come out and the title song became my anthem. That magic foursome, with their funny accents and outlandish uniforms, seemed like beings from another dimension. A picture of them naked, their bearded groins and faces cavemanishly dark against a Day-Glo background, hung in the basement, and I often looked at it, wondering at their potent strangeness.

Paul McCartney came to the house, and Ringo Starr, but I don't remember John Lennon or George Harrison there. When my mother bumped into Lennon in the hallways of The Beatles' production offices in Abbey Road, he flirted outrageously with her, confessing that he'd had a pin-up of her in his room 'as a lad.' (My mother as the young Lennon's jerk-off fantasy: not half bad.) She was present at what would turn out to be The Beatles' last concert, standing on the roof of 3 Savile Row in the blustery cold, unaware that this was the end not only of an era but of Ron's gainful employment. But while it lasted, Ron's stint at Apple gave us an impregnable base in London and my mother constructed her extravagant life around him.

30 South Street. My new home. Its front is black, its steps are white, and the front door is shiny black with a big brass knob. Inside, the floors slant and creak because they're so old. The tight stairs zigzag all the way to the attic, which is where I sleep.

I love Ettore. Ron brought him from his house in Switzerland to make us pasta. He smiles a lot and has very white teeth. He wears a white jacket like a naval captain and his skin is very tan.

London is at war. Mummy says the miners are angry and there's no coal to make electricity. When the lights go out, Ettore lights the candles and his face goes warmer and browner. He says, 'Attenzione, attenzione…' as I climb the stairs with a candle like in the olden days.

One day we all go to Ringo Starr's house in Hampstead. He shows me a 'groovy ornament' – a lava lamp: a see-through box that see-saws and makes a blue wave that rolls slowly back and forth inside. I could look at it forever. Then there are fireworks because it's Guy Fawkes night. Ringo tells me about the time a firework he let off in the garden looped the loop and came back into the house, setting it on fire. His son Zack is bigger than me, with long blonde hair, and he teaches me to ride a bike. He pushes me down the long gravelly drive so I can get a little balance before I pedal off.

My favourite house to go to is where Roger Moore's son Geoffrey lives. It's big and in the country. Geoffrey came to my fifth birthday, which was a clown party, and now he's my best friend. Our favourite game is Escape from Colditz. We run into the big garden maze that goes on forever and hide from the Germans. Then we creep inside the house and pretend it's Blofeld's. The wooden chairs are shaped like hands and the old staircase reeks of cigars. Blofeld has beautiful shoes, too. Geoffrey puts them on and slides around the bathroom laughing at himself. Roger is filming *Live and Let Die* which Geoffrey says is going to be the best Bond ever. He takes us to see him making it at Pinewood Studios, and it's the train scene where Bond fights off the bald man with the mechanical arm. Jane Seymour is there, too – almost as pretty as Mummy.

At weekends we go to Auntie Jackie's. She lives at the top of a skyscraper. We ride up there and the silver elevator doors slide open like in *Star Trek*. She wears blue jeans and a big brass belt just like Mummy. Her dog is called Charlie. He's so happy to see us and wants to rub Mummy with his naughty pink lipstick. She runs away and everyone laughs. Mummy hates dogs. There's a huge patio and I run out on it to watch the jumbos flying in. They go in and out of the big cloud caves and fill them with sound. Some of them are coming in from Los Angeles, which is where Daddy lives. I like my cousins because they're all girls and let me ride their tricycles. Sometimes the Khashoggi boys come over and bring their Rolls-Royce pedal car; but they won't let me drive it. After tea, I go into Auntie Jackie's library and look at her books. I open one of hers – she's a writer – and I read about a woman who is on her knees and hungry for a man. Jackie's picture is on the back. She has flower eyes like Mummy's and a bullet that dangles from a necklace between her bosoms. It must feel cold. In her bathroom there's an exercise machine with a strap that goes around you and makes the fat wobble off. I turn the dial way up and sing a note that turns to fizz in my throat. Then I weigh myself and look at the photographs of her friends: some of them are in bathing suits, some are wearing furs, but they're all smiling.

We were often there. On the weekends, my mother didn't know what to do with us, so she took us to her sister's. It felt like family, the first we'd ever had. But then we'd go home again.

Life with Ron at South Street was geared toward entertaining. His Mayfair townhouse was a few turns away from Mount Street, where Doug Hayward had his luxury men's tailoring shop. With its rich furnishings and Edwardian hunting tableaux (not to mention the flirty shop girls always ready to refresh your drink and laugh at your lame jokes), Doug's shop became *the* destination for the alpha males of the day. Doug received his customers like Buddha, sipping his G&T with an amused hangdog expression, processing the latest scandal with a chuckle and a priceless one-liner, before repairing to his workroom to cut cloth with Mozartian elan. He and Ron became good friends; and, with my mother pulling the party strings, South Street soon became the go-to pad for Doug's A-list customers and their equally glamorous girls.

I was allowed to stay up late and watch the guests arrive. Dodi Fayed slinked through the den in his maroon Hayward cashmere, young and slim, fresh to the London scene at twenty-three; followed by Pedro Rodriguez, a Formula One driver for McLaren, soon to race at Silverstone. The danger of the impending Grand Prix hung over him like perfume and made an intoxicating mixture with his natural charisma and matador good looks. Michael and Shakira Caine, Roger and Luisa Moore, Peter Sellers and Britt Ekland, were all regulars, as was Johnny Gold, the larger-than-life manager of Mummy and Ron's beloved Tramp.

The South Street parties were warm, candle-lit affairs, with guests lolling on suede bean bags around a glass table piled high with art books, while a smooth, proto-disco sound thudded from the Bang &

Olufsen. The women sported bangles, Pucci scarves, and cowlicked hair; the men were all suede-swathed, gold-chained and tanned. Ron's big, harrumphing laugh was the party's territorial marker. With my mother on his arm, he was the happiest bloke in London.

She understood the hippy scene to perfection, but never indulged its spirit; never smoked pot or grooved to Ravi Shankar or read a book on Eastern mysticism. It was the look she loved. Whenever Tara and I went out, she dressed us in matching black leather pantsuits with brass belt buckles. The leather made me feel dangerous and I loved the sweetish stink of its cure. She was mad for Art Nouveau and ransacked the antique stores of the Portobello Road, bringing home gigantic sculpted candles, flower-embossed cigar boxes and all manner of *objets d'art*. There were Tiffany lamps, like tantric blooms on iron stalks that shed a blood-orange light through their porcelain shades; and practically every glass shelf in the house exhibited a chorus line of Chiparus statues, their ivory faces and hands set into dark metal bodices.

After the pulsing, hypomanic, high-summer sixties, the seventies were autumnal and calmative. Rust oranges, Indian yellows and russet reds made an arboreal canopy over the mellow scene. Our velvet walls were hung with curvist Erte watercolours of svelte goddesses embodying the four seasons. Jasper Johns was emerging as the big new artist and Ron proudly displayed several of his signed prints in the den. A number 9 lithograph from Johns's famous series – white on black, the numeral loosely but expertly brushed in as an open hieroglyph – had pride of place over the fireplace. There were also numerous prints by Vasarely – the poor man's Albers – that were the perfect stimulant to a 'good trip', with their vanishing colour perspectives and fishbowl dioramas of geometric colour.

I revelled in it all and wanted to stay up all night, but after a kiss from my mother, I was made to trudge upstairs in my all-in-one pyjamas. The throbbing music rose three floors to agitate my bedsprings and I crept on to the landing to savour the exhaust plume of laughter, cigarette smoke, and perfume. Mummy was in heaven. That much was clear. I heard Ron laughing and knew he was holding her and looking at her with sparkling eyes. I never saw Daddy do that.

Next morning, I wandered through the den trying to smell the vanished party through the cleaning lady's antiseptic: cigarettes, spilled brandy, clove incense, chocolate mint... I slipped an After Eight from its dark sheath and let it dissolve in my mouth as I studied the Chiparus statues. They'd seen it all – the Tinkerbells of this Peter Pan scene. I marvelled at their windblown garments modelled in lead, as they austerely leashed Afghan Hounds or balanced on one leg in perfect equipoise. I sat down in a suede armchair and fingered the table ornaments: little metal balls clicking in tandem; a whiskery bouquet of fibre optics stroked by coloured light; the wriggly glass tube with vermilion liquid in its seed bulb. I warmed it in my hand and watched the bubbling liquid rise and pee warmly into another chamber...

*Where am I?*

The clock ticks and the sepulchral light of London entombs me. I cannot see the world from space – the relation of continents and oceans; how everything turns and comes round. All I know is rooms – a succession of rooms – with the thinnest of narrative threads joining one to the next. At any moment, the thread could break, the rooms could come apart and leave me adrift in black space. I feel the loss of my father, but I do not ask for him or demand to know where he is.

I start lashing out in random fits of temper that make me a difficult kid to understand. I develop a lisp, and then a stutter. I am quiet and docile, but then, by turns, a little strongman who won't budge. Hence I become a problem for a succession of au pairs from Scandinavia who quit after a few days and leave my busy mother perpetually in the lurch. While she is trying to get on with her new life I am finally and inconveniently acting out. I climb the stairs at

South Street obsessively, fantasizing that I am scaling a mountain-side. My anxiety has adopted the vertical form of the house and I climb up to keep it down. I am equipped with imaginary ropes and pitons to hammer into the unyielding stone. It takes me all day sometimes. I pause every three steps to inspect the towering cliff that rises before me. Beyond it, the peak is always there, orientating me in time and space.

Long days are conquered this way, my ropes taut, my resolution sure that the peak will eventually be achieved. I pause to take stock from the second-floor landing, a perilous ledge from which I gaze out over the misty mountains dissolving into the distance. My mother jogs past me and asks what I'm doing. I tell her about the mountain and the climb and she just chuckles and continues on to her room.

When I get to the top floor, body-rolling on to the landing with exhaustion, I allow myself a moment of reprieve to admire the blue dome of heaven above. Clouds drift majestic and slow, combing my face with shadow. I am free of all anxiety.

The climbing drama has stayed with me – a way to process tension that I rely on to this day. My paintings progress in granite increments that give me just enough satisfaction to persevere. The workmanship must be perfect, or I risk slipping into the abyss. I'm convinced that nothing works unless it has met the mountain and paid the price. The rest is approximate striving, lacking depth and purpose.

Eventually, I grow bored with the stairs. I must push further. I force open the attic hatch and pull down the steps for my final ascent. The attic wraps me in musty darkness, but I don't take fright. My eyes adjust, and I see the bell shape of dirty windows, spaced along one side. I stride the ceiling beams and crouch in a pool of daylight. There's nothing to see through the dusty pane. I hammer the ancient seals and push the window open, thrilling to the cool, louvred air. London fills the attic with sound; a thronging

*Climbing Arrows*

*Man Meditating*

*Stairs*

ocean-roar of life. The city dissolves in waves, moving away, from black to blue to misty grey. Taxis squeal like gulls. I look up and imagine white birds wheeling about my crow's nest. My voyage is complete. I must join them and fly away.

I monkey down the rigging, get back on to the stairs and clamber down the mountain. I look into the kitchen. A kettle is whistling, but Ettore isn't there. I go to the front door and pull it open. Brightness and cold. I get my coat, close the door, and step lightly down the white steps. Freedom feels good to my five years. My puppet-cords twine and I head east down South Street. At Waverton Place I turn right and head to Hill Street. There I turn right again, until I am walking up behind our house. My tummy is growling. Ettore will be putting tea on the table, Jaffa Cakes and shortbread on the Wedgewood china…

*What am I doing?*

I pause to consider my expedition. I have no food, no water, no shelter against the impending night. I am looking at the back of the house now – its quivering TV aerial picking up *Jackanory*, my favourite kid's programme. I see the coloured shapes of *Jackanory*'s opening, hear the sweet tinkle of its theme music, and my resolve vanishes. I am a child. I must go home.

Mummy says she is going to have to get us a proper nanny. We had one from Germany before the last one, who left because I was a bad boy. The Kraut made me eat spinach, and dried her laundry inside the house. The smell made me sick. And now I'm moving to a new school called Hill House which is very strict. It's right behind Harrods and the boys have to wear uniforms: mustard-coloured sweaters and burgundy shorts. It makes us look like 'poofters'. And I don't care for the teachers, either. Mrs Frost lives up to her name, and we have to march between classes like soldiers because the headman is a major. Today I was bad and the major made me face the wall and clench my hands behind my back like a prisoner.

After school I went outside by the front railings but no one came to pick me up. Then I saw Daddy walking down the street toward me with a big smile. I ran and jumped into his arms and he lifted me up. High. It felt so good.

It had been a whole year. I don't know why he was suddenly in London. Maybe for preliminary talks on *The Good Old Bad Old Days* – his last musical with Bricusse. He took Tara and me back to his suite at the Connaught, where we stripped the pillows from the sofas to build a show-jumping course. We cantered around on our fantasy steeds, jumping the stacked pillows as my father put on his cheesy American voice and announced my entry as 'Ralph Nader on his gamy chestnut, Pronto', at which point I collapsed in hysterics and couldn't continue – the name Ralph Nader for some reason nailing my funny bone.

After horsing around, Daddy moved us on to a discussion of meditation. He had recently discovered Zen Buddhism and wanted to share his bliss. Tara and I paid close attention as he showed us a red rose preserved inside a glass paperweight. He told us that the rose would reveal the magic of its beauty if we could look at it with total concentration – not the kind we used at school, but a concentration that wasn't forced, that rode in on successive waves of breath and deepened until the rose blossomed for us from its deepest core. This was Daddy's magic trick and we couldn't manage it for ourselves, not yet – but we sensed how important it was to him and we wanted to show him that we kind of understood.

The next day he flew back to Los Angeles.

# 4

## Fat Sue

STRETCHING WEST TO EAST ON A WIDE SWATH OF SANDY CLAY above London is the ancient parkland of Hampstead Heath. It covers almost 800 acres and embraces numerous ponds and woodlands. Constable painted his famous cloud studies there, brimming with his raw perception of nature's wildness. Keats, a long-time resident at Welsh Hill, first heard the sonorous notes of his signature nightingale while pausing for thought and refreshment at the Spaniards Inn; and Karl Marx, a veteran picnicker with his family, took brooding walks during the course of composing his great work, savouring the grand vistas of evil, capitalist London.

You cannot walk there without wanting to write, think, create; and if these inclinations fail to clamour about you, the Heath will leave you richly disturbed by an intimation of life unlived. I first walked its rolling hills and lost myself inside its gothic groves when I was six and its hold on me hasn't weakened since. Much as I visit 1106 looking for lost connection, I frequent the Heath whenever I'm in London for some potent reverie, travelling back in time to when I actually lived nearby.

Highgate Village rides up and over the eastern hump of the Heath and spills its traffic down the long curvature of Highgate Road that skirts the Heath's northernmost edge. Sheldon Avenue is one of many somnolent residential streets that feed off it: a wide, smoothly-tarmacked avenue lined with costly homes of diverse design. Some recall country manors with their Tudor facades and curving gravel drives; others have the modern, architecturally ambitious look of glass and steel – evidence of the area's popularity with artists and designers in the sixties and seventies.

Number 42 Sheldon Avenue sits behind a steep, semi-circular drive. The steps to the forecourt are hard to see; and I remember the night Johnny Gold, arriving late for my mother's thirtieth birthday, failed to break in time and plunged down them in his brand-new, mint-green Jensen, smashing the transmission to smithereens. I waited outside with him while he cursed a blue streak, until eventually the tow truck came. I savoured the tell-tale scrapes on the steps forever after.

The house is fronted by a robust growth of ivy that camouflages its essential ugliness and turns the oversize bungalow into something almost grand. My room sat behind one of the two 'eyes' in the house. There I brooded on drizzly afternoons, gazing at the empty avenue and trying to conjure up my mystical window at 1106.

We moved there in 1971, after my mother finally surrendered and agreed to marry Ron. South Street was kept as our town residence, but Mummy and Ron said we needed a bigger house in which to 'start a family'. At least that's what Ron wanted. My mother worried that having another child would further alienate Tara and me, but Ron allayed her fears, assuring her that we'd make it work as One Big Happy Family. Looking at him in the funhouse mirror, she saw an honest man.

As a stepfather, Ron was a non-event. He had walked out on a wife and three sons in Switzerland, dropping them wholesale for my mother, and was in no moral position to father anyone, let alone the son of another man. We bonded exclusively over cars. My first words had been: 'CA! CA!' and I could pretty much name the make and model of any car on the road by the time I was seven. Ron took me for a few thrilling top-down drives in his Maserati (the very car that had scared me witless at Summit), and to the pits at Silverstone, where I was photographed with Pedro Rodriguez shortly before the British Grand Prix of 1971. Other than this, he remained a virtual stranger to me. I was left with a gaping hole where a father should have been.

Tara was equally poleaxed by the paternal absence. But she dealt with it differently. She filled her Daddy-void with knick-knacks and diary entries, building an interior world of disaffected girlhood. We had drifted apart since the divorce. The choice was to survive together or go our separate ways on the desert island and we chose the latter course, unconsciously mimicking our parents.

My mother was flying blind with Ron. She had overlapped their affair with her failing marriage in a bid to free herself emotionally from my father, and therefore hadn't taken the necessary alone time to know herself – or Ron – before the next plunge. The need for a constant male presence in her life was in all likelihood a bad habit traceable to her father – the emotionally glacial and self-important theatrical agent, Joe Collins – who never gave his perfect little daughter the time of day. Every relationship thereafter became a quest for the father's love. But the old man wasn't listening; he'd long ago left the theatre, indifferent to his daughter's acting out.

Living with this painful truth informed her consciousness as an actress, and the awareness of her fear of emotional collapse helped her to develop the iron-clad persona that would eventually make her career.

In addition to her role in *Lo stato d'assedio* – an execrable Italian homage to Godard in which she had to bare her bosom – she did some films for TV, *The Persuaders!* among them, with Roger Moore and Tony Curtis, and then landed a recurring role in the long-running *Hammer Horror* TV series, for which she was crowned queen of the horror flicks. Her penchant for an outsized method of acting, with overly theatrical gestures and heavy timing, suited the genre. To look suddenly left and right with mounting dread was cinematic stuff she could sink her teeth into. She knew well how to portray a woman facing lurking threats, with trust always just beyond reach.

Ron purportedly offered her security and a release from anxiety. He was utterly head-over-heels with her; and she, in turn, basked in the glow of Total Love, which was something she had never experienced before, sensitive as she was to her father's coldness in a man. And like a good actress, she convinced herself that she was equally in love with him.

After Apple folded, Ron got it into his head to become a movie producer. Two efforts were trotted out in succession: *Melody* with Mark Lester, and *The Optimists* with Peter Sellers, neither of which did the slightest business. Undaunted, he had the attic at Sheldon Avenue painted blood-red and turned into a cinema. There Tara and I danced to the old jukebox my mother had shipped from 1106 (Alan Price's 'Simon Smith and His Amazing Dancing Bear' was our standby) and watched a few Clint Eastwood flicks and some blaxploitation films like *Shaft* and *Cleopatra Jones*. The Corvette-driving, machine-gun-toting heroine of the latter made a huge impression on me with her massive Afro and deep cleavage sheened with vixen sweat. Tara was convinced that the screening room was haunted by a ghost whose hands she could sense undulating in the window of the projection booth. I didn't believe her, but stopped going up there alone to mooch around and look at the framed stills of my mother's movies – all thirty-six of them hung in a chronological row.

My mother soon established herself and Ron as *the* hip Hampstead couple with a coterie of chic nether-London friends. Their marriage ceremony took place in Jamaica in October 1972. Tara and I were not invited, but were treated to the photographs. My mother looked stunning in a white gypsy dress with plunging neckline, and Ron was all shiny-cheeked happiness in a cream three-piece suit. Shortly afterward, she announced to us that she was pregnant. The mummy hormones did the rest and after all the disappointments of recent years, she was back on the Yellow Brick Road to happiness. She started filling photo albums with pictures (her favourite pastime) and the new, heavily edited version of life on Sheldon Avenue took fantastic shape: there were birthdays and picnics on the Heath, location jaunts on her films, tropical getaways with Ron...

Sifting through these albums now, I see that the colossal grey eminence behind all this fun has been cut from the story. My mother and I fill the frame in the foreground, smiling in our party hats, while the principal caregiver of my youth, the atlas of my world, blurrily exits or enters in the background. And yet, without her, the whole edifice would have crumbled. Ron might have posed happily beside me for a photograph but I don't remember *his* hand on my shoulder, ever. The presence that fills the frame of my heart to bursting is that of a very big woman from Bristol called Sue Delong.

New York City, 2007. I woke up one morning with the feeling that Sue was still sitting on me, squashing the life out of me. I had to throw her off my back. It felt like a matter of life and death.

I started the painting soon afterward. It was a very literal expression of what I was feeling, and had been feeling, for thirty-five years. The humungous lummox was shutting me down. The confidence and self-belief I needed to succeed as an artist was always just beyond me. I couldn't climb the mountain with Sue still astride me.

As I worked on the painting, my burden morphed and metastasized. I kept adding flesh, making her bigger and bigger until she threatened to spill over the sides of the canvas. I was now a man of forty-two, reimagining the terror that had plagued me as a little boy – I was dragging myself kicking and screaming back to the age of six. When Sue's carping voice boomed in my skull, all the helplessness and impotence overwhelmed me again.

I laboured on the painting up until the morning it had to be shipped to London for my exhibition. Later, as I hung it in the gallery I felt elated that I had finally told the truth about something. But at the opening, my mother passed it by without comment. I was astonished. Did she not recognize the giantess from my childhood? I was about to say something but stopped myself. The giantess said not to. She had always protected my mother from me.

Where's Mummy? I'm so hot. I want to be sick. The red wallpaper is full of gangster voices, calling me names, wanting to kill me. Huge numbers fall on me like a waterfall, pounding me down, one, two, three, four... The gavel bangs, the judge demands silence. He leans down and looks at me; his eyes are big and scary. I roll over... the sheets hiss and boil... I see an oil tanker sitting on its blade. The sea has pulled out. Hot and dry, the land ticks. Now the tanker groans, inclining my way... A shadow gains across the land, picking

*Self-Portrait Carrying the Fat Lady*

up speed… I can't move… moan of cramped steel as I brace for impact; one, two, three, four… the fat lady is coming… The door bursts open and there she is, all of her, shushing me, telling me to be quiet. I can see her eyes flashing in the dark. She tucks me in tight and leaves me to the darkness; the TV in the next room, the gangster voices calling me names: little shit, sonofabitch, we're gonna get you…

Of course they were mine, those voices. They had no one to blame but myself. *I* was the cause of my missing father, my nervous mother, my interminable roll-call of nannies – and they were going to kill me for it.

The assassin arrived in the spring of 1971. She answered the ad that my mother had placed in the papers for a long-term nanny, and had come to Sheldon Avenue for the interview, which took place as I kicked a ball around the garden. My mother told her about my problems, my broodiness alternating with anxiety and the big lady knowingly nodded. She had helped bring up five younger brothers and knew the drill – she could handle difficult boys. My mother was impressed by her resolve and felt that she understood the kind of all-encompassing help a working actress needed.

When Sue waddled toward me across the garden, arms semi-lifted by the fat spilling from the sides of her bra, she smiled as if she already knew me. I saw my mother watching approvingly from the top window; and so, when Sue asked me to, I passed her the ball. We booted it back and forth for a while, and she surprised me with her sense of fun. She was too fat to lean and use the top of her foot and could only punt the ball with her toe, which sent it repeatedly flying over my head. I got tired of fetching it from the bushes and announced that I was going to climb a tree.

'Go on then,' she goaded.

I clambered on to the branches, and my mother shrieked from the window.

'Don't worry,' said Sue, 'I'm watching him.'

My mother paused momentarily at the window, then disappeared inside. And that, without much fanfare, was the day my life passed into the care of Sue Delong.

Sue has short hair. Her accent is pure Bristol. She has big bosoms and calls them Bristol Cities, which is cockney rhyming slang for titties. I have a lot of fun with her. She likes cars as much as I do and she drives fast. One time, in Oxford Street, we were in traffic and she got mad and drove up on to the pavement to get around the buses. The shoppers scattered and dropped their bags. Another time we were going to school in the Mini and had a crash. We were late and crossed the intersection and a car skidded into us. Sue was angry because I tipped forward and almost hit the windshield.

I like wrestling with Sue. I can hit her really hard and she doesn't feel a thing. But sometimes I hit her in the Bristols and that hurts a little and then she takes my hand and bends the fingers back until I scream. She smiles then with sparkly eyes. Her laugh is very big and climbs in galumphing hills until she sounds like a man. She is a bit like a man, come to think of it, but her feet are very small, and she wears white Adidas. Her slacks are spandex for her thick legs and when she walks they chafe and tick with static. She smells a bit, a sweetish stink of fat, but I don't mind. She likes hamburgers and milkshakes as much as I do. She takes me to the Hard Rock Cafe on Park Lane and we love the loud music. She says she likes everything about America and hopes we can go there.

Sometimes Sue and Mummy argue and Sue goes to her room and slams the door. She puts on her red earphones and listens to Earth, Wind & Fire and Barbra Streisand and The Carpenters. I like The Carpenters, too. I understand why that lady's voice soothes Sue so.

She would emerge from these sessions with Karen Carpenter refreshed and ready to submit to the yoke of servitude. She made my meals, took me to school and picked me up, bathed me and watched TV with me. She set my boundaries and freedoms. I would depart from her schedule only for weekend photo-ops with Mummy and Ron and return to it with a mixture of dread and consolation.

Her arguments with my mother were mostly about me. My mother felt that Sue was infringing on her authority. Sue felt that my mother was in no position to judge what was best for me. There had been an unspoken pact between employer and employed from the beginning: *I cannot deal with the emotional demands of my children; please lock them down.* But my mother reserved the right to take back the reins whenever she wanted to. Only Sue couldn't let go. In that, she was unprofessional. Her commitment to me was obsessive. I was HER boy.

Counting backward I figure that she was born in 1949, as she was twenty-one when she came to work for us. The rest is sketchy. I know she was adopted at birth and grew up in a poor part of Bristol. Her adoptive father left and she was raised by her mother, who married again and had four boys in rapid succession. That father also left, and Sue grew up as the elder sister of the brood. She had no so-called higher education. Her first job was driving an ice cream van in Bristol. I was her second.

She was intelligent and intuitive and generally buoyant in mood. These high spirits were marred by frightening downbeats, during which she would disappear. Perhaps that's when the self-medicating and the binging occurred. She must have had an eating disorder, because there's no other way to account for her bulk. At five-foot-two, she weighed well over 250 pounds. But it wasn't a lumbering mass. She could move quickly, even balletically at times. She prided herself on that, and in contrast delighted in pointing out my mother's heavy footfalls, pounding across the floor above.

She didn't think much of Ron and made sure he knew it. He was intimidated by her – and his stutter grew perceptibly worse in her presence. She didn't respect boundaries, which was refreshing or scary, depending on how you looked at it. Ron rarely dealt with her directly. I can still see him patting his pockets for car keys, desperate to flee confrontations with her. That's how Sue succeeded in becoming indispensable to us. She saw the man-hole at the centre of our family and filled it with her blubber and concrete presence.

With her butch haircut and her predilection for dressing in shirts and trousers, she was probably – given the mores of the time – lesbian. There was never a trace or a hint of a boyfriend during the whole time she was with us, but a few lady friends would routinely drop by for a glass of beer and a chat. I felt her energy as male and didn't question it. I even welcomed it, because I had repeatedly asked my mother for a brother, and was, of course, missing a father. But what made her so engulfing to me was her emotionalism. She loved movies and music and beauty. She certainly wasn't cut out for any normal, commonplace job, despite her salt-of-the-earth self-reliance and British-working-class vigour. She had gifts. She knew she had; and I felt it, too. But she had no way of expressing them, beyond her nurturance of me.

Despite her levelling attitude to class and rank she was star-struck and loved basking vicariously in the limelight when so-called Big Names came to the house. When Streisand showed up one day, she went bananas, and begged my mother take a photograph of them together. In the cherished shot, Streisand wears a laconic smile as Sue, flushed and sweaty, edges into the great diva's aura with a look of explosive, button-lipped happiness. The photo graced her bedside table from that day on.

On the rare occasions that she wanted to, she could achieve a surface polish of presentation, right down to stunning diction and the most calligraphically perfect penmanship. Her voice could be soft and sensitive, but was more comfortable at the crude end of the spectrum; and her laugh was an enormous, wobbling affair of explosions and stentorian yelps.

She could size up a person at a glance with her quick, dark eyes; her pupils merged with dark-brown irises and had that Picasso look of depth penetration. She loved to slip back into Bristol dialect to make me laugh. 'You can't, can you?' became, 'Thou casn't, cast?' and 'It isn't in the tin', the madly alliterative 'Tain't tin tin.' She would frequently adjust her Brobdingnagian breasts with a proud, upward scoop of her bra, quipping 'Just adjustin' me overflow.' Then, with dulcet tones, she would become Mary Poppins again, sending herself up and making me wonder at her surreal nature. Perversely, when I would swoon with love for her, she would bring me up short with a dinner knife cocked my way, growling: 'Finish that plate NOW or I'll brain ya!!'

Her discipline was administered with a guillotine – you did what she said or off rolled your head. I had several what felt like near-death experiences at her hands, the blood pressure pounding in my skull as her wheezing bulk ground me into the carpet. Something between a laugh and a scream escaped my lips as she repeated the latest line of discipline: 'You won't do that again, will you, Kiddo, no sirree, Bob, now let me hear you say it…' and so on, until I recanted and the pressure was released. At that point, I almost levitated off the ground. Earth gravity was nothing compared to eyeball-squashing Sue-gravity.

Sitting on me was not her only method of control. She had finer instruments in her torture arsenal. Dead legs, as she called them, were administered with a customized fist, her middle knuckle set forward like a battle flint. This bone-point was pounded into the soft tissue of my thigh, causing me to spontaneously collapse, as if my motor cortex had been disabled. Dead legs produced the juiciest bruises: large purple affairs with a swollen brown centre that lasted through a fading blue-green iris for weeks. To gently press the bruise and release a pain-pulse became a fetishistic pleasure for me – battle scars recollected in relative tranquillity. The 'noogie', so popular in American schools, took this same painful knuckle jab to the head. This entailed Sue taking me in a flailing arm-lock so she could concentrate her efforts on the crown of my skull. Round and round went the fat ballpoint of her knuckle until my skull burned with a thousand torn follicles. This produced slow-building screams that crested in a gurgly silence.

Our wrestling had been witnessed by my mother and Ron and passed off as child's play. But these more pointed assaults on the child were reserved for drizzly afternoons when my mother was away on location, Ron in London, and the lonely house could freely resound with my blood-curdling screams.

I fought back with all my little might. But there was another kind of force in me – as mysterious as it was defiant – that Sue didn't understand, and could only address combatively. Had she been able to speak to this place in me, she might have discovered a child alive with conjurings and inspirations. As it was, she was unsettled by these glimmerings, and the jobbing disciplinarian in her elbowed forward to interpret my creative energy as insubordination. No wonder I made the unfortunate connection between self-expression and slamming judgement that afflicts me to this day.

But I did have my little victories. One enchanted evening, I actually knocked Goliath out cold. There she lay, at the bottom of the stairs, while I jabbered with panic and ran to the kitchen to fill a bucket with water. She woke as I held the slopping bucket over her and her revenge was swift. She picked me up and began imagining what she could make with the long balloons that were my arms and legs. Inspiration struck. She put me on the floor to brace her effort and ripped off my shoes and socks. Then she bent my legs back until my toes caught in my belt loops. I howled and rolled around like a legless gimp. Then she picked me up by the waistband and marched me through the house to the front door, opened it, deposited me on the prickly mat and shut me out.

There were also pleasurable interludes. Sue's pleasure mostly. She was plagued by back pain – the cumulative strain of carrying around those enormous breasts – and ordered a massage device from some catalogue. It goes without saying at this point that I was pressed into service as her masseur. She stripped to the waist and lay face down on her bed. I tucked in my pyjama top and mounted up, Ahab on the white whale. I was confronted by a twelve-hook bra. The first few hooks were easy pickings, but as I proceeded down, the pressure of all that constricted flesh incrementally increased, until the final two hooks seemed fused together.

'What's taking ya, Kid?' she complained.

I took a deep breath, keened close with trembling elbows, and managed to disengage the truculent hooks. Her bra whipped open and her width suddenly doubled across the bed. She sighed, and settled into deeper, calmer water. Fully in charge now, I shook the white, modular device from its Styrofoam packaging and unwound the power cord. Which massage head should I use? The French Tickler? The Hard Node? The Claw? I plugged in the power cord and mounted back up, John Wayne before the charge. I unholstered the special lotion and squirted a cold zigzag across her back. She shivered with pleasure as my fingers splayed and worked in the grease, buttering her hump. I dried my hands and held triumphantly aloft the Vibrathon 2000. I turned it on and slowly lowered it into position.

The Claw sucked and gummed on to her flesh, getting in amid the fillets of muscle. She moaned, and urged: 'Harder, harder… that's good, oh…' I held my love machine firmly in place, letting my energy find its way deep into her trouble. Then I moved intuitively, seeking out the knots and burrs in the flowing grain of her back. I found a dimpled nerve and worked it through. She snarled with pleasure as I ploughed a straight furrow up her spine, pushing the bulge of tension till it exploded through the top of her head in a long sigh.

Mastery. This must be what John Wayne felt like when he rode the tied-up baddie into town past the falling arms of the gunslingers, agape at his audacity. I looked at her squashed profile, the lips a drooling figure eight. I could kill her now if I wanted to – draw a long sword from under the bed and finish her off. I switched off the machine and listened to her snoring. I observed the pearly stretch marks, like snail-trails, converging on her armpits, the expanse of her back a slab of slimy dough.

I rolled off her, and one eye opened: 'Where you going?'

'I thought you were asleep.'

'Go on then, hop it.'

I crossed the landing and climbed into my bunk bed. I lay there inhaling the smell of her oil. I dreamt of a deep swim with her, like a whale calf, holding to her side as the bubbles skittered across us. *My blue mother, where are you going, and how will I ever grow in your shadow?*

'All right Kiddo?'

'Yeah.'

'How was your day?'

'All right.'

'Mummy called from location today. She really misses you.'

'Can we watch *The Waltons* tonight, Sue?'

'No, that's Thursday; tonight's *Panorama*.'

'I don't want to watch that...'

'Shut it. You have to learn about the world... And don't forget your bath tonight, and a letter to your Dad tomorrow –'

'But Sue –'

'Oi!! What'd I tell you?! You have to write your Dad. Capisce?'

'I never know what to say...'

'Just draw a nice picture and say you love him. That's all he wants to hear. All right?'

'Yeah.'

'Good boy.'

In the photos by her bedside we appear happy together. I pose in my tracksuit before soccer practice, her leg-of-mutton arm around my shoulder. We stand in front of Sheldon Avenue next to Mummy's gold Mercedes. At Longleat, we smile from the safety of our Mini as baboons clamber over it.

I don't know where she ends and I begin. She's in my space all the time – she *is* my space – and when she isn't, I'm empty. She attributes my sadness to absent parents. She resents them because she was an orphan herself. Now she has a chance to reverse her abandonment through me. I am not allowed to be sad or melancholy because it triggers Sue's pain. Nor am I ever able to confess my need for my own mother. This would be tantamount to saying I didn't need Sue. So I am marooned between two mothers, unable to reach out for, or feel safe with, either.

Green and white and gold – the colours of Mummy's room. Sue said I shouldn't go in here, but I'll be careful not to move anything. The brass bed frame is grand and woven with fronds and fruits. I press my cheek against the cold metal and use my sleeve to polish it. The knobbly white bedspread is pulled tight, the pillows fan out in perfect order. On the bedside table: a tissue box sheathed in silver; and Mummy's eye mask, crusted with night cream. I open the bedside drawer and find her blackcurrant pastels in their golden tin. I open the flashing box and take one; the pastel melts and stains my mouth with purple syrup. I breathe in, savouring the fruit.

The wallpaper is full of leaves and flowers with strands of pearls woven through. The pattern repeats across the strips, but doesn't quite match. I inspect closely, wanting to press and push to make them blend.

In Mummy's mirrored bathroom I toggle the lights on and off. My face repeats down an endless curve of mirrors into infinity. The closet sighs open in a wave of scent. Deep and dark inside. I let the cloth flow over me. I twist the dresses and feel their patterns: chilly beads, sharp-edged sequins, tickling feathers. Jewellery hangs in coral bunches; spiky shoes march up the wall in rows. How can she walk on claws and pins?

I take a toy car from my pocket and run the bidet. I kneel down and drive my car against the flow. Then I push it along the marble bath. Here Mummy strokes and bastes herself with a coral sponge – dry and hard now, still smelling of lavender. With this foot stone she rubs off toughened skin and with this razor she smooths her foamy legs. Here's the golden bath oil that anoints her, its pearly gobs floating in the steam.

On her dressing table everything is in perfect order. I twist out a lipstick that smells of pasty roses. The nail polish is dark, like dragon blood. And here's the magic crystal that holds her smell. I squeeze the bud and watch a puff of dandelion scent roll out to nothing. I swipe it back and inhale her; then, too late, realize: Sue will know I'm covered in Mummy's flowers.

I go to the garage to change my smell. It's cold and damp where Mercedes and Maserati sleep together. The man-car is dreaming – it wants to race. I run my hands over its white streamlined curves. I kick the tires, capped with stars and kneel down to finger the gleaming spokes. The roll of tire flab pressing the cold floor is like Sue's thigh.

I throw the latch and heave the bonnet open. In sudden light, snaking pipes seethe and tighten around the engine block. The smell of rubber and oil is the ooze of their activity. They drool and stain the floor, hungry for the road. I can't resist; I pull open the heavy door and slide inside. A breath of alcohol mixed with leather banishes Mummy's scent. I grasp the mahogany wheel, transfixed by the Maserati trident in its pearlescent dome. My fingers find the wheel's ribs; my hands squeeze, knuckles whitening, as the engine revs. The gearshift is trembling to be touched. I tease it back and forth and find the perfect fit of first gear. The clutch comes out gently, the garage opens its gaping mouth and I roll outside. I turn the stiff wheel and coast down Sheldon Avenue. I step on it and the dragon-car wails. It wants to find a way out of London, so congested, so unfriendly to my feelings. We cannot fly until the buildings lie down and the road peels open before us: the wide strip of the M1 going north, the polished blue tarmac and pulsing white lines.

I feel the engine heat creep back through the car, burning away the body to show the frantic pistons underneath. Mummy's Mercedes speeds alongside, but cannot prevail. My mouth makes an ultimate engine sound: fifth gear, pedal flat – a white-hot whine in my head as the chequered flag sways and gives me the victory. In my child's mind's eye, the crowd goes wild. I wave from the Maserati on a victory lap. Then the garage door bangs open, shattering my win: 'Ey! What the bloody 'ell you doin!'

Sue comes up from behind and pulls open the door, 'Didn't I tell you about playing in the cars, ey?' She yanks me out, 'You'll ruin the bloody transmission. D'you know how much this car is worth? Do you? Answer me! A bloody lot. Now get to the kitchen, go on, hop it – NOW!!'

I have no appetite. Tara has finished her meal and been excused, but I must sit over my cold fish fingers and baked beans – a disgusting spill, like frogspawn. Sue jabs her knife at me: 'EAT!'

I push my fork under the peas and take a dry, pasty mouthful. I look at the pictures of trains on the walls made of different kinds of pasta, but they don't please me any more. Sue chews, looking blank, and swallows heavily. She cuts and forks up with her right hand, but her left is clasped over the table in an effete gesture that irritates me.

'Can I watch *The Waltons* tonight, Sue?'

'You've got a lot of bloody nerve…'

'Sue, please.'

She takes a slug of coke, sucks on her molars, then pounds the table: 'FINISH YOUR BLOODY DINNER – OR I'LL FINISH *YOU*! CAPISCE!?'

I climb on to her bed and get comfy. Sue wears a caftan, with her Flintstone feet poking out. We cuddle up. *The Waltons* starts, the music bouncing along and making everything cheerful. The mountains and the pines and the dusty roads are old and beautiful. All the Waltons have clear eyes and feel things very deeply. John Boy has to think a lot because he'll be a man soon. I wish *I* was at the centre of a family with everyone looking up to me.

The father has the bluest eyes. His creases and lines are from experience, and when he smiles, they all gather round and that makes his smile bigger. That's what being a Walton is about: how you get through the hard things in a big house where everybody says goodnight to each other.

Sue lifts me into bed and I can tell she's happy. Her voice is high like Mary Poppins's. 'I'm taking you to Bristol tomorrow to meet my Mam and brothers. Excited? Good boy!'

The next morning, the world is white. I look at the carpeted avenue from my window and fog the glass with delight. The snow stays all the way up to Bristol. Everything is coated – included in the whiteness and softness – even the church spires. Bristol gets suddenly ugly near Sue's house. The streets close in and the houses are small and poor.

'This is where I went about in my ice cream van,' she says. 'Seems like a hundred years ago… And there's the corner where I turned it over, going so fast I was… I loved that sodding van!'

We turn a corner and there it is, Sue's house, like a pile of dirty plates. We walk up the cracked drive and see a boy in the garage working on a car. He's a friend of one of Sue's brothers and she punches him hello. We look at the car – lime green with a black stripe. He tells us that he painted it himself. I look closely at the black stripe and see a botched edge where the tape came away. The engine hangs on a chain overhead. He reaches inside up to his ear and pulls out a dirty engine part he's going to replace. He turns it under my eyes to show the damage. His oily-black hands are beautiful.

'Allo…' says Sue's mam, leaning in the doorway. She looks at me with folded arms and tight lips. We follow her into the kitchen, which smells of old grease and disinfectant. The pipes are peeling and there's moss bubbling up the walls. She talks with a cigarette stuck to her bottom lip. Her white face is angry and her red hair goes up in a fuse. She scares me.

In the front room, the brothers wrestle and knock things over. Sue yells at them to stand up and be polite. Their names are Stephen, David, and Fats (because he's so skinny). Stephen is the eldest and has pimples and whiskers. He works in a factory. I say my name and shake all their hands and the hot room seems very small. I go to the window and look out. There's a slice of worn grass and a clothesline with pegs and a little tree tipping the sky. A train goes by and makes the crockery tremble.

Then we have Sunday roast. Mam brings in thin slices of beef in watery blood and potatoes. The boys eat like gentlemen and Sue asks them about school and work. She's very proud of them. Mam smokes and looks hard at me. Then it's time for *Mastermind*. We sit around the TV, and a friend called Jez comes over from across the street. The quizmaster asks a question about Shakespeare and Jez gets it first: 'Julius Caesar.' Everyone punches him and Sue knocks his glasses off because he's so sodding clever.

At bedtime, Fats gives me his room and extra blankets. I feel strange getting into his bed. I pull up the covers. They're so thin, like aeroplane blankets. I look at the gas fire making wobbly lines in the dark. I like it here, even though it smells funny. For some reason I dream of the house going up in flames.


Katyana Kennedy Kass was born in June 1972. Ron turned to jelly; my mother, to butter. Sue boiled the formula and changed the nappies. Contractors and decorators had turned Tara's room into a nursery and constructed a new room for her over the garage. There she sat, surrounded by guardian tchotchkes, scribbling in her diary. I lingered in her doorway, hoping for connection, but she peered beetle-browed over that infernal diary to which she was no doubt confiding, *Sacha is at my door again, the shitty little pest, I wish he'd go away...*

She knew I'd developed crushes on all her girlfriends: Jane Pample, Jacqui Hawler, Lisa Guild. I was always on hand to pad out their make-believe with my renditions of a tight-lipped Indian brave, a donkey, a rampaging monster – anything in exchange for my not being, for a few brief moments, an irritation to be endured. I left Tara's doorway and wandered over to the nursery where Sue was dealing with a soiled, bile-green nappy. Katy's eyes scanned the room and her fingers reached out to infinity. She was the new, supreme value in the house.

Overcome by paternal feeling, Ron tried to mend relations with the children he'd abandoned back in Switzerland. They joined us at Christmas and for summer holidays in Spain: three sullen, dark-skinned boys who spoke mostly Italian and resented us for stealing their father. My mother's Christmas card that year shows us all by the pool of our holiday villa in Marbella: five bewildered children, two ferociously smiling adults, one cradled baby. 'Christmas is a time for kids,' reads the card. 'Have some of ours!'

The sentiment was not lost on us. Our holidays ran parallel to our parents', but they were on a separate trip. All childhood trials and tribulations were automatically referred to Sue and word of them was rarely allowed to reach the ears of the basking, poolside whales. The Kass boys may have been back with Dad, but they were under the jurisdiction of Sue. When Robert, the middle one, refused to change his bathing suit for lunch, he received swift justice. Sue went after him and he ran toward the pool, thinking, silly boy, that he could elude capture by jumping in. The look on his face was priceless as he danced on his toes in the shallow end and realized: *No, she's not slowing down; in fact, she's accelerating... Oh shit!* He tried to wade to the steps but it was too late: fully clothed, Sue launched into space and came down upon him in a cataclysm of foam. Poor Robert enjoyed a few gulps of air before she forced him under and keelhauled him back and forth underwater. He came up coughing and spluttering for mercy, which never worked – Sue *liked that* – and she forced him under again with renewed vigour. When she was finished with him (his vomiting gouts of water and offal may have convinced her that the lesson was complete), she got out of the water, shook herself dry like a massive bulldog and laughed all the way back to the house. Robert sat on the shallow-end steps, shivering and convulsively sobbing. I tried to comfort him but he batted my hand away. *Welcome to the world of Sue.*

Sue is really good at cooking. She makes potato cakes with onions and peppers, and huge jugs of sangria for the grown-ups. I love the Nutella she gives us for breakfast. This morning I caught a lizard and its tail came off in my hand, still moving. Then I put my hand in a flower and got a bee sting. Sue was actually sorry about that. She gave me ice to put on it. Mummy is really good at Scrabble. She beats the men. She sits there in dark glasses and concentrates really hard. I like that she's so clever and can put down long words that score high. Everybody says she cheats, but she just smiles and lifts her shoulder. Sometimes she argues very hard and you could swear she doesn't cheat but then you remember that she's an actress.

Ron likes to put Ambre Solaire on her. He slips off her bikini and smooths it on in big loving circles. It looks like marmalade but goes on clear. Sometimes Ron sits with the baking foil under him and gets really cooked. He looks so happy and hairy with his gold medallions.

Mummy doesn't like troubled water so she waits till we're all out of the pool before she goes in. She does the breaststroke back and forth and never gets her face wet. She wears a big hat so the sun won't get on her face and make her old.

When I first saw Sue in a bathing suit, I almost died. She appeared in a black one-piece, waddling past the disgusted faces of my mother's guests. In the pool, we children quickly lined up our inflatable canoes, chanting: 'Sue! Make Waves! Make Waves!' She broke into a run and plunged. The surge she created was stupendous. We rode it with rodeo yelps and begged for more. For such a big woman, she was indefatigable, repeatedly hauling herself out of the water to renew the charge.

Let's watch in slow motion as she turns about at the far end of her run-up, flicks the spray from her hair and launches into another spectacle of ballooning breasts and rippling arms, charging past the slim and nut-brown bodies of the schmoozing grown-ups, her oatmeal thighs a shocking concussion of gyres and blubbering up swells, her garish smile building in a knowing compact with what she is about to do: entertain the kids, fulfil them as she fulfils herself... There she goes now, launching into space, the legs brought forward to ride the air in a sitting position, the toes and fingers splayed, the mouth agape as the children paddle in place and watch her land. What a blast of whiteness and splitting atoms... what a superhuman being.

On hot afternoons, as the sangria-stoned grown-ups snored by the pool to the murmuring accompaniment of Sergio Mendes, Sue sensed that the kids were drifting. She'd grab the car keys to the gold Mercedes and take us on long drives into the Spanish countryside. She'd always manage to find an unmarked mountain road and drive us up to where we could gaze at the sea from a lonely peak, or lose ourselves in dusty forests of pine. On one of these forays, I made the mistake of pleading for an unscheduled pee. Re-emerging from the bushes, I found myself all alone. The car had quietly moved off downhill and was fast disappearing. I yelled and sprinted after it, my espadrilles slapping painfully on the hot tarmac, until I saw the brake lights wink on and gratefully slowed for breath. Tara and Robert giggled in the back window; I could see Sue's eyes in the rear-view, patiently regarding me as I got closer. I went for the door but she sped off again – to Tara's squeals of delight. She got me down the mountain like this, leashing me with false hope until I was stumbling around like a drunken puppet. That was the cue for the game to end.

On another outing, by the sea, we chanced down a dusty track and discovered a deserted beach. The waves sucked and plunged. Sue cajoled us in with her and we waded forward against the ferocious pull. She lunged ahead, breasting the surge; then suddenly lost her balance. She turned, pale-faced, slipping in the undertow, shouting: 'Go back… get out – NOW!' We tried with all our might, but the current swept around us and carried us screaming toward her. She put her arms out and caught us like leaves in a drain. Head down, Samson between the pillars, she strained against the current. Seaweed whipped past me, lashing my legs. Tara screamed and choked as the tide bilged over her face, while Sue panted and gurgled and cycled against the dragging grains until her feet got a purchase and we slipped the bonds of the elastic surf, lurching all together on to the sand.

We sobbed and clung to her dripping thighs, looking up at her heaving chest. I knew she had just saved my life; what I couldn't accept was that she had endangered it.

Out of boredom we turned to amateur theatrics, raiding my mother's closet for costumes. At her dressing table I made myself up as a clown, like I'd seen Daddy do, with thumbed black eyebrows and a blackberry nose. Tara was a butterfly with delirious purple eye make-up flecked with glitter.

At curtain time, Mummy and Ron gathered in the doorway of our bedroom. The portable played 'Live and Let Die' as Tara flew back and forth, dragging my mother's Pucci scarves. Robert got into the act – from atop the bunk bed, wearing a wig and pulling at his braids, he implored: 'Romeo, Romeo, wherefore art thou…?' At which point I flushed the bathroom toilet and rushed out breathlessly. Big laugh.

In the evenings, Mummy and Ron dressed for yet another night at the Marbella Club. Ron wore white slacks, loafers and a blue shirt to set off his tan. My mother was all flamenco-chic, with glossy lips and bottomless eyes of danger. Ron couldn't quite believe his luck: his boys back in the fold, Katy in the manger and this beautiful creature his loving wife. It didn't get any better than this. And it never would.

The matador came out very proud and everybody cheered. He looked at Mummy and swept off his hat and bowed. Ron didn't like that. Mummy smiled back and then quickly covered her mouth because the bull was charging. The matador did a dance that made fun of the bull and the bull got angrier and angrier, and made so many charges at the silly red dress he was wearing. The matador was good at tricking him, like he was holding candy and pulling it away at the last minute. I wanted the bull to have the candy but I knew that would mean the matador got killed, so then I wasn't so sure. Mummy said Picasso was there but she didn't show me where. Ron was filming as the bull stumbled about. Then the picadors appeared and stuck it from all sides with spears.

Then the bull came close and I saw its scared eyes. But something kept making it put its head down and charge after that stupid red dress. Then it got so tired it just stopped. The spears stuck out all over its back. The blood was oozing out like maple syrup. The matador looked like a ballerina in his slippers. He was pleased with himself now that the bull was on its last legs. It was honking as it breathed. The matador had a sword by his head, long and curved, and he was aiming down it. Sue pulled me back as the matador swooped and the stinger went in and the bull crumpled. It shook its ears, then laid its head down low and died. The matador was walking around with his hat off and his face lifted high and everyone was cheering. Mummy threw a flower and then Picasso stood, applauding – an old man, very small – and everyone was roaring and clapping for him, too. Then men on horses came and dragged the bull away and it made a long red line in the sand.

# 5

# King Alfred's

HAD I BEEN ENROLLED AT THE AGE OF SIX IN SOME STUFFY, conservative, rule-driven school, I think I would have caved. As it was, the hippy, art-saturated atmosphere of King Alfred's in Hampstead gave me air to breath. We called our teachers by their first names (even the headmaster: Frank) and spent our days manipulating clay and papier mâché. Christmases were festivals of invention during which the school mess hall was transformed by us kids into a cave of delights: striding giants of tinsel with helium-balloon heads, fat Santas with tethered puppet arms chasing looping strings of reindeer. Little as I was, I played a big part in the creation of these phantasms – kneeling on the floor, painting on faces or cutting out paper pads that could open into long accordion strips. It was my first intimation that art was a form of magic – 'white magic', if you will, unfurling its miracles in full view, without deceit.

Unfortunately, the school's whole-hearted embrace of creativity left little room for the three 'Rs' and I quickly developed age-inappropriate deficits in all these areas. My writing and reading were below par (I would eventually learn to read simple sentences from street billboards at the advanced age of nine) and my maths skills were non-existent.

But what we Alfredians lacked academically, we amply made up for in other ways. The school's goal was not so much to mould character as to set free whatever character we had, along lines unique to each individual. Now, many of my friends could only be described as feral. With Marcus, the most reckless of these, I once, tremblingly, shoplifted. (It was a Twix, and it turned to ashes upon my conscience-stricken palate.) Peter could turn his eyelids inside out and draw the most amazing air-battle scenes with ruled, stutter-gun aim. Saul, a precociously verbose and bitter kid, once called down to the defunct handball courts where we were having a gang meeting, 'Time for class, you fucking fascist pigs.' Nice, coming from a boy of seven.

The greatest expenditure of our energy was reserved for Kiss Chase. Feelings and dynamisms between the sexes were encouraged at this progressive and, indeed, propulsive school; and Kiss Chase was seen as a healthy expression of this. I was very keen on a little brunette with a baby voice and a demon intelligence, but she spurned me. To my mounting horror I became the object of affection, and the gazelle-like prey, of a Sue-sized girl. She would run me down with aplomb and smother me with repulsive, slobbery kisses. As accustomed as I was to enormous controlling women, this was too much.

British Bulldog was a sort of pitched battle between the upper and lower schools. We would stand at opposite ends of a turfy, torn-up field and run at one another, rending the air with the blood-curdling cries of medieval field troops. The object was to get to the other side without being caught, lifted, and smashed down on the ground. The criss-crossing traffic slowly thinned out, until there were only a few heroic souls left to make the charge and try to wriggle through. We would trudge back to our classrooms bloodied and muddied and resume work on our frescoes and woodwork houses and papier mâché heads. It was a thrilling, rough-and-tumble sensorium of a school, and it encouraged my connection to something wild and untameable in myself.

Dawn is my teacher and I love her. She's tall and wears purple tops. I can see her bosoms and they're small, not Bristols like Sue's. She speaks low and soft and breathy and has straight brown hair that curls under. Her jeans are faded and they swish as she moves about.

I like that sound. Behind her fringe her eyes shine. When she looks at me, her eyes hold me. Her words push me where I want to go. I draw for her and she always says, 'That's good, Sacha, that's really wonderful, do more…' I do dragons and birds, and sometimes I do black boats in silhouette on a calm sea. I'm always happy when I'm drawing for Dawn. She smiles when I make the rickety spikes that go up a dragon's back, or the orange fire that comes wriggling out of its mouth.

I use Copydex glue and I hate it. It smells like sick. But I like how it dries in yellow gobs that frill the tin. I like to pull them off and snap them. Then I pour a cool spill of glue from inside and watch it spread across the coloured paper. I draw it out into white spikes that soften as they spread. When the paper goes down over them it sticks and stays put. I cut flower petals and stick them down, or giant spines for my dragon. Before the leftover glue dries, I rub it quickly with my fingers till it gathers into little dirty roly-polies that blow away.

The powder paint is in tight tins that Dawn helps me pry open. The powder inside is dark and rich and ready for water to draw out its scarves of colour. Now I can paint Sue with a big round shape and stick legs. I put myself in, too, holding her stick hand. Then I put the sky in, high, high above us, a blue strip that will never come down.

I love clay most of all. The grey sacks are stacked in heavy piles, covered in plastic to keep them moist. I like untying the candy twist and freeing the smell of damp earth inside. I reach in and tear off a chunk and work it in my hands. I add water, so it gleams and goes slimy. I make dinosaurs, with slabs for the body and columns for the legs. I make one to take home and guard my room at Sheldon. I lacquer him in bottle green, and put him on my windowsill. The soles of his feet have no glaze, but they have my initials scratched in and the date I made him. His head has the mark of where I gripped him and the eyes I dug with sticks are full of hate.

I wish Daddy could see him – he says to send a picture. The phone is a boring colour, beige with a grey dialler, and I press the coils of the wire together and let them spring apart while I'm listening. He says he just wants me to be happy and doesn't care what I do when I grow up. If I want to be a street sweeper, that's OK, as long as it makes me happy. He tells me he loves me very much and can't wait to see me when I come to Los Angeles this summer. I say 'Bye Daddy I love you' and hand the phone to Sue.

I go into my room and think about being a street sweeper as I play with my soldiers. They want to fight my teddy bear. I'm not sure I want to ruin my teddy. Then I realize that teddies are for little boys, and I'm seven now. I use a red felt-tip pen to make bullet holes in him. It's exciting to see him getting red all over. Then I stab the pen into him, hard, and it feels good. All the while the soldiers are getting closer to his furry feet and winning. The red felt-tip is drying a bit and I have to stab deeper to make my point. Poor little Teddy is getting wobbly on his feet and about to fall. The soldiers climb all over him like ants, and Teddy whirls on one foot and then… CRASH. The soldiers swarm all over him and put in more holes for good measure. Then it's all quiet in my room. I put on my tape of James Bond music and fast-forward to 'You Only Live Twice' with the violins going over the waterfall. The sound makes me woozy and I go to my window for dreaming.

Nothing happens here on Sheldon Avenue. I look at the driveway and the parked cars across the street and nothing is happening there, either. I wish I could part the clouds and see blue sky; but the grey folds go on forever and the curtain refuses to rise. I stroke my dino and the light wiggles over his shiny back. I can see my face in him, small and far away.

At school I feel big. All thanks to Dawn. I paint and sculpt and I'm really there. I can do anything. At recess I climb a tree and see a rainbow, bending its colours like a big slinky. The gym teacher calls me down but I want to stay up there. Then he blows his whistle and gets mad so I come down. I go to the sandpit to play, but it's too grainy and wet, and full of leaves. A girl is wriggling and crying because her tights are full of poo. Then the milkman comes with his cartons and soon I am sipping the creamy milk through a straw. We have a nap after that, but I can't sleep now, I'm too old. And I'm thinking about the fight I had with Monty. I called him Monty Python in the sandpit, and he tried to strangle me and I started hitting him, and everyone said fight, fight, fight... so then we had to keep going because everyone was watching, and I got him down on the ground and started bashing his head and it felt very good, like I was Sue.

The clock says ten to four and I really have to piss. My body is getting tingly, but I know everyone will laugh if I explain why I need to be excused so I just wait. Then I can't wait any more and the teacher says 'seven more minutes' and it's already too late. I see it by my shoe, spreading like cooking oil.

Sue cleans me up when I get home and then sits me down and makes me write to Daddy. I never know what to say. She makes me walk back and forth seven times to my bedroom desk to rewrite it before she says 'OK' and licks the stamp for me.


I'm in middle school now and I miss Dawn and Kindergarten. The only thing that's better is the lunch. We had roast beef and Yorkshire pudding today. And then semolina – I like to squirt in the red jam and mix it all up pink.

Then we watched the general election on TV. I'm rooting for Jeremy Thorpe. I like his black hair and his young face. Wilson is a scaly old toad with a pipe. Mummy says if Wilson wins we might have to leave England.

I'm learning the recorder in music class, but I can't seem to get the hang of the thing. It's made of plastic and sounds like it. There's a black boy who plays the silver cornet. His hair is big and full, like a dandelion. His notes are silver and strong, and he smells like hot spit. I wish I could play like that.

My stutter is getting worse and I get sent to see a speech therapist called Olive. She's very tall, and nice, with white hair. She stands over me saying 'friendly' – FRI-ENDLY – with her big, spreading mouth. I try to follow but the 'F' has an edge I can't get past. I try to explain to Olive how it gets stuck in my mouth and how that feels. I don't like words. Pictures are what I like. I wish books could speak in pictures only.

Mummy gave me some horror books. The Wolfman is my favourite, with his little beady eyes and combed fur, and the Neck Muncher, with his one creamy eye, feasting on the lady's neck. And the Brain Bug – a big alien thing with antennae that closes over the head of a screaming woman.

Mummy screams like that and real sounds come out. I've seen her do it in horror movies. She let me watch one where she's alone in a country house, with a crazy Santa Claus looking in the window who wants to get in and kill her. But tonight she's in my room kissing me goodnight and I feel close to her. Then she turns the lights out and I take out the watch she bought me, the one that glows in the dark, like James Bond's Rolex. I can't sleep, so I turn the light back on and thumb through my marine biology book with the picture of a giant squid pulling a sperm whale down into the deep, dark depths. There are a lot of strange creatures down there. The Lanternfish has huge teeth and a light dangling over his mouth to lure in unsuspecting prey.

It was only natural that this gruesome cast of characters should follow me into my dreams and wreak havoc. By day, they popped up in my drawings. My favourite doodle was a wolfman with dripping fangs. Was this a self-portrait? The little monster that Sue did battle with and had to tie down? Or is that too pat? It takes a monster to subdue a monster. This was logic that even a child, perhaps especially a child, could understand.

For my eighth birthday dress-up party, I declared, 'I want to be a monster.' My mother complied, taking me to Harrods where I found a rubber Frankenstein's monster mask and matching gloves. She stuck hair to my bare chest with eyelash glue and gave me one of her wigs to wear – I was Frankenstein's monster with hair extensions. Then she photographed me for posterity – laughing so hard the camera shook – before I thumped downstairs to my party. The rank smells of hot spit and rubber inside my mask gave me the monster brainwave: *I am dangerous, I will kill you.* I roared at Sue, then posed with my mother beside the birthday cake. This photo went right into the album for 1973: 'Sacha's monster party. We had fun.' The next page features her again, on location with Jack Palance in *The Cry of The Wolf*. (No, she never went to bed with him.)

*Self-Portrait with Hairy Beast*

The monster in me would grow larger and larger until, in my late thirties, it took total control of my work. I executed a series of paintings devoted to the grotesque, culminating in my portraits 'The Seven Deadly Sins'. With them, the exorcism was practically complete. In *Self-Portrait with Hairy Beast*, the eponymous creature regards me and the viewer with open aggression and barely concealed insanity, but he and I have already come to some sort of understanding. By painting myself in next to him, holding his hand and sitting patiently while he fidgets, I am sending a message of acceptance deep into his thick head. I am prepared to be seen with him, ready to own and acknowledge him as my own. I have begun the slow and painful process of civilizing him, turning him from an insensate brute into the magical wild man who can give me back the secrets of my nature.

Those secrets were spirited away from me as a child and locked in Sue's strongbox. The key was under my mother's pillow, but I hadn't the strength or cunning to steal it, to pipe up and say: 'Mummy, you must extinguish Sue, you must put her out, and give me back my fire!'

I had no choice but to love the damn beast.

At the middle school Christmas party I watch, transfixed, as Humphrey Lyttelton performs with his jazz quintet. He lifts his trumpet and blows an enormous golden bubble that drifts wobblingly overhead... I look inside this sonic globe and see a knot of sizzling snakes – a magic voltage. At home, I lay aside the childish recorder and demand a trumpet from my mother. She readily acquiesces. In no time we are on the fourth floor of Harrods, asking for the music department. I hold her hand and stumble excitedly along beside her as she stalks toward it. Beyond the pianos, I see a trophy wall of mounted brass instruments. The trumpet is there: a golden sound-gun, twisted by love and patience.

The shop assistant takes it down and lets me fondle it – trophy-heavy and cold. He shows me how to pump the keys to get the oil over them. I feel a horsepower in my hands that is new to me: a testy animal raring to go. I fill my lungs and lift the trumpet for a first kiss. The silver mouthpiece fits my lips so snugly. I crowd my skull with effort and gently exhale... a windy nothing. Then my air seems to catch and open, and a hot, pure growth of sound struggles through the trumpet to be born... It rings out loud and true on the fourth floor of Harrods. Shoppers turn in their tracks.

My mother smiles at the clerk and says, 'We'll take this one.'

He nods, 'Very good, Madam,' and then his professionalism cracks as he blushes and asks her for an autograph. She dutifully signs while he turns to me and blathers about the trumpet accessories: the green, velvet-lined case it sleeps in; the spare silver mouthpiece that slips in with a satisfied sound; the oil to keep the keys active and alive; and the soft cloth to polish its gold. My mother hands over the autograph and the cheque in one practised gesture. I put my new trumpet in its case and carry it out of Harrods like a man handcuffed to treasure.

I'm in Trumpet Heaven. I worship my instrument. I take it on holiday to the Bricusses' place in Acapulco and play 'God Save the Queen' every evening, with utter seriousness, as the sun sets over the Pacific. Back in music class, I sit next to the black boy with the silver cornet and profuse hair and patiently work my scales. I feel like a plodding donkey next to his dressage, but I aspire to surpass him.

At home, I spread my sheet music on a stand and practise for my Grade 3 diploma. My examination piece is a simple trumpet air (it still goes lilting through me) and I am steadily mastering it. The notes stand bolt upright as I press and squeeze the wine from their little black heads. When I finish the tune, I start over again, walking up and down the melodic line like a drill sergeant, testing and sweating every note until it's deep-set in the ground of my knowledge. Sometimes my fingers won't obey and I scream in frustration. I must learn to relax – count my heartbeats on my fingers, trot out the right notes so I can pass the bar with ease. Only then will I struggle and wriggle through my trumpet – its intestinal twists and turns – and be reborn as Music. Because I have a terror of getting lost inside its maze and expiring there, I practise until my mouth is sore and puckered and numb. Exhausted, I accidentally drop my precious taskmaster and dent the bell. Sick with anguish, I dream of a wolfman mangling it, then turning to me, grabbing me up and tying me like balloon sculpture until I wake screaming.

On the day of my examination, Sue drops me at King Alfred's. I walk the campus, trumpet case and music in hand, but can't locate the examination room. I am too embarrassed to admit I'm lost and to ask for help and time is fast running out. I sit on a log by the playing fields and go slack. I let go of the handle. That is the end of all the golden notes and all the patient striving. I'm just not good enough for Grade 3. I put the trumpet away in the back of my closet and never touch it again. Sacha is a child spoiled by too much and too little.

The silver room at Sheldon Avenue is for entertaining only. I'm not allowed in. But it's cold and quiet now, the perfect place for me. I turn the dimmer down. I want it gloomy. The silver things cast their own light: silver-jointed crabs and crayfish; silver-stalked and silver-petalled flowers; silver boxes and silver frames. Outside, the clouds drift over the sun, making the silver walls glow and fade. I sit on the floor and listen to the clock ticking. The silence is long and lean and burnished. I notice where the vacuum has gone in zigzags.

I have plenty of hiding places like this. There's a closet under the stairs I've turned into a space capsule. I close the triangular door and power up my craft. I go through my checklist: boosters, stabilizers, hydraulics – check. Oxygen, food, sleeping tablets – check. Sue yells it's time for supper and I freeze. I hear her chafing thighs approach and keep very still. She pounds up the stairs and screams for me, but I keep quiet. If I answer from here, there'll be one less place to hide and feel safe. Her thighs swish past, crackling with static and I wait until I hear her banging in the kitchen to resume take-off. I point my torch to ignite the stars, one by one. Orion's belt is my bearing as I count down to blast-off. The rumbling starts in my mouth, then broadens and expands until the whole capsule is shaking and my cheeks cave in with g-force. I'm leaving Earth-pull; Tara wants me back now; Mummy and Sue want me, too – let them want me. I break the atmosphere and breathe. It's hot in my capsule. I enable the air-conditioning system and savour the cool breath of my imagination. I see the blue cheek of Earth through the frosted pane and lie back floating.

Inside my glacier, time stops. Life outside moves under glass. I don't seem to hear when people speak to me. Even Sue's taunts fail to reach me. My mother goes to a lunch with her girlfriends and breaks down: her son is becoming a deaf mute. They counsel her to consult a child psychologist, but she recoils at the idea.

A few days later, walking with her hand-in-hand past a pet store in Knightsbridge, I suddenly perk up. I speak. I say, 'I want a dog.'

Pirate is my new love, a Dalmatian pup with black markings over one eye. He's warm and quivery and dear. I love to rub my face in his fur. I love the smell of him. He has a little peepee with a twirl of hair on the end, and whenever I pick him up he licks me hello.

When I play with him in the house he gets rough. He likes to chew the tassels off my mother's lampshades. She tells me to keep him outside, which I don't like. Every night I have to abandon him to the cold and the dark. I lock the garden door and see him turn in circles and make a silvery sound like a flute gone wrong. This kills me. I go upstairs and get into bed and think about him so weak and delicate outside. I can't sleep.

After a week, the matriarchal edict is lifted and Pirate gets to stay inside. I go to bed happy that night. I've made up a bed for him in the spare room by the kitchen. There's a bowl of water and some dry kibble for his night snack. He licks my nose as I kiss him goodnight.

In the morning, I bound down the stairs, excited to see my puppy. Sue is standing at the door of the spare room, her face as sour as the stench. I walk over and look inside: Pirate has outdone himself – the small room is a minefield of pooled crap. He's expelled enough shit for the two of us, my voluminous complaints and unexpressed hurts all over the floor along with his. And to top it all off, he's mutilated a Tiffany lamp – its ravaged silk shade hangs by a thread from the stem. My little piebald hero looks up at me and wags his tail.

'Sorry, Kiddo,' says Sue, and shuts the door on his face.

The next day he is returned to the kennel. There is no question of appealing the decision and I don't even try. I just stop talking again.

# 6

## Daddy in Wonderland

*My Father in the Beautiful Land*

MY FATHER DRIFTED AFTER THE DIVORCE. HE DID SOME TIME in therapy and broke the seal on his abandonment issues, but the deep spadework never got done and he fled back to the surface. He still craved a film career and, despite the fiasco of *Heironymus*, he had enough clout to land the directing job on *Summertree* starring Michael Douglas and produced by Kirk Douglas. By his own admission, he never really understood the piece, a coming-of-age story about a conscientious student who objects to the Vietnam draft. Brenda Vaccaro was the love interest and her intense off-screen romance with Michael Douglas may have exacerbated my father's bifurcation. Here was another one he couldn't seduce. The ghost of Sandy Dennis!

The film sorely strained his relationship with both Douglases and came and went in a puff of mixed reviews. In four short years, my father's dreams of a movie career had soared and plunged on waxen wing. He salved his wounds with girls and opium-laced grass and supplemented his income with a string of ridiculously lucrative cabaret dates – he was very famous and commensurately loved. His entourage of advisers and yes men kept the feel-good factor high and stage-managed his trysts. Then he clapped eyes on Danielle Mardi. Tink, as he nicknamed her, was the perfect foil to his Peter Pan. They met in Vegas while he was performing at Caesars and she was dancing for Tom Jones. The affair took hold, breaking his pattern of one-night stands and weekenders. His entourage grudgingly opened to make a buddy-space for her. Tony felt special about this one, though: she had depth and brains, he insisted – she understood him.

That was true. Most people loved Fabulous Tony; she loved all of him – especially the little boy. In her eyes, he was the *poèt maudit*, the great 'sick one', drawing inspiration from an underworld of pain and self-loathing. She would cure him – pull man and boy together and make him whole. They became children of the meadow, plucking the daisies of lust and partaking of huge narcotic blooms. Erotically, their dynamic was the equivalent of what my father described in songs like 'Candy Man' and 'Pure Imagination': an eye-popping world of plenty where dreams came true and coming was all.

Those songs, from *Willy Wonka & the Chocolate Factory*, for which he co-wrote the score in 1971, were a testament to the fecundity of his partnership with Bricusse. The clever buggers managed to finish the score without ever spending time together in one room. Lyrics were mailed back and forth and melodies hummed over the phone to Ian Fraser, who translated them into notes and passed the results to Walter Scharf for arrangement. Bricusse and Newley literally phoned this baby in – but what a call! 'Candy Man' went gold, enriched by the vocal talents of Sammy Davis Jr, while 'Pure Imagination', which my father and Bricusse thought would be the hit, became a sleeper classic, only now mounting into the pantheon of their time-tested creations.

With these successes, more golden eggs came tumbling into Tink and Peter Pan's basket. Thus fortified in body, mind and pocketbook, they set about finding another 1106, another hilltop Shangri-La in which to live large. Presto magico, a perfect English country house – complete with cracked stone facade, traceries of ivy, and storybook eaves – materialized on a ridge overlooking Coldwater Canyon. 9477 Lloydcrest was such a house as Tennyson or Swinburne might have revelled in – but transported to twentieth-century Los Angeles. My father filled it with antiques and ephemera from the curiosity shops he loved to frequent. One room was devoted to a collection of porcelain hands that detailed the art of palmistry, another to the eighteenth-century pseudo-science of phrenology, the practice of reading the traits of character from the skull. The plaster and ceramic heads stood in stern, judicial rows, their bare braincases mapped by lines long and lateral, denoting Humour, Genius and Prophecy.

The rosewood library smelled of must and binding leather and contained luxurious coffee-table books on astronomy and the microscopic world, not to mention stacks of magazines that kept my father abreast of every 'fascinating' discovery in the sciences. He was an ardent amateur scientist himself, a throwback to Goethe's time, when science and art were bedfellows. The house mirrored the jumble of his psyche. On a table below a wall of gold records were displayed hairy tarantulas and rainbow scarabs in perspex boxes. His Grammys shared shelf space with silk and velvet display cases of pinned butterflies. For me, a sense of wonder and discovery pervaded the house, as if every room held a new find to spark the imagination. I learned that knowledge didn't have to be dry and dusty, but could be bound up with mystery and magic.

I'm going to see Daddy in L.A. Sue drives me to Heathrow and I can't keep still. She leaves me in the care of a nice lady in uniform who smiles a lot and walks me to the waiting room. It's for kids like me who are travelling unaccompanied. I sip orange squash and munch on biscuits while I watch the planes take off. The jumbos are big like their name and that's what I'll be flying on: TWA, with the long red stripe and a black patch over the nose to stop the sun glaring in – a pilot told me that when I peeked into his cave of buttons. The smiling lady in uniform says it's time. I walk to the jumbo on pins and needles. Inside there's a spiral staircase that I long to go up, but the stewardess sits me down and plies me with ginger ale. I look out the window: the luggage men and the men with pipes are pulling away. The door closes. I can't get out now.

Then we're out by the runway, turning for take-off. The stewardess straps me in, then herself, and smiles at me just the way Dawn would. The engines whine higher and higher, like Pirate locked out and we begin to move. Now it sounds like a million Pirates whining as we go faster and faster. The jumbo is too heavy to fly, I feel it in my body, but a big hand lifts us from under and the ground peels away. The plane tips and turns over London, scaring me. Then it levels off, and cheery sunlight moves through the cabin. London's now far below, rough and grey, with long whiskers that go everywhere into the green countryside. Clouds tickle the jumbo, making it giggle and bounce. The wings are flapping like a duck. I'm scared they'll snap! I look at the stewardess, but it's Mummy I want. She's somewhere under the sky I'm bouncing in. Now the plane steadies and the stewardess smiles again. We go into pure blue above the mashed-potato clouds. I take out the sticker game Mummy packed for me and make pictures on the glossy blackboard for a while. We're completely still now. How can we get to Los Angeles going so slowly? There are crystals on the window – heaven must be very cold.

We arrive in Los Angeles, and they take me to a special waiting area with unclaimed bags. The laminated sign around my neck reads: Unaccompanied Minor. I swish my feet over the polished floor and count the beige bits in the white tiles. After two hundred, I give up. People come for the bags but nobody comes for me. Finally a limo pulls up. The driver comes in and approaches with my name spelled wrong on a card. As we cruise into Beverly Hills, I drop the power windows and count the palm trees gliding by. Then I stretch out on the back seat and caress the cool creases of the black leather. The driver's neck is thick and he sits extremely still, balancing his black hat that looks like a teacup.

We turn off Sunset and head up Coldwater Canyon. No palm trees here, just tall pines that seem to touch overhead and make a tunnel. We turn again, on to Lindacrest, a narrow street that climbs steeply into the hills. The limo takes the bends slowly, splashing through garden run-off; a wall of brilliant bougainvillea smears the black interior with colour. 'Almost there,' says the driver. My belly flares with excitement as he takes a hard left, the power steering wheezing, and the gates shudder open to reveal… Lloydcrest.

My father comes running out and lifts me in his arms. He covers me with kisses, then holds me away from him, the better to regard me. I wrap my arms around his flowing hair and cry. He carries me toward the house, through the front courtyard, and past the mossy bubbling fountain. The den smells of incense and baking. There's a big charred fireplace, and a tobacco-store Indian, and medieval saints carved in wood. In the kitchen Grandma Grace is rolling pastry amid the hanging pots, and Daddy's girlfriend Tink comes at me, all smiles and perfumed silk.

Waiting for me upstairs is a brand new bed, shaped like a racing car, with chiselled-tread wheels and a sloping front end emblazoned with Number One. And that's exactly how I feel. I step outside and dip my hand in the blue pool, warm for swimming, and see, beyond a low wall of potted flowers, the City of Angels, moored in its ochre haze. I follow my father down curving stone steps on to the wide plane of the lower garden, which rides like a magic carpet over the tips of the canyon pines. Its sloping expanse is bordered by lemon trees and culminates in a circular rose garden criss-crossed by redbrick pathways. Bees weave their way across it and birds blitz it with song.

My father lifts me so I can twist off a lemon and inhale its sweet skin. 'Do you like it?' he asks, putting me down again.

I run across the garden and throw myself down. I roll on to my back and watch, barely breathing, as a solitary cloud tears itself apart to make two.

I felt like I'd regained paradise; like I was back at 1106, although pale and Sue-haunted, barely able to speak. Gradually, the balm of Lloydcrest unlocked me. I babbled away in Tink's arms, wondering aloud why one side of a butterfly's wing was shiny and the other matt. It had something to do with flying dust, Tink explained, no doubt enchanted by this mini-facsimile of her divine lover, so serious and interested in everything.

On movie nights, we huddled together as Daddy threaded the projector in the booth behind us – a small room between the den and the garage he'd fitted out for the purpose. A hinged painting swung wide to expose the projector glass, and a portable screen did duty at the far end of the room. I always loved to go back there and watch him thread the film through the toothy chicanery of the projector gears, blowing away dust and frowning with a technician's concern. He had a library of 16mm prints, most of them illegally procured through a contact at the studios. There were pirate copies of all the Disney classics: *Fantasia, Pinocchio, Sleeping Beauty* – and a complete set of Jacques Cousteau documentaries.

My favourite pirated Disney, for obvious reasons, was *101 Dalmatians*. The flight of the puppies from Cruella de Vil struck a deep chord and I longed for them to get away and live happily ever after with Roger and Anita. At the same time, I was slavishly in love with Cruella – her angularity, her vicious elegance. She was just the sort of woman I would find myself pursuing throughout my early manhood, in a classically doomed attempt to procure my mother's love.

*Dr. Strangelove* was my father's favourite film. He showed it to me one night, chancing the content on an eight-year-old. I didn't get any of it, of course – except, unfortunately, the searing image of Slim Pickens riding the falling bomb like a rodeo horse to whiteout detonation.

But the deepest impact was made by Jacques Cousteau. His documentary voice-overs, with their beautiful Gallic cadences inflected by passionate concern, were for me a kind of poetry – a human evocation of nature's mysterious agency. I felt sure he spoke for the whales that swam freely and majestically in the projector's spotlight; for the white, cruising sharks; for the swales of silver salmon that pressed ever northward to spawn and die. He was like God, commenting on His own creation, warning off the desecrating legions of man – his favourite derogation of humanity. Cousteau's rapturous distress was the first intimation I had that something was wrong, not just with me and my little world, but with the world, and humankind, in general. We were lousing up the planet at cartoon speed.

My father was a total convert. With a natural distrust of authority engendered by a missing father, he was one of the first to champion the green beliefs we now take for granted. On aeroplane flights he would routinely direct my gaze downward to the immense natural canvas riddled with rivers and etched by the fernlike reliefs of mountain valleys. Here, like some mad scientist, man had run amok, he explained – violently and perversely carving up the natural flow of things into squares of cultivated land. 'Look at what we've done, Sachie,' he would say in a rapt whisper. 'Our boxes and bar graphs are obscene...'

I would nod, in thrall to his sense of mourning. The city lights that pinned and needled the edges of lakes and rivers – the mad, neural net of roads and highways that choked up to the dark mountains and glutted the seaboards – did, indeed, seem like some infernal disease the planet had contracted, slowly drowning out its once sovereign peace.

It was a lot to unload on an eight-year-old, but my father felt I was ready. His study of Zen Buddhism had convinced him that a child's mind was no less valuable than an adult's; that, in fact, it was more precious. The crowded, overdeveloped consciousness of an adult – with all its superimposed data, prejudices, and opinions – was like that desecrated terrain below: too busy to recognize and receive the truth. He was genuinely interested in my utterly innocent take on things – the 'uncarved block' of my 'beginner's mind'. When I asked him the standard childhood questions about phenomena, he responded at length, encouraging me to interrogate him until he was all out of answers. At which point, he felt, he might actually begin to learn something from me. Later in life, when the habit of intellectual debate had become ingrained between us, he would often say, cajoling and half serious, 'When I grow up, I want to be just like you, Sachie.'

'Dad, where do clouds come from?'

'It's evaporation from the sea, caught by gravity.'

'What's gravity?'

'The pull of the Earth.'

'Why does the Earth pull?'

'Because it's so big – its mass is enormous.'

'The sun is big, too, so why don't we get pulled into that?'

'Because we're on our orbital path, going round and round and round.'

'Who got us going?'

'No one in particular. The Earth formed out of clumps of gas that circled a young star.'

'Are the stars all suns?'

'They are.'

'Are there planets like Earth around them?'

'We don't know for sure – let's just say it's a mathematical probability.'

'Are there people out there like us?'

'Maybe… something like us – poor buggers. What do *you* think?'

In the pool I pondered the question, idly fanning my arms and watching the water disperse in glossy ripples. Could any of this – could, in fact, ALL of this – be happening somewhere out there as well? I looked up at the dormant moon – dead, like ash. But maybe somewhere beyond it there was a place like Earth, where a boy like me sat in a pool pondering? If it was happening here, why couldn't it happen out there?

The screen door banged open and my father appeared by the pool in his red-and-green trunks printed with female faces. A girl, not Tink, followed him out, hot on his heels, blonde and tanned, wearing a bikini.

'Sachie, this is Jenna,' he said; whereupon the girl giggled, caved her shoulders, and gave me a little wave.

They dived in and swam up close.

'Hi,' said Jenna, venting her warm breath all over me and shedding diamond droplets of water from her lashes.

'Hullo,' I replied, and ducked underwater, swimming in one breath to the deep end. I looked back and saw them giggling and rubbing noses, then kissing deeply and slowly submerging. I got out and ran for my towel. They were at the bottom now, pressed against each other, undulating.

'Dad.'

'Yes.'

'Where's Tink?'

'Shopping.'

'Who's Jenna?'

'Just a friend.'

'D'you like her more than Tink?'

'Why d'you ask?'

'I dunno…'

We were in his bathroom now, towelling off after a shower. I forgot all about Tink as he dried my hair with an oatmeal towel, an electric heater behind us, a tree at the window. I closed my arms around his head and inspected the coloured threads in his hair: red, white, fawn, in a sea of black. I was amazed by the variety – there was always more to see if you looked hard enough. Down by his right eye, a renegade hair sprouted like a watch-spring.

'Dad! Look!' I turned his face to the mirror.

'Good God, that wasn't there this morning…'

'It's a monster eyebrow, Dad – it's… it's… an eyebreenie!'

A thunderclap of laughter. 'That's it, Sachie, that's exactly what it is – from now on they'll always be eyebreenies!'

'It's a reticulated python,' I said, trembling with excitement as the snake wrangler draped it around my neck. I knew this from my snake book. Dad smiled with pride, photographing me as the serpent levitated out of my grasp, its head the size of an avocado. I couldn't stop talking about it all the way home from the petting zoo, and a few days later, Dad being Dad, he bought me my very own snake: a ribbon or garter snake, black, with yellow pinstripes running the length of him. He was about as thick as a nickel and as long as I was tall. I dubbed him Thaxsted.

I pose for my father with my namesake coiled around my neck. The way he moves – his urgent, sinuous way – is my way. He's quiet like me and licks the air to taste before moving. I thrill to his tender musculature as he inches and throbs through my grasp. I put him down in the grass and lie on my belly, watching him seethe toward me in an endless iteration of my first initial.

At the dinner table, I want to wear him around my neck, but Tink draws the line, so I place him back in his tank where he promptly curls up in a bowl of water. I feed him dry, turd-like compilations of insect bits; the feast I long to serve him is a real live goldfish, but Tink seizes up at the thought. All through dinner I imagine him swallowing the fluttering red ruby, slowly passing it down his length as his digestive juices work it down to a smaller-and-smaller lozenge. I've read about this process in my snake books: how the python unhinges his lower jaw and inhales the paralysed warthog; how on day two he lies sunning himself on the savannah, the absurd lump halfway down his body; how on day three the bubble slowly deflates, juicing him with energy. It's an intimation of nature's strangeness and surreal facility. If only I could swallow Sue this way!

After dinner, I run out and release Thaxsted in the twilit garden. He thanks me with a flick of the tongue, blurring and fanning its litmus strand to read the living air. His eyes, fixed and expressionless, transmit the snake signal of total vigilance. I love this robot side of him. Daddy comes out and lies down next to me. Thaxsted strives toward us, crushing his path through the bending fibres. I wish I was bug-sized so I could part green curtains and watch his monstrous tube crashing by like a freight train.

Under the microscope, Daddy and I inspect a dragonfly's wing. It has silver veins like a leaf. The colour is purply-blue and turns goldeny-green as we rotate the scope. Daddy adjusts the focus knob and we blur down to deeper clarity. I see roads and branching highways, like I'm up in the jumbo looking down. Daddy's voice is warm and crackly at my ear: 'Everything has this pattern, Sachie – trees, rivers, even the veins in your body.'

'But *why*, Daddy?'

'Because it's the best way to spread information: to get blood to every cell, to balance the load on a dragonfly's wing, to bring traffic into the suburbs... it's the tree of life.'

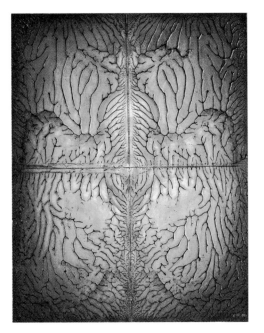

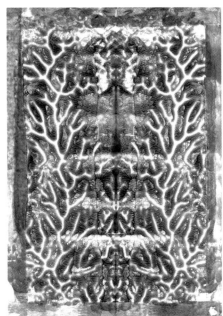

*Firebird*                                          *Purple Fractal*

We switch slides to a dust mite. His legs are bubble jewellery: little crystal balls on a string of dried blood.

'Who made him, Daddy?'

'Evolution.'

'What's that?'

'Nature tinkering and working very hard over time.'

'Why, Daddy?'

'Why what?'

'Why does it have to work so hard?'

'Because it needs to create.'

'WHY?'

'Why do *you* like to draw? Why do *I* like to sing? It's a bloody mystery, that's what it is.'

He uncorks a test tube and carefully spills a droplet on to a fresh slide. 'Look at this…'

I startle at the whizzing bugs. 'It's like bumper cars…'

'Every organism has its own unique way of moving. The most common thing in nature is originality.'

'This one looks like a jellyfish and that one's like an X-ray of Mummy's purse.'

We chuckle at a Chaplinesque worm, whiplashing his way forward, but making little progress.

At night, Daddy turns his telescope on the moon and I see to the bigness beyond. The moon is a 'fossil planet', he explains, with a distant memory of 'meteors falling like rain.' Its white disc trembles in my scope, the Sea of Tranquillity a grey expanse that holds my breath.

'One day we'll grow crops there,' says Daddy. 'There'll be domed cities and playgrounds. The human seed will jump across and start another tree.'

It's time to put on my Unaccompanied Minor sign again. All the way home to London in the jumbo I think of Thaxsted, coiled in his little dish. Will he be properly fed and looked after? Will he miss me? Does he know how much I love him?

Sue meets me at the airport and roughs up my hair with a fat hand: 'Hey Kiddo...' Now that I'm back, I have to switch my scope to normal magnification. On the ride home to Sheldon Avenue, I contemplate Sue's thigh, wrapped in brown spandex, bulging over the side of the seat. I put my hand there and feel the vibration. I know she'll be crushing me again in no time, rolling me in the wave of her strange, potent love.

A few weeks pass before I'm told the news – passed from Daddy to Sue – that Thaxsted had tried to escape from his tank, slit his throat on its edge and bled to death.

# 7

# Snakepits

LOS ANGELES, 1998. I SIT BROODING IN MY STUDIO. I'M totally out of gas. The portrait I'm working on is propped on the easel – an Indian lady. I've been working on the decorative brocade of her sari for weeks now. I'm suffocating from the concentration. I need to breathe.

I take out a blank canvas and start making marks and shapes: squares within squares within squares, telescoping down to a central box in the middle of the canvas. It looks like a target grid – and that's what I feel my head has become: a weaponized device for compacting information.

If nothing else, the painting has told the truth. So I rush to do another, and another… the box paintings slowly deepen until I burst through into an interior space of writhing anxiety, a seething snakepit of lines. What's this? The quantum field? The id? The unconscious? All of the above? None of the above?

Browsing in a bookstore, I come across a tome on yoga and read about kundalini, the sacred serpent energy coiled at the base of the spine. The purpose of yoga, says the book, is to awaken the kundalini and gradually lift it up the chakras, opening them one by one, until reaching the head, where it detonates the thousand-petalled crown chakra of ultimate enlightenment. Musing on this, I realize I've awakened my kundalini alone, without the necessary precautions of an ancient practice – a process fraught with danger. I soon make a series of miserable decisions in my relationships and find myself demoted from the snakepits into the pits of hell. The only escape is to paint my way out. By coincidence, I am commissioned by a collector to commit to canvas my interpretation of St. George and the Dragon – that ancient tableau involving a man, a maiden, and a fire-breathing dragon – and immediately recognize a subject that's had my name immemorially on it.

Mrs Benet's office sits at the top of a four-floor walk-up. It's my mother, not Sue, who accompanies me on the climb, so I know this is important. Mrs Benet answers the door herself and smiles with eyes schooled in patient understanding.

''Allo, Sacha,' she says with a French accent. She's small, with olive skin, and reminds me of Alice, our beloved cook and caretaker from 1106.

*Tail-Wrapped*

We follow her inside to a waiting room and she and my mother confer in low voices while I look at a framed poster of a man with a bandaged ear signed Vincent.

My mother kisses me goodbye and Mrs Benet bids me follow her down a short hallway into her office. It's panelled in red wood. She sits me down in front of the desk and takes the other side. She laces her fingers and looks at me intently.

'Would you like to tell me a little bit about yourself, Sacha?'

I say nothing. There is nothing to say about myself.

'Perhaps you have some hobbies you'd like to tell me about? Your mother tells me you're a wonderful artist.'

I say nothing. It's easier.

'You don't want to talk today, do you? I understand. Sometimes I don't like to talk, either. You know what I do when I don't want to talk? I read. Would you like to read?'

I look at the kids' books along the walls, and stay silent.

She clasps her hands and leans forward confidentially. 'I'll tell you what. Why don't I leave you alone for a bit and you can think about what you want to do. Here's some crayons and paper, if you'd like to draw. You can do whatever you want. I'll be in the next room, not so very far away. All right?'

I nod, leaning forward in my chair to watch her as she disappears somewhere down the hall. I hear pencils being sharpened, papers being rustled, then silence. I glance at the paper and crayons. They're closer than the books, so I pull them over. The crayons are brand new. I open the carton and inhale the friendly waxy smell. I tip them out and consider the rainbow colours. The red is deep, like the walls of the office. I take a sheet of paper and look at it hard. The whiteness expands and breathes me in. The crayon wavers in my hand. Little magnets in my head are pulling the tip this way and that. And then suddenly I'm drawing...

Nothing at first, just wavy lines; then I see I've made two snakes weaving back and forth. I close off their bodies and give them bubble dialogue: they're going to work and hissing 'top of the morning' as they slither past each other.

Next page. I make a curly snake, like a tornado whirling, and bring him to rest in a deepening coil of black. I give him yellow eyes and a broad, lipless grin. Next page. A green viper, hanging from a branch, his purple eyes ringed with fire. He appeals to me and I make his pupils super black. 'Don't mess with this snake,' I hear myself say aloud. Next page. His long yellow lines are slightly wavy, his black scales diamond-shaped. I work until the whole length is black and the crayon is worn to a nub. 'Thaxsted,' I scrawl at the bottom.

Mrs Benet picks up the drawings and admires them. 'Very good, Sacha. I love these... Who's Thaxsted?'

I can't really say.

'Can I put them up?'

I nod.

Next session, they're all there, taped to her office wall – my little exhibition. Mrs Benet's already in the next room, sharpening pencils, rustling paper, and there's fresh paper and crayons laid out for me. I waste no time: she wants more. I comb through my brain and snag a thread – a vibrant snake-end. Must be a rattlesnake. I pull him out and coil him down again like a pastry chef carefully squeezing out his cream. He must have brothers and sisters and they must all have rattles. I make a quivering bowl of snake spaghetti and lick my lips. Then a big-daddy rattler, diamond-blue and black, packing the page intestinally, his fat rattle poised like a grenade. Then one standing up – a skyscraper snake, collared in cloud and extending to the sun.

Mrs Benet loves these, too. Next session, I see that she's given *The Skyscraper* pride of place. She's taken down all her citations and diplomas to make more space for me. So I sit down and make an accordion snake ten pages long – gold, with floating purple stars. My yellow wears down and I have to finish with orange. I tear off the paper sheath and work it lengthways until my arm aches. Next I make big bandy snakes that split from a festering knot and go everywhere. And circus snakes, weaving in a mutual macramé – a playful copulation of curves that I colour turquoise and red and accent with bright pink. My harlequins thrill me and I tumble forward, eating up pages and exhaling imagery: happy snakes with clown colours and bad snakes with vermilion eyes and preposterous fangs; brooding snakes stacked like racing car tires and frantic snakes pinballing inside the page. A seraglio of snakes for Mrs Benet, and me the happy conjurer at their seething core. I hear her coming down the corridor and wind up my catapult snake, forced back on congestive coils, springing like an arrow over London…

'That's marvellous, Sacha, really beautiful.' She holds it up and smiles. 'See what you can do when you let yourself go.'

I love you, Mrs Benet. You have given me the gifts of time and space. In my snake trance, I am happy – smooth and lean and utterly stutterless. My snakes are lined up for miles – links in the monumental chain that extends before and after me: my lifeline, my signature without end.

So it goes. Every Thursday at four, the fresh paper and crayons, the empty office, the burgeoning exhibition of my work. I have covered three walls and am working on the fourth. When my snake room is finished, I will finally exist in the world. My mother comes to review my progress. She sees the snake room and is unimpressed. She's paying thousands of pounds for this? Mrs Benet patiently explains that she is earning my trust, that this will take some time.

Next Thursday I'm on my third drawing when I hear the phone ring down the hall. Mrs Benet answers it. 'Oh, hello, Mrs Kass…'

I concentrate on my pyramid snake, his squared-off coils building to a summit, his tongue hoisted like a banner…

'…A little longer could be really beneficial. I feel he's almost ready to open up to me. And his stutter is definitely improving…'

My snake tongue wavers, fading away like smoke…

'…I realize it's frustrating, but we must be patient. Yes. Yes of course…'

Green for the eyes, with an orange iris around the slit pupil…

'The bill, yes, to 42 Sheldon Avenue. Thank you, Mrs Kass. Goodbye.'

She re-enters with one end of her smile turned down. She sifts through my drawings dutifully enough, but I know it's over. I will never finish my snake room. After my mother terminates my therapy with Mrs Benet, my snakes go back inside me and simmer there with rage. With Sue always ready to sit on me for acting out, I have to somehow keep them from flaring up. My play rituals become obsessive, and feature a compulsive need to repeat. Doing a thing over and over and over again leaves no room for serpentine chaos. I hold my bowels to gain the same control over my body, and when Sue does sit on me, I rather welcome the pressure, because it helps me hold everything inside.

In the midst of my repetitions I feel an eerie calm. My snakes whirl in unison and make a magic ring of concentration. I can see back through them to the 'perfect' world of my childhood. How happy I appear to the cursory, maternal eye: little Sacha riding his bike in circles, climbing a tree, bouncing on the trampoline, practising his trumpet…

My compulsiveness reaches perfect pitch at Christmas with the unwrapping of gifts. Tara watches in a fury as I gingerly unpeel the tape from the wrapping paper and spring the flaps. Her presents lie strewn about, discarded in a chaotic frenzy of paper ripping, while I patiently unfold my luxuries, enjoying the origami of the process. I remove the paper in the manner it was applied; I even smooth out the wrapping and fold it afterward, which inflames Tara no end. We all pose for a smiling picture under the tree, and it has the desired narcotic effect. I must say I look happy. Perhaps I am happy. After all, I have seen a therapist and she has seen me.

I spend hours in the driveway showing off my tricycle to an imaginary press corps. They *ooh* and *ahh* as I point out the air intakes and the extra-soft seat and the knobbly handlebar grips. On the surface, I, too, aspire to be an ultimate prototype: the perfect son. But deep down I ache to unloose my snakes, disembowel Sue, dismember my family and burn 42 Sheldon to the ground.

*The Good Old Bad Old Days* opened at the Prince of Wales Theatre in London in December 1972. Ill-starred from the beginning, it exacerbated the strained relationship between my father and Bricusse. The songs had come as easily to them as ever, but the book always was another matter. This one went through numerous drafts before falling resolutely short of their gifts and their ambitions.

My father billed the show as a 'pantomime for adults' about the great questions of existence. As with *Greasepaint*, it was driven by an argument between high and low – privilege and poverty. In this case, Sir and Cocky are reimagined as God and the Devil: the one, a fractious and bullying patriarch; the other, a winningly roguish and sympathetic underdog.

The story starts off well. Having despaired of his attempt to create man in His own image, God (aka Gramps) wants to cut his losses and destroy the planet. The Devil (aka Bubba) is up in arms – not least because he'll be out of a job. Like some infernal defence lawyer, Bubba argues on man's behalf that man is more a victim than a perpetrator of history's crimes. Bubba invokes all the great and tragic moments of human history as testament: Ancient Rome, the Renaissance, the French Revolution (Bricusse and Newley got there first, *Les Mis!*), the Age of Shakespeare and so on… all processed and presented in theatrical shorthand by the Bricusse and Newley sausage machine. The bottom line is that Gramps doesn't even understand His own creation. He, Bubba, is mankind's true friend, closest to him by virtue of the fallen state they share.

The stage is set for my father to perform a winning song-and-dance on mankind's behalf. This smacked of the romantic propaganda he smuggled into all his shows: the 'little guy' is really the 'big guy'. Bricusse bought into the act: after all, it was Newley who was treading the boards. But beneath all the high-concept architecture, it was my father's forever-unresolved issues with *his* father that propelled the drama:

BUBBA [desperately]: You've never given a tuppeny damn whether I lived or died!

GRAMPS: We've been through all this before, Bubba!

BUBBA: Right from the beginning, it was always good boy, Abel, that's right, Abel, well done, Abel! And then it was Noah, then Abraham, then Moses – all your other arse-licking Old Testament favourites! Anybody but me! … Was I so hard to love?

The vitality of my father's performance kept the show running for a perfectly respectable 100 performances. It also garnered an Ivor Novello Award for best song for 'The People Tree'. But my father never even showed up to accept the award. He was drained by the emotional expenditure of the show. He told Bricusse in no uncertain terms that he 'didn't want to do it any more.'

'Newberg,' replied Bricusse, 'it's six years since you were last on Broadway. Isn't it high time you hauled your cockney arse back there?'

'Brickman,' my father interrupted, 'if you were getting a million dollars for eight weeks at Caesars Palace, would *you* give a rat's fuck about Broadway?'

Bricusse thought for a moment and replied, 'If I wanted to still be getting a million dollars for eight weeks' work five years from now, then yes, I would, because Broadway's what got you there in the first place.'

My father returned to Vegas and took the money.

Daddy is the Devil. The Devil is half-man, half-goat. The goat part is hairy. At night I watch Daddy getting ready. He puts on the leotard first. It's black with red feathers and has a knobbly tail growing out of it with a fork end. He peels an apple with the sharp edge in act two and everybody laughs. He wears shoes that look like hooves and a black cape. His horns are blackened at the base like a goat's and made of plastic. They have a comb in between to keep them in place. When Daddy twists back and forth, his tail whips me and we both laugh. Then he gives me a big devil smile and a hug. I smell the make-up on him and the rubber and these are devil smells.

The last thing he does is rev up his voice. He takes a sip of warm honey and lemon and closes his eyes. A bumblebee sound starts low in his throat; his hand swirls as the bee climbs higher and higher, till it's singing like a mosquito and stings him at the top of the head. His eyes open then and he breathes. He's ready now.

The speaker says, 'Five minutes, Mr Newley.'

Daddy takes me by the hand. We walk under the stage, past the props and the waiting actors. I can hear clapping overhead, and imagine the weight of all those bums on seats. Then we're at the devil cage and Daddy climbs inside. The propman gives him the pitchfork and Daddy leans down to kiss me goodbye. 'I love you, Sachie, you're my special boy.' And then the propman closes the door. I look at Daddy through the bars as he puts the shiny red devil mask over his face. Then the music booms overhead and he lurches up. I watch him disappear through the swirling smoke and red light – the trap door closes and he's gone.

Onstage, the Devil ascends through a seething morass of women. For a moment he stands there as monumental as Rodin's *Balzac*, then slowly lowers his sequined mask to reveal the eyebrows haughtily flexed, the mouth twisted in an unspoken quip.

Under the stage, the boy is led away from the scene of his father's nightly disappearance. Reg, the chauffer, drives him home while the Devil goes into his first number. The boy peers out of the blue Jag at the streets of London bathed in orange lamplight, the car windows streaked with drizzle as, back at the theatre, God questions his father about mankind's fitness to survive.

At home, he brushes his teeth and goes to bed. By this time, his father has completed a musical evocation of the Renaissance and is leading into the taking of the Bastille. The boy lies awake, thinking of the moment the cage closed and his father went up in red smoke. He feels happy because he knows he'll be there to see it again tomorrow night, and the night after that.

He's falling asleep as his father takes his bows and goes backstage to undress and shower – wearily wiping off his make-up and reflecting on all the holes in the show. Bricusse senses them, too, but he doesn't have to carry the whole fiasco night after night, and this stokes my father's resentment toward his clever father figure and stalwart collaborator. *This is the last time,* he tells himself, *I can't do it any more.* Reg is waiting at the stage door to drive him home to his townhouse (rented) and new girlfriend (eight months pregnant).

Jenna was not the only Playboy Bunny in Tink's seemingly picture perfect meadow. Whenever she turned her back, another one would spring from its secret rabbit hole. My father's world was riddled with passageways of deceit. One day, Tink skipped home to find two sets of ladies' shoes outside the master bedroom at Lloydcrest. Cries of ecstasy issued from within. She went back downstairs for a good think. How much did she love him? She tried to rationalize that his inability to be faithful was because he had no faith in himself. But that didn't mitigate the hurt. She had no choice but to leave.

My father was rudderless without her. When the next girl came along he was ready for dreaded Commitment. Cathy Price was a stewardess for American Airlines who had happened to be on the same flight from Washington to Los Angeles. He was heading home from a cabaret gig with his old pal and comic sidekick, Buddy Hackett. She had been assigned to economy, but came up front to say hi to Hackett whom she had met before, and he introduced her to his handsome, famous friend. There was instant heat between them; she was twenty years his junior, and as her lissom figure sashayed down the aisle, my father strained for a backward glance. Hackett egged him on to cash in on some of his star capital.

Later in the flight, he invited Cathy upstairs to the lounge and kissed her, deeply.

'Mr Newley,' she said breathlessly, 'you're going to get me fired.'

'Then I'll hire you the best lawyer money can buy.'

He made her promise to watch him on Carson that night. Huddling with her stewardess friends in a motel room, she heard my father inform a vast TV audience, 'I think I've met my next wife...'

Cathy screamed – at which point, as if she'd been teleported into some Frank Capra farce, there was a knock on the door and the manager presented her with three bouquets, 'From Tony, with love.'

From there it was full steam ahead. My father would wait, sick with lust, for her to fly back to Los Angeles from Tulsa or Palm Beach or Detroit. Her stewardess uniform was obligingly left on so he could have the pleasure of peeling away the corporate skin. She was no fool, and knew how to use the itinerancy of her job to keep him hooked. Eventually, he prevailed upon her to come down to Earth and settle into life at Lloydcrest.

After Tink's loving indulgence, my father found Cathy's no-nonsense approach to things refreshing. His long-playing, self-pitying monologue about his missing father occasioned the rebuke, 'Why not shut up and try to find him?' He decided to hire a detective.

George Kirby had been a bit of a Dapper Dan and ladies' man in the pre-war Clapton neighbourhood where he ran a clothing store with his wife, Nell. She was much older than he and no oil painting, but she had a head for business and looked the other way whenever George strayed. Enter Frances Grace Newley. She had been born in 1902 into a family of thirteen. By the age of eleven, she was cooking and slaving for the whole miserable brood, as her mother, an alcoholic and erstwhile harlot, was usually down for the count and her father was off fighting at the Somme. Young Grace grew into a dreamy young girl, but never lost her heart – until George. He twinkled at her as she entered his clothing store, looking to buy a suit for her father. He showered her with attention and sent her home with two suits on approval, slyly suggesting that she make a weekly payment of two shillings and sixpence on the one she chose. Seeing her so often would give him a chance to reinforce his spell. It was obvious to him that Grace found his slicked hair, fine voice and overall good looks irresistible.

When Nell, oblivious to her husband's latest shenanigans, offered Grace a job as a 'tweenie', or between-the-stairs maid, at their big house on Greenwood Road, the love-struck girl readily accepted. She and George were now free to consummate their attraction behind closed doors. One afternoon, while Nell was out, they had a go on the living-room carpet. A child was thereby conceived; and as soon as she began to show, she was unceremoniously dismissed.

George lined up a backstreet abortionist, but in the event the procedure didn't work: the little embryo had big things to do in life and hung on in there. As her pregnancy advanced, Grace stayed away from home, not wanting to burden her family with the scandal. She lodged with the Salvation Army and, for a time, with a distant cousin. The trysts with George continued on the sly – on fog-enshrouded bridges, behind railway stations, in the backseat of his Morris Valiant where he could cop a cheap feel and relieve some pressure. 'Mimi,' he affectionately called her, after the heroine of La Boheme. He was an opera fan, and in addition to the few bob he'd slip her now and again, he'd sometimes throw in an opera ticket.

There she would sit, alone and heavily pregnant, in the upper stalls. The music enfolded her as if it were an earnest of George's tenderness. When she first heard Mimi's aria from the end of act one, she was struck by how nearly the poor little seamstress's circumstances mirrored her own. Yet from her consumptive throat pure heaven poured, striking a chord in something – someone – inside Frances Grace Newley. Or so it is comforting to surmise.

On the eve of the birth, George sent his solicitors to Grace with a proposition: if she agreed to absolve him of his paternity, he'd set her up for life. In a fit of pique, she refused. Anthony George Newley was born on 24 September 1931, in Homerton Hospital, up Marsh Hill – a decrepit institution that my grandmother always referred to as a 'workhouse'. These were truly Dickensian beginnings for one whose work and life would be doggedly hounded by poverty and yet undone by plenty.

My father was gobsmacked when the detective he'd hired called back only a few days later with a mess of details: address, medical records, bank accounts. He suddenly had every statistic on George Kirby. After all the conflicted longing, not to mention the wistful, bitter songs that had reached out in vain to a shadowy someone on the far side of the spotlight, all my father had to do now was pick up the phone.

He and George exchanged a few letters before arranging to meet. He flew to London and prepped for their momentous encounter by taking Tara and me on a trip down memory lane. Oswald Street was just another dingy byway in London's East End, but for my father, it was klieg-lit with memories. Reg turned down the street – a dismal stretch of row houses, leaning against each other like starving derelicts in a bread line. It reminded me of Sue's old neighbourhood in Bristol. Here my father had grown up an only child – gone hungry and dirty in these streets, picked up hot shrapnel from these pavements after German bombing raids.

As the shiny Jag moved along, Tara and I were uneasily aware that my father was being overwhelmed by surging recall. He named aloud the childhood mates who had originated in those houses: 'That was Joey Hackstead's place... God, Sid Miller lived there, awful bully... and Doris Stokes... Oh God, Dottie Stokes... my first and fastest hump...' And there, at street's end, was the house in which he had grown up with his mother – unchanged, he said, but for a lick of blue paint on the windowsills.

He rang the tinny doorbell and introduced himself to the stunned, sour-smelling occupants. Given the run of the place, we explored it like pilgrims at a shrine. In my father's old bedroom, he cranked his 16mm Bolex to film me standing at the window he had stood at as a poor, no-prospects boy. Below was a postage-stamp-sized garden enclosed by spears of rotten wood fence. Wormy hopelessness was in the air. My father walked about in a trance of sensations. He finally took my hand and said, 'What are you thinking, Sachie?'

I considered the house, the claustrophobic garden under a leaden sky with its overgrown borders and broken greenhouse glass panes: 'It's sad, Daddy,' I said.

He nodded and squeezed my hand a little harder.

Two weeks later, the moment has come. The shiny Jag merges off the motorway at twilight and enters a dreary suburb forty-five minutes north-east of London. It turns down a street of low, pebble-dashed houses darkened by sickly-yellow windows. Behind them, an open field of wasteland and a railway where a late commuter train mournfully shunts along.

My father leans forward and scans the numbers, counting down to fourteen. 'This is it.'

Reg pulls over and we get out. My father takes Tara's hand, then mine, and we walk down a short path, through a low gate, to the front door. The bell sounds its depth-charge of anxiety. I look at the pebbly wall under the porch light – a reptilian skin I long to touch.

The door opens on a gust of warm light and hermit smell, and there he is, smaller than I thought and uglier, blinking in his National Health specs.

'Oh, hullo, son,' he chirps.

'Hello, Dad.'

They embrace. George looks at me and offers a knotty, disfigured hand: 'You must be little Sacha.'

I nod as his dry hand encloses mine.

'And you must be Tara.'

She smiles with the same polite misgivings.

We follow the cardigan and the slippers into a hobbit's nest arranged around the TV. There's a brown armchair with a doily, and a gas fire. The walls are crowded with framed posters and yellowed clippings. George fidgets uncomfortably as we take it all in. My father puts his glasses on and moves closer to the crammed walls. 'Good God,' he murmurs. Now I see it for myself: the little room is a shrine to Anthony Newley – framed eight-by-tens of my father as a young man; clippings of his chart-topping songs; even a still from *Heironymus*.

'Dad, this is incredible,' says my father.

'I've kept up with everything,' says George, rocking on his heels. My eyes go to the dirty-green phone on the sideboard. The stooped old man never thought to lift it and try to contact his world-famous son? Or did he?

'Biscuit?' says George, advancing and offering me a plate of ginger snaps. I take one and bite into it. As it comes apart in my mouth, I see my father's mask cracking. I go over and take his hand, restoring our connection and his strength. He smiles at his father and tells Tara and me to go out and play so they can talk. We leap at the chance.

'What d'you think?' asks Tara.

'I don't know.'

She nods. 'I don't like his hands. Or his ginger snaps. They're stale.'

When it gets pitch-dark my father calls us in. We climb back up the grassy bank with big, tired strides as he watches us come, standing with his arm around his own father, who smiles mildly, hugging himself.

Now there's a great nervousness and desperation to be gone. The old man is a robot of tics and thwarted movement as he offers us a box of Quality Street chocolates. 'Thank you,' says Tara, mechanically taking one. He shakes the box: 'Have a little more, I got them just for you.' Now he offers me some, and I take a load, filling my pockets with guilt chocolate. 'That's more like it,' says George, and shows us to the door. My father kisses him, promises to come back soon and we're suddenly through the low gate and into the waiting Jag. Reg steps on it and a fluid spurt of speed takes us away. I look back and see George standing at the door.

'Bye, Dad, I love you,' my father calls through the window, and the old man waves one arm and refolds it across his chest. I keep him in my sight until he turns and closes the door.

Our father holds our hands in silence as we merge on to the M1 going south. Orange shards of lamplight rake his glasses. I can't see his eyes, only sense their fixity. I imagine George, in his kitchen, sipping tea. Perhaps he has turned on a football match. Or is he like our father, just sitting and staring?

The two men are officially rejoined, but now both understand why the silence was important. My father is probably the more lost. Finding this unremarkable man instead of his fantasy father has knocked down another of the supports that buttressed his strangeness in the world: *How did I ever happen? How is it that this man made me?*

There's no answer. Even Freud gave up explaining it. So much forgettable human music, and then a passing phrase or melody that moves us to tears, that makes all the tedious listening worthwhile.

Strangest of all, soon after my father informed his mother of the reunion with George, she separated from Pops and began a correspondence with her long-lost love. There was so much to forgive, but also a desire to meet again. My father flew George to Los Angeles. He and Grandma were waiting on the tarmac as the plane pulled up. When George appeared at the top of the steps, Grandma didn't recognize him at first, then gripped my father's arm. 'Tone,' she gasped, 'he's so old!'

There's a picture of the three of them together at last, sitting by the pool at Lloydcrest, smiling and raising their glasses to the camera. My father is in the middle, enjoying the novel sensation of being balanced between 'Mum and Dad'.

He flew them out to Las Vegas to watch his show, and stopped it halfway to let the spotlight find them, as he told the astonished audience the story of their miraculous reunion and how he finally 'felt complete'. There wasn't a dry eye in the house. Afterward, George broke down in my father's dressing room, and they sobbed together. Grandma filed for divorce from Pops and, Cathy having found them a house in the Pacific Palisades, George moved in.

My father was ecstatic. His life finally made sense to him. The two halves that made him were whole again. And he was in love, perhaps for the first time. He confided to his diary that Cath made him so happy 'it's almost scary.'

Catholic Cathy wanted him to marry her, but she was savvy enough to know you couldn't impose wedlock on an avowed bohemian like my father. So they came up with a New Age compromise: a druidic love ceremony. They invited all their friends to Lloydcrest for fine wine and grade-A weed to witness them swearing undying love for each other under the spreading eaves of the garden elm. Wearing his gold ankh and a floor-length shawl, my father murmured his specially written vows through hobbit sideburns, his eyes barely open under the death-stroke of ganja.

'With my seed, I thee love… With the gift of my art, I thee honour…' he burbled.

Cathy gleamed in triumph as he symbolically handed her a scroll of his music tied with red ribbon.

I doubt she knew what she was getting into. The magic and the pain in Newley would remain a mystery to her, as it had to my mother. Perhaps that's the way he wanted it. His mother had abandoned him during the war – for his own good, she insisted – sending him away from the Blitz to the relative safety of the country. There he had been billeted with an old crone in a one-room flat. She washed naked in front of him, and they had to share a bed. Once in the middle of the night she rolled over and almost suffocated him, contributing to a life-long fear of bed sharing. Woman was not to be trusted, in other words.

His love child with Cathy, Chelsea Andora Newley, was born in London during *The Good Old Bad Old Days* – my father's third bundle of joy to arrive during the run of a show.

Tara and I greet the birth with the same ambivalence we felt on the arrival of Katy Kass. We go to visit at the manger and stand around awkwardly – we are not the magi of the painting.

The two beloved infants impress upon us the reality that life has begun anew for each of our parents, that our existence is marginal and belongs to an earlier time – we are an experiment that failed. We understand intuitively that we must be happy for them, but can't gloss over what we feel. In the photographs my father took of us in Chelsea's nursery we appear at our most beautiful, as only children can when they are unhappy: the smiles at half-mast, the eye-pits deep and inward-looking.

Mummy says we have to leave England. She says Labour has it in for rich people. We're going to have to go back to Los Angeles, which makes me actually cry. I don't want to leave the Heath and all my friends at King Alfred's. Sue is tickled pink about going to

America because it's where all the movies and hamburgers and milkshakes come from and everyone drives around in Cadillacs. But England is a little sad, like me; I belong here. I get on my bike and ride to the Heath. London is far away and looks like a smear of blue paint with little exclamation points in it. The Post Office Tower has dishes on top that send out signals. The Waltons come from there, and Daddy's phone calls. I sit against a tree and hold a poo. I feel the roots under me; big hands, clutching the ground. If these trees could speak, they'd have a deep voice, hundreds of years old and tell everyone, including Mummy, to let me be. I don't want to go home. The boxes will be there, filling up with our things.

Instead, I get back on my bike and ride to the sweet shop. I go too fast for the pavement and slip on to the road. The handlebar tassels whip my hands; my ears roar like seashells and I'm crying straight lines around my face. At the zebra crossing I squeeze the brakes and get off to walk. The sweet shop is just across the road. There's traffic waiting at the light, but I can make it. But halfway across, the lights change, the traffic starts up, and my legs root down into the ground. I can't seem to move. I'm a matador stuck in the wrong place and the bull is charging. He comes with his horns low and digs out my bike and chucks me over. I turn in space, screaming. The sweet shop goes upside down and I land heavily, with a tire skidding to a stop inches from my nose. When I get up, my hands are dancing like I'm playing the piano. I'm laughing, too, and blood is squirting out of my head.

There's a lady standing on the pavement with her two daughters and their mouths are open like three black caves. The lorry driver climbs down with a white face and walks toward me. Then someone comes from behind and puts their arms around me. It's another lady, very worried, and she's trying to stop the blood. She puts me in her car, a green MG, and asks where I live. We speed back to Sheldon Avenue. I'm getting blood all over her leather seats but she doesn't seem to mind. Sue answers the doorbell. The lady tells her what happened and Sue just laughs and clips me round the ear, saying, 'Silly bugger.' Then closes the door on the nice lady's face.

My skull X-ray discloses a concussion, and they send me home. I bend over the tub and watch crimson water drain away as Sue washes the blood from my matted hair.

'You're lucky,' she says. 'You've got angels watching over you.'

Later, as I lie in bed with an awful headache, Ron looks in and asks if I'm all right. Yes, I say, and he nods quickly and withdraws. Sue has decided to play down what happened lest it reflect badly on herself. Nor does she report the near-fatal accident to my mother, cautioning me to do the same and not 'worry her about it.' She quickly disposes of my leather jacket, all stiff with dried blood and dumps my bike in a builder's skip – the front wheel twisted like a pretzel.

Days later my mother returns from a junket in Japan where she's been promoting the Italian comedy *Playing the Field*, and presents me with a kimono, which I proudly belt and pose in for her. The big scab on my head is still there, but when she runs her hands through my hair she doesn't feel it.

# 8

# 1011 Chalette Drive

I'VE ALWAYS BEEN STYLISTICALLY DIVERSE AS A PAINTER. THIS might have something to do with the fact that my childhood was so nomadic. My work has reflected that malaise, and taken advantage of that opportunity.

In 2000, I was in the middle of yet another stylistic shift. The spirit of my roving childhood was very much upon me as I moved from Los Angeles to New York. I settled into a studio in Harlem, and began making some experiments in gel pouring and paper crushing – even using a hairdryer to push watery pigment around on paper. After working for a while in this abstract vein, I had a strong desire to do a figurative drawing. I took a large piece of toned paper, pinned it to the wall, and the drawing *Traveller* literally leapt out at me. I had no idea who this hooded figure was – he just came out of the woods, as it were, and proposed himself with the modesty of an old friend.

Looking at it now, I see all too clearly that it's a self-portrait. I was excited enough at the time to feel I'd hit a seam with *Traveller* and I continued exploring the subject. The next work – a painting – I called *Lost*. Even though it follows in the series, it really predates *Traveller* in significance. It's because I had felt so lost that I became a traveller. It's because I had always been troubled by a sense of displacement that I reconceived of my life as a pilgrimage. This is the alchemy of all art: turning darkness into light, a sense of exile into one of adventure. It's also the primal meaning behind the expulsion from the Garden of Eden. We leave home in order to gain the universe.

*Traveller Drawing*

*Lost*

We are all, no matter how blessed our childhoods, exiles from the perfect garden – that paradise of early life when the world came to our doorstep and settled like a butterfly. Just as we paused to inspect this miracle, it up and left us, fluttering away for no apparent reason. Instead, there was homework to do, garbage to haul out; the world outside the garden called.

We joined the river of exiles and it was flowing. The river was called time and history, and there were dips and rapids as a matter of course. But where were we all going? That is what the child always wants to know: where and why. The question is never answered. There is only the non-answer, 'I don't know.' And to turn that 'I don't know' into a jubilant cry is the work of art.

*Fellow Travellers* followed *Lost* as the third work in the series. Our hapless exile is now at peace, attended by a knowing friend – that is, a friend who knows the way. But who is this ghostly other, who looks at us with a slight smile of reservation?

When Dante descends into the underworld, Virgil is waiting there to guide him. Nowadays we might say that Virgil is one's higher self – or perhaps the voice of the therapist exhorting the patient to confront his so-called demons. Or we might say, borrowing the original meaning of the word guide, that Virgil is his *genius* – his *genie* – the magical spirit that grants his wish for self-knowledge. My experience of genius came early, through watching my father perform. It was a veritable masterclass in the ways of the *inspired one*.

In my painting, the guardian spirit cautions us not to judge his charge too harshly. True, this man of clay is childish and ridiculous – a fool easily led astray by temptation – but in the hands of the spirit, he's a minstrel, a poet, a sacred vessel for the transcendental statements of art.

How early did I feel that hand on my shoulder? Certainly, my father's hand was there first, and left its lasting imprint. But there were so many times when he was absent, and times when I wandered away from him or went against him – and still I found my way. What was this instinct that made the unknown a friend to me, that turned the threatening forest into a grove of magical possibilities?

'Eternity is in love with the productions of time,' Blake said. I want my *Fellow Travellers* to express that beautiful truth.

*Fellow Travellers*

1974. The English papers were accusing Labour's Denis Healey of 'soaking the rich.' Exorbitant wealth taxes were draining away what little money my mother had left. She'd come home to England to start a new life and find herself – again. That much she had accomplished. Now her acting career was stalled. England had theatre, but that was not her calling, in the way that Hollywood always was. An opportunity was opening up for Ron in Los Angeles with Atlantic Records. And so we became revenants.

At Heathrow, the photographers fired off pictures, backtracking frantically as we walked to the plane. So another home-grown talent was jumping ship. 'Why you leavin', Joanie?' was the refrain.

'Healey's a pig,' my mother snapped. 'He's destroying the country. I'm just trying to earn a crust!' They laughed as one and pleaded for a family picture, but Tara and I cowered behind Mummy as she majestically breasted the flashbulbs.

Ron met us at LAX in a brand-new drop-dead Cadillac Eldorado convertible. Gold. It was the most glamorous thing I'd ever seen. 'Not bad, eh?' he said, as the electronic roof cantilevered down and stowed itself behind the rear seats.

I just nodded, admiring the white-wall tires and the king-size hood. We loaded as much as we could into the trunk, and a waiting van took the rest. Heading up the 405 freeway on an adrenalized high, I lifted my windblown head into the wide blue sky of Los Angeles. The Cadillac seemed to roll on a bank of air. When we merged off the freeway and came to a stoplight, it pitched forward, then reared up again like a boat on liquid shocks. I ogled the shops and the fancy cars as we entered the precincts of Beverly Hills. Ron smiled in the rear-view mirror. My mother's arm was around him; her headscarf was blowing – everything was picture perfect.

We turned off Sunset and started a steep climb up Trousdale Drive. There was a warning sign there and a deep gravel pit by the road.

'What's that?' I asked Ron.

'For cars that have lost their breaks – to ditch in.'

I nodded as Ron floored the gas and the Eldorado's golden tonnage sped upward past the clipped driveways. The car could only manage thirty-five miles per hour on the incline – its 6,000 ccs of power muffled to a gravelly roar by the smog converter. We were entering Shangri-La – or Shangri L.A. Mansions encrusted the hillsides like so much jewellery, shelving down velvet contours to enjoy magnificent views of Beverly Hills. The wide road was flanked by perfectly spaced pines and signs that warned of brake failure on the downward gradient. Near the top, we turned left, and Ron pointed up a steep bank of ivy to the spreading white facade of our new home: 1011 Chalette Drive. I clung to the side of the car as we lurched up the drive and came to rest outside the house's slick fifties facade.

'Here it is…!' said my mother, sashaying toward the monumental double doors. They seemed to sigh open by themselves on a long, air-conditioned corridor.

'Wow!' exclaimed Tara and I in unison, running down the corridor into a vast empty space carpeted all in white.

'This is the living room,' said my mother, smiling delightedly. 'There's no furniture yet, but it's going to be great!'

We ran outside and tested the temperature of the kidney-shaped pool – already warm! And then we discovered the tennis court – complete with nightlights. Tara and I dervish-whirled in ecstasy as Sue lumbered on to the court and clapped her hands for a group hug.

Over the ensuing weeks, Eugenio – our virile if bejewelled decorator – added the bravura touches to a house that was essentially geared toward entertaining. The bar was covered in a mirrored skin of segmented glass. Silver lamé palm trees camouflaged the support columns; vast lengths of interconnecting white sofa hugged the walls and broke up the space for conversation. It was like the bungalow of a visiting Arabian prince – or a white slice of cruise-liner kitsch, sailing past the Hollywood sign. It was all designed to make a statement: I am successful; I am *not* desperate for work – and fuck the budget.

The living room took up roughly sixty per cent of the house; the master bedroom, another twenty. The remainder doglegged down by the pool area, with three rooms for us kids off the corridor. The master bedroom with monster closet faced the downtown view. It was papered and draped in the same pattern of palm fronds and flora that famously graced the interior of the Beverly Hills Hotel and furnished with a four-poster king in matching fabric. The jungly effect was slightly suffocating. By contrast, Sue's room, up at the far end of the house, was a dark little nook that adjoined the garage and smelled vaguely of damp and gasoline.

From the huge balcony carpeted with AstroTurf and bolted to the front of the house like an afterthought, I surveyed the smoggy sea of downtown Los Angeles and wondered at the nature of my latest voyage. After the excitement of arrival, my old sense of disorientation had returned. It didn't matter that Eugenio had decorated my room in the wake-up-and-go yellow, orange and ultramarine that I had requested, and that I now see anticipated the spunky palette of my first paintings. My sense of displacement was bound up in the house itself. The living room had a plastic walkway across it that I was told to keep to at all costs – woe betide me if my errant sneakers strayed on to the pristine desert of shag (Sue couldn't wait for *that* infraction).

The very spaciousness of the house was a heartache to me – it was like I wasn't even there. Its acres of fitted carpet oppressed me with the dry, antiseptic spirit of an airport waiting lounge. I gazed over the white expanse of the living room, not having the guts to leave the plastic walkway, as if I was the living inhabitant of a controlled exhibit that only came alive at party time.

Also out of bounds were whole areas of my mother, roped off from my interference. I watched her pass back and forth in agitated dressage: a beautiful, spooked, thoroughbred desperate to clear the hurdles and resurrect her tumbled career. I sensed she was battling a tortuous headwind, trying, with her jewellery, charisma and rapier wit, to get through. She persevered through the days because she was Mummy: amazing, inspired, indomitable.

Something of her spirit is captured, I like to think, in my first portrait of her, painted when I was twenty-eight. It depicts the immense psychic force straining under the surface of her loveliness. It's the jagged undercurrent that makes that loveliness angular; makes it darkly beautiful – as in fairy-tale conjurings of the Wicked Queen.

This is not a portrait of Joan Collins the actress and public personality, but of her being as it manifested itself to her only son at all stages of his development. It is therefore *my* truth, not hers. The little boy, through the medium of the painter, asks: why can't Mummy relax and love me?

On seeing the portrait hanging in the dining room of her London house, Michael Caine remarked: 'Fuckin' A, it's the picture of Dor*een* Gray!'

I knew nothing of my mother's real troubles and vulnerabilities. She had succeeded all too well in shielding me from the problems she was facing. As a result, I could never gain access to her warmly protective, inner sanctum; I could not hide inside her from my own doubts and fears. When she asked me what the matter was, I couldn't say – I had formed no habits of confession. So I grew hard with strength and denial. Although I longed for her affection, I could only mirror back to her the lack of affection I felt. I didn't know it then, but it was the same spirit of withholding that she felt from casting directors every time she failed an audition. It was the prevailing negativity of the industry that she was unconsciously handing down to me. It formed in me a hatred of Hollywood that persists to this day. The little boy has never forgiven Tinseltown for toying with his mother's heart.

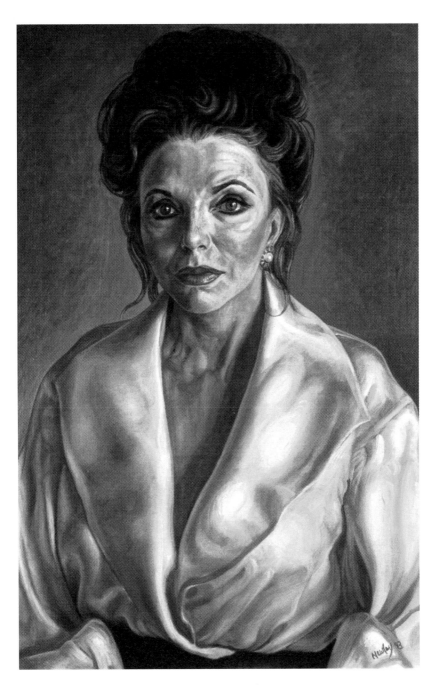

*The Artist's Mother*

Her first months back in town after five years away were a nightmare of demeaning casting calls and other embarrassments. Secretaries mangled her last name calling her 'Kullens' or 'Connings'; young punk producers put the moves on her. She soon realized that her time in England not only had not helped her but had actually damaged her prospects. Nothing she had done in the years 1970 through 1975 had registered on the Hollywood radar, and the successes she had enjoyed in fifties Hollywood as a tenured starlet at Fox were long forgotten. There was no TCM to keep her past achievements streaming under the noses of the young execs, who in any case were now hopelessly into the brute realism pedalled by Peckinpah and his ilk. Hollywood had entered another Golden Age, but one utterly without Glamour. My mother's star turns in *The Girl in the Red Velvet Swing* and *Land of the Pharaohs* were interred in studio vaults. It was as if she had lived and done her work in a past century, and had now, by some tragic mistake of time travel, turned up, aged forty-two, in 1975.

Her agent advised her to lop off a few years and take whatever she was offered – mostly TV. She did an episode each of *Starsky & Hutch* and *Police Woman*, and then a more up-market gig on the *Bing Crosby Show*, where she was paired with that burbling curmudgeon with the pipe for the first time in twenty years (she had worked with him on *The Road to Hong Kong* in 1962). This was followed by a favour from her other co-star on that film, Bob Hope, whose televised variety show gave her a brief purchase in the Monday night line-up. At least she was marginally professionally alive – the casting agents and ratings hawks saw that she was back in town and still kicking, and looking like ten million bucks. Nevertheless, her personalized license plate – 'Joan Who?' – remained all too stubbornly apt. She was like a character in one of her sister Jackie Collins's novels: a gutsy survivor looking for the big break in all the wrong places. Every morning she read the trades and called her agent.

'Anything, Tom?'

'Honey, what can I say… There's just not a lot for a woman of your… experience. We could do *Tattletales* [the famous couples' gameshow]. It's money and they'll give you a free appliance.'

'I'm not doing that shit again.'

'Ron likes doing it…'

'Of course he does, it's easy – all he has to do is sit there and let loose with my intimate secrets.' She looked at the snoring lump beside her. He would invariably have tossed and turned all night, until a 4 a.m. fudge binge knocked him out for good. She hung up with Tom and went to put on her face. Joan Collins, aka Kullins and Connings, was about to do something unthinkable: go down to the unemployment office.

On the way there, she considered an extreme solution to her financial problem: settle for a smaller house, put the kids in public school, let the nanny and the maid go.

Hell no! She wasn't ready to accept defeat – there was no point in living if she couldn't live large. She was damned if she was going to accept anything less than a glamorous life after all the hard work she'd put in. One way out – or rather, back in – would be to write her memoirs.

God knows, she had many tales to tell and enough writerly flair to pull it off. With a word-wizardry acquired from untold hours of poolside scrabble, she was a born contender in the kiss-and-tell stakes. Her book agent, Irving 'Swifty' Lazar, a legend in Hollywood, had championed her since her early days in town and was gearing up to go to bat for her with leading publishers.

In line at the unemployment office, she struggled to stay positive. The wait was interminable. She was going to have to draw on her dwindling reserves of patience. The line was full of unspeakable people. How much longer would it be, she grimly wondered, before she became one of them, loitering with the kids at the corner of Sunset and Vine, rattling a tin cup? Her imagination, usually a strong point, was a liability at times like this.

At last her number was called and she stepped forward to a sullen black lady bent over her forms.

'Name?'

'Joan Collins.'

'Social?'

She gave her number.

'Profession?'

'Actress.'

The lady looked up for a second. 'Go fill out the forms and come back.'

'But I've been waiting in line for forty-five minutes!'

'I know, ma'am, we all have to wait...'

'How long till I get the money?'

The lady blinked, perhaps noticing for the first time that the desperado before her was beautiful.

'If you're approved, about a month or two...'

'If I'm approved?!'

'That's right, if. Next please...'

In the parking lot, my mother slumped over the wheel of her gold Mercedes and wept bitter tears. It was all too much: the pressures of career, of motherhood, of a souring marriage. Lifting her tear-stained face, she saw a billboard promoting the film *Network*. Faye Dunaway was in that – Faye who had cut her dead at a party the night before. They had come up together through the ranks, but now Faye was riding the crest of a wave while Joan was bottom-feeding. Her past rose up to torture her: if that little girl in St John's Wood, pasting beloved film stars into endless scrap books, had been able to conjure this future moment – sobbing over the wheel in the parking lot of the unemployment office – would she have changed course and relinquished her dream of stardom?

Not on your life. She drove home and called RJ Wagner. They'd been the greatest of friends (they'd been dating, for Chrissake, when my father entered the picture and scooped her up), and now RJ was Hollywood royalty after marrying Natalie Wood. He listened sympathetically to her problems and promised to help. He invited her over with us kids; and we splashed around in the pool while she and RJ sat on sunloungers talking Hollywood Survival 101. RJ threw her a lifeline, offering her a one-off cameo on his hit show *Switch*, and lectured her on the importance of 'fuck-you money' for the years ahead.

'Capisce,' she said, 'but I need it now. Even a little "excuse-me money" will do.'

Ron was useless. He had studied accounting but his talent was for cooking, rather than balancing, the books. Whenever my mother wailed about money, he calmly reassured her. His home office on Chalette, with its huge desk, high-backed leather chair and sprawling view of downtown, oozed liquidity, while in fact he was struggling to stay afloat in the recording industry, flapping and fussing and robo-calling to little effect. After the belly flop of his film-producing ambitions, he took care to perfect his smoke-and-mirrors act while basically vacuuming up coke. He must have had something to do with Rod Stewart's album *Atlantic Crossing*, because Rod showed up at a few of our parties, but that seemed to be about the extent of his work for Atlantic Records.

The Kass-Collins family was in economic free-fall. The ground that the big white house stood on no longer existed. I instinctively braced for impact, but the adults around me seemed endlessly expansive. The house throbbed with parties and hullabaloo. A rhythmical bit of fluff called The Hustle was the musical craze of the moment and I was allowed to join the party line-up and hold hands with the grown-ups, moving back and forth across the white carpet in serried rows, doing The Hustle. The plastic walkway was rolled up for these occasions. On the carpet of clouds, I felt weight-less and free. The laughter and all the mirrored surfaces worked on me like a drug, and as for my mother, she seemed the happy goddess of this enchanted demesne.

Sue was in pig heaven. America, principally Hollywood, had lived up to her wildest expectations. She embraced with open arms the splendours of its vinyl emporia and loved every manifestation of its tackiness: the strip malls, the drive-ins, the gross display of material wealth – everything felt right. Subtlety was anathema to her. She liked things plain to the point of crudity, and beyond. The California sun shone sympathetically on her brassiness and she loved to wear her Ray-Bans and hang a fleshy arm out of the window of the Mercedes as we sped down the boulevards, pounding the wheel to 'Jumpin' Jack Flash'. The emotional terrain around her was always in upheaval. She was either shouting or laughing, angry or impassioned; about a movie, a song, a TV show, a movie star. Every drive with her had this adrenalized feeling. She was coked up on American sugar, and even her Bristol accent started to melt around the edges and actually *sound* American.

We took long drives down Sunset together, our heads radar-tracking from one marvel to the next. It was my first experience of the carnival and carnage of greater Los Angeles. As a sheltered toddler on Summit Drive, I had never ventured beyond the miniature golf course that was Beverly Hills, but now I saw the full sprawl of L.A.'s prefabricated ugliness. This outland became our world of adventure. We travelled east to where the palm trees ended and the billboards began. This was the beginning of The Strip, as Sue loved to call it. My eyes became lost in a forest of signage: Tower Records; Whisky a Go Go; strip clubs; burger joints; mean motels that lined Sunset on its descent into the first circle of Hollywood, where the world became even more lurid and filthy. We stopped for the obligatory bag of Famous Amos cookies and scarfed them as we watched movies under the crenelated roof of the Cinerama Dome. At Grauman's Chinese Theatre, I put my mitts in the big prints of Steve McQueen and Sue sucked down her vanilla shake, staring in happy delirium at the bristling, oriental facade. This was such a long way from Bristol and the house of stacked dishes, the tussling brothers, the mother with the frightful face – she must have felt it like a heavenly afterlife.

She mastered the freeway system in no time and we went on long desert drives to Disneyland, Knott's Berry Farm and Magic Mountain. We were there for the opening of The Revolution, the first upside-down rollercoaster, and went on it seven times in a row. Sue screamed the loudest, her Bristols lifting in zero gravity as we looped the loop. Then we posed for pictures to go in the perspex picture-blocks by her bedside – more moments in the sun with 'her kids'.

At day's end, ravished by our time in the sensorium, we would repair to our favourite drive-in: Tiny Naylor's, where the waitresses roller-skated to your car just like in *American Graffiti* – and fastened burger trays to your window. We unwrapped our burgers and added the Tiny Naylor's special sauce, which was Thousand Island dressing with chopped pickle. The mixture made a wonderful slurry in our mouths, and we looked at the strobing lights through half-closed eyes and were warm and grateful.

That spring, Tara and I started at Hawthorne Elementary School. The campus took up a whole city block in the flats of Beverly Hills. The main buildings were modelled after a Spanish mission, with a blue-domed bell tower in the centre. The heavy stone walls kept the hallways cool in summer and framed the central courtyard where we gathered for school portraits. Aged nine, I can be seen sitting cross-legged along the bottom, a third grader, while Tara stands tall and spotty in fifth.

The school was exclusive and is still attended, I would imagine, by the beautiful children of actors and actresses, and the not-so-beautiful children of their agents and managers. We started there in 1975, on the eve of the American Bicentennial; and were quickly force-fed on a pablum of founding fathers and first principles. Every morning we had to face Old Glory and put our hand on our hearts to say the Pledge of Allegiance, which I can still recite without a hitch. In contrast to the loosey goosey atmosphere of King Alfred's, I was now in a far-right propaganda nation: 'republics' and 'upstanding individuals' replaced creatives and soul-diggers. The Heath, with its lush enclosures, had been succeeded by Fields of Waving Grain. This was America, and I must admit I liked it jolly well.

Every kid in my class seemed to be Jewish: Silverman, Shapiro, Goldberg, Mirisch, Stern – it was like the rollcall of a blue-chip urban law firm. A few had inherited the boorishness and egoism of their Hollywood fathers. I was among the quieter kids. It didn't help matters that King Alfred's had grievously underprepared me for the demands of a proper school. I was soon demoted a grade and frequently kept after class to work on spelling and penmanship while my classmates streamed out to the sun-drenched playground. My slipshod academics roused the ire of our dictatorial principal, Dr Rowan. He convinced my mother that I needed extra help – and so, even at home now, I was made to labour away under the beady eye of a tutor in half-moons.

I love you, Dana Pepp. I wish I could talk to you. You're always so far away, at the other end of the hallway. Sometimes I watch you walk past, talking to your friends, playing with the tinkling charms around your neck. Whenever I hear that tinkle, I freeze in anticipation.

I feel invisible around you. This has its useful side – I can observe you without discovery. Your tanned skin is so smooth. Your brown, feathered hair, shaped into a perfect bob, has a velvety smoothness I want to touch. There's more to you than meets the eye. There's a power in the air around you and it humbles my own power.

I've had this feeling before, around my sister's friends, but this time it goes deeper. Dana Pepp is the light that pervades my days. Sightings of her flood me with adrenalin. I watch her pass, my head moving like a sunflower tracking the sun. She pulls me out of myself and into her space, making me live and yearn. My sick-puppy heart goes bounding after her.

I have what they call feelings for Dana, and guilt and shame attend the fermenting crush; at the same time, I am full of joy and longing. For some reason I imagine that by walking pigeon-toed I will be more appealing to her – and she might even notice me. Perhaps it's because *she* walks like that, with her toes slightly turned inward. My mimicking her is a show of body empathy: seeing me loping past, she can't possibly fail to recognize me as her mate.

I practise: head slung low, arms swinging. I am apelike, but have a 'Pepp' in my step like her. As soon as the opportunity arises, I do my walk, passing right in front of her. But she *still* doesn't notice me. The necessary conditions of unrequited love are therefore met: I don't exist for her; I am invisible while she, the love object, fills my field of vision.

Watching her, I have the same feelings I will presently experience in front of a portrait subject, or a landscape, or a still life I'm paint-ing. The overwhelming reality of 'it', of the Other. The sensation causes, in the initial instance, a moment of anxiety during which all my instincts as a painter are held in suspension. I feel that it's impossible to capture what is there, that it's reckless to even try. And yet the brush goes to the canvas and begins somehow to trace the lineaments of what I feel.

And then, a moment captured, the fall into unknowing merci-fully arrested: something has been held back and understood. And with that zero sum of fixed information, I begin to assemble my discovery; slowly, over days, I excrete the sticky mass of my concen-tration and build the web within which the thing is held quivering. If I have succeeded in catching the butterfly without maiming or killing it, now I must be careful to provide enough oxygen while sealing off its escape. Be careful not to over-paint, I tell myself; leave enough negative space, enough untreated canvas, to let the thing breathe. 'To define is to limit,' said Wilde. Tread along the hair's breadth of that paradox and do not fall...

By this point it should go without saying that my first experience of unrequited love began long before Dana – with my mother. That was the primal wound that would ultimately make me a portrait-ist, prefiguring how my heart goes out to my subject, how I must capture them so they'll never go away.

After school, in Sue's gloomy room by the garage, I watch *I Dream of Jeannie* and imagine that the interior of Barbara Eden's genie bottle with its wrap-around velvet sofa and Moroccan throw cushions is the capsule in which Dana and I will one day sail away. We will drift through the universe in an ecstasy of wanderlust and eat cake and drink Kool-Aid and gaze into each other's eyes, never tiring of what we find there. I ogle Barbara Eden's legs through the diaphanous silk of her genie pants and feel an ache of association: Dana's legs are like that – shapely, long, and tanned. I'm almost ten now – in that Arcadian pause between childhood and the onset of masturbation.

As a fifth grader at Hawthorne, Tara was already being subjected to courses in sex and drug education to shield her from omnipres-ent temptation. She showed me the textbook pictures – a cutaway pregnancy with the foetus lodged sideways for delivery; a fertilized egg, radiating sperm like sunrays – and it all made me slightly queasy. When she returned from school with a watch list of all the illicit drugs available on the open market, my mother took it the wrong way, concluding that her eleven-year-old daughter was now thoroughly indoctrinated in all the possible ways to get high. She ran to Ron with her concerns (not a smart move – the man was a walking pharmacopeia). Did he really think L.A. was the place to bring up children? Wouldn't it be better to return to the decency and restraint of England? And besides, Hollywood hadn't exactly delivered on its promise of a career jolt.

Ron demurred. Things, he insisted, were about to happen for him – as always. He had been befriended by Edgar Bronfman, the

CEO of Seagram's, a premier liquor firm, and felt he was about to be offered a senior position in the company – it would just take a little more schmoozing.

For once, he was right. My mother's anxieties were allayed for the time being when, only weeks later, Edgar Bronfman did take Ron on. It was an ersatz position – he was to be more of a glorified PR man than anything else – but it gave him the excuse to print large amounts of headed stationery. His first job was to talk my mother into marshalling her Hollywood connections for a huge party to celebrate Edgar Junior's twenty-first birthday – the kid was looking to get into the business and this would be a perfect way to introduce him to the town's movers and shakers.

So, on Edgar Senior's dime, my mother got busy, sending out a Hollywood APB to all her friends and lovers of decades past. They in turn spread the word, and the party soon ballooned, inflated by the appeal of getting oneself in on the ground floor with the young wannabe mogul.

Three days before the bash, tables and tent poles began arriving. I watched excitedly as a Big Top was erected over the tennis court, and a black-and-white floor laid down to turn it into a dance pavilion. Black and white was the colour scheme and everything had to match, right down to the black-and-white napkins coiled together, and the bursting bouquets of Calla lilies and painted black coral on every table. There was an army of men perched on ladders wiring crystal chandeliers and a constant thrum of work and anxiety as the bare space was transformed into a fairy-tale pavilion of candle-lit tables and jungly ferns, heating lamps and swathed fabric. Caterers and culinary specialists were on hand to carve out huge ice sculptures of swans and crabs and to adorn the buffet tables with banked displays of seafood worthy of Harrods' food halls.

Dressed by my mother in Gatsby chic – white pants, black-and-white plaid jacket and polka dot bow tie – I wandered through the party tent in a happy daze, observing final preparations. Sue saw me and remarked, 'That's show business, Kiddo!' I nodded. It was like a spaceship was landing and enclosing us in its throbbing, star-lit interior. We weren't on Planet Earth any more.

Inside the house, I found my mother fussing – plumping pillows, wiping ashtrays and screaming at lacklustre waiters. It was impor-tant, this business of making a show.

She stopped at a mirror to check her make-up and I saw my chance. I walked up and said, 'Mummy, can I help with the party?'

'No, Darling, but thank you for offering…'

I had a brainwave: 'Maybe I could stand by the door and take the coats?'

She looked at me and smiled: 'Yes. Yes you do that. I'm sure the guests will be charmed.'

I went running to the tall double entrance doors and stood at attention, a toy soldier, waiting to receive. Perhaps I'd grow up and be like this, wearing white gloves and tails, my hair slicked in a zigzag cartoon shine. A Stutz Bearcat pulled up with gleaming pipes and a beautiful man and woman got out and walked jaun-tily toward me. 'Rod and Alana Stewart,' whispered Sue over my shoulder. I took a deep breath and stepped into their path: 'May I take your coats?'

Alana cooed and slipped off her mink. Rod unwound his scarf and gave me a laddish slap on the back. I toddled to the closet with the suffocating fur, inhaling the sweet morphia of her perfume and barely reached the hangers. Then came Tony Franciosa with his heavy suede jacket; and Angie Dickinson with her pink feather boa whose stray tendrils got inside my mouth and made me cough. My mother passed by, pulling on a cigarette: 'Darling, you're doing a smashing job!'

I was a hit. Tara might look demure in her sheer silk pinafore, my mother and Ron might rival F. Scott and Zelda in the glamour stakes, but I was delectable and cute.

As the party powered up and the arrivals started coming in a steady stream, the closets filled up and I had to build a foaming pile of furs and feathers on Sue's bed. Hurrying back and forth, I passed into a sort of trance: the beauty and excitement of it all, along with my mother's evident pleasure, gave me a contact high of ecstasy. I was stoned on perfume and glitter and red lips and white teeth.

When the gong sounded for dinner, I followed the guests into the tent. With the space full of milling bodies, my hallucination was complete. We were the chosen ones, the elect of the elect. The spaceship was taking us away to bring light and laughter to the rest of the cold universe; the rumbling orchestra was our jet propulsion as we left the Earth. I caught Mummy's eye and she came over and showed me to my seat, next to hers – I had to force myself down into it like a helium balloon. I speared a prawn from my cocktail and the fishy taste exploded in my mouth as Mummy lifted her champagne and sipped.

Then after dinner there was dancing. I dived in amid the slithering bodies. Mummy clapped and looked coyly over her shoulder as I advanced toward her with a threatening display of funk. 'Kid's got rhythm,' Edgar Senior said, as I muscled him aside. My mother laughed and got into my groove. My magic was bubbling to the surface. 'Go Sach!' she said, as my gyrations accelerated. The space around us cleared. The grown-ups hooted and clapped accompaniment, and I put out coiling arms, then chivvied in place, elbowing my way down into the baseline. Jeeves had morphed into Travolta.

This was *my* party now. I owned it. I was known here and my dancing loved. As I wandered between the tables, acknowledging the smiles of admirers and savouring the bionic flexing in my legs, I came across a young man sucking on a cigarette and looking happily nonplussed by it all. With his straggly hair, Lennon specs and fuzzy beard, he struck me as a waiter.

'Hi, I'm Edgar Junior,' he said and offered me a puff on his cigarette.

I sucked in the acrid smoke and retched a plume.

He laughed and ruffled my hair. 'That's your first cigarette, kid, but not your last…'

I felt myself sinking as the party emptied out with kisses and long goodbyes. I began to lose my high. This was punishment for having gotten carried away. The spaceship had come back to Earth and dumped us all out on the ground. I had no heart to give back the coats – I left that to Sue – and disappeared down the long corridor to my room. I lay there in the dark and listened to the tent poles clanging and the stray laughter of staff as the party emptied out. When I woke the next day, it was all gone: the dream had been rolled up and away in a big wave. I repaired to the kitchen and found Sue wiping down the breakfast table. She served me a bowl of cornflakes, which tasted like ashes. My mother and Ron slept till noon and woke to hangovers and a call from Edgar Senior, who thanked Ron for a wonderful party, then fired him.

# 9

# A Tale of Two Houses

Lloydcrest was only a fifteen-minute drive from Chalette, which put my father almost too easily within reach after the privation of being 3,000 miles away from him.

Our time with him was always high-key. We would run through the butterfly garden, swiping our nets over the monarchs and golden moths and then ogle our beautiful captives in specimen jars. Daddy was there to puncture the lids so they could breathe, and especially to help us draw them. We always released them afterward, wondering why they lingered inside the jar until Daddy flushed them out with a puff of air.

When Tara and I both came down with a twenty-four-hour bout of flu, Daddy cancelled all his appointments to nurse us through. We were so drained from vomiting we couldn't even get off the bathroom floor. I can still feel his presence, stroking and flannelling my forehead as I melodramatically croaked, 'I want to die.' He carried me back to bed when the nausea abated. I remember how safe I felt in the bower of his arms.

Tara embraced Cathy as the mother she'd never really had. They'd sit together by the fireplace at Lloydcrest, Cathy with her cigarette and glass of Chardonnay and rehash Tara's problems. It always circled back to the same thing: 'Mummy doesn't understand me... Mummy is never there.'

No, but Cathy was.

When we went east on our summer holiday, her stature only grew. My father was doing a string of gigs with Burt Bacharach and had rented a rambling colonial house in the horse country of

Mount Kisco, New York. There Cathy presided as earth goddess, tweezing out horse ticks, cooking ample roasts and fearlessly flushing a garter snake from the shade of the pool heater. The image of her brandishing the writhing reptile overhead, before releasing him, became instantly fundamental for me – erotically charged with myth. Even the actor Mike Lipton – my parents' best friend and soulmate from the sixties wonder years – softened towards her after a delightful practical joke she played. He was sitting alone in the dining room, sipping his soup, when she led a horse up to the open window behind him and manoeuvred its great head inside. Mike felt hot wet breath on his neck and spun around. The horse whinnied and almost gave him a heart attack.

We returned from Mount Kisco a family. Cathy took over the running of Lloydcrest and my father signed the cheques. (I once observed him signing a stack of them with his secretary; he didn't even want to know what they were for – he just couldn't wait to get away from these tiresome practicalities to some dreamtime with a lyric.) She possessed all the male attributes he lacked, and then some. When gophers started digging up the lower lawn, she astonished him by picking them off with a rifle held at waist level. She loved cars and was soon the squealing recipient of a brand-new Pontiac Firebird that sported a flaming avian on its tumescent hood. It was a sex machine all right – a testament to how my father felt about her. And it was succeeded by a silver Porsche (in which she would proceed to have a near-fatal accident) and then by my own favourite, a first-off-the-line Cadillac Seville.

Chelsea was her precious gift to *him* – a perfect little angel complete with button nose and big brown eyes. Her fourth birthday, celebrated in the butterfly garden, was a storybook carnival of clowns, five-tier cakes and dappled sunlight. As one guest remarked, 'What do you give your child after this – Cuba?'

So glorious was Chelsea that she received her very own eponymous song: a swooning ballad smothered in lush strings and

pre-recorded birdsong, the backing vocalists crooning 'CHEL-
SEEE…' as my father sang his saccharine lyrics and Chelsea babbled
away in the background about 'budderflies and puppy-goggs…'

So where was *my* song, Daddyo: *Sachaaaa* – with its macho evoca-
tions of me on the soccer field? Did my father ever toy with composing that one? Tara was similarly passed over, while Cathy eventually
got hers, a dubiously entitled number called 'I'm Learning to Love
You' (the bloom was off the tiger lily by this point); and even my
father's agent, Sandy Gallin, and his best friend, Howie Greenfield
(writer of such classics as 'Love Will Keep Us Together' and many
others in Neil Sedaka's hit parade), were the gratified recipients of
songs written expressly for and about them.

Tara and I had gotten used to our paradoxical place in the Newley
scheme of things. We were deeply loved, but then so was everyone
else in my father's orbit. He seemed to love *everyone* deeply.

Except himself. He once confessed to me that there was a time
in his mid-forties when he couldn't think about anyone he loved
without a big fist appearing in his mind and striking them down.
This, he maintained, was his inner child remonstrating: *How dare
you love another when I'm still waiting!* The torment drove him to
therapists, psychics, and assorted other healers. He found an old
photograph of himself aged eight and made it the centrepiece of a
shrine to this aggrieved child (bristling with candles and childhood
mementoes: a bit of shoe leather, a piece of wartime shrapnel, a
rusty whistle), propitiating him with prayers and devotions whenever the blackness came over him. It seemed to help. A little.

Then he hung a punchbag from a tree at Lloydcrest and pounded
it mercilessly every afternoon to get out what he called his 'hostility'. As I watched him, I repeated to myself this strange word,
*hostility*, so uncomfortable in its bag of skin. I fancied I could almost
see it leave my father's body as he dodged and faked and furiously
threw punches. I wondered if I had it, too. I didn't have to wonder
long – he bought me my own headgear and gloves and encouraged

me to work the bag. I liked having him behind me, breathlessly goading: 'That's good, Sachie, good! Go on, get in there, really work it...' I grunted and flailed until my arms were boiled limp and he had to take over, throwing neat little jabs and chuffing air through rhino nostrils. This was very satisfactory father-son stuff. We had missed that phase and now were making up for lost time with a vengeance.

His license plate says 'Zen Bug' because Daddy's big on Zen Buddhism. This is his third Corvette and they've all been silver with black interiors. The leather's so cold against my legs it makes me shiver. Daddy slides in beside me and pretends we're in a cockpit. He goes through a checklist of buttons, making a chirping sound. I laugh when he says: 'This is Zen Bug flight 4567, requesting permission for take-off.'

The front end of the Corvette rumbles and grumbles and emerges into full-throated consciousness. Then it dies. Such a large engine dreams heavy and balks at getting out of bed. It's a sullen teen with way too many hormones. Daddy keys it again and guns it. The garage resounds with the angry roar of twelve cylinders coughing up phlegm and getting trumpet-clear. Already carbon monoxide is seeping in and we must back out. The garage door opens and the Corvette swings around in the glare. Daddy points its shark nose at the gates and they shudder open. We scrape down on to the canyon road as he looks right and left. The Corvette gurgles and gulps air and the thick black coffee of its circulating fluids – its adrenalins and gisms and hot fuel. The car is all cock and we ride in its sack, our asses barely six inches off the ground. I feel all-powerful, and very joined-at-the-hip with Daddy.

We get to the turning for Coldwater and the Corvette farts and dies again. Its unreliability is part of its temperament, its irascible maleness. 'Come on, come on...' says my father, juicing the engine and sparking the plugs. Another explosion jolts the stalled pistons into a steady, drumming rhythm. When the coast is clear, Daddy really steps on it. Our ribcages compress as we leap into the lane and accelerate to steady speed. Daddy smiles. His brown shades deflect a steady stream of curving light. I open the window and inhale cool blasts of piney, lifting air.

At the playing field, I put on my studded boots and kneepads in a blizzard of nerves. I take my position on the right wing and feel Daddy looking at me, willing me to succeed. My team, the Rovers, is in sixth place, and sorely needs a boost. I have football in my veins, but I'm uncomfortable on this California grass where the boys chase after the ball like Keystone Cops and never stay in position. The whistle blows and the centre passes to me. I'm determined to go all the way and move through the scrum of boys, following a preordained pattern, a branching tree of possibility that wrong-foots everyone and brings me to the mouth of the goal early. But at the last second I decide to give the ball away – passing to my centre, who tries for it, and misses.

My father shakes his head, cupping his hands and shouting: 'Put it in the back of the net!'

My next opportunity is similarly fluffed, and disastrously embarrassing. I am perfectly placed, leaning for the shot and bringing my leg forward when, instead of the ball, I kick the ground. My toe staggers forward and only just taps the ball, which rolls forward at a snail's pace. The goalie watches it and watches it and watches it and, for some reason known only to the universe, lets it go past him. (Perhaps he, too, was clapped in the kryptonite of his father's gaze.) My team leaps up, but I'm too bewildered and ashamed. I come to the sidelines for the half and suck on an orange while my father tries to take me in hand: 'What's wrong, Sachie? You get all the way to the goal and then you pass to somebody else. You're the best player on the field, but for some reason you don't want to *finish it.*'

For my tenth birthday, he comes up with a novel idea: a Children of the World-like gathering of freedom and equality on the lower lawn at Lloydcrest. I'm slightly mystified when, instead of my friends, a bunch of Mexican kids show up – the offspring and extended relations of our gardeners, Jesus and Ramiro. All huddled together, they stare back at me with dark, mistrustful faces. I try to engage them with hoops and balls, but the kids won't lighten up. I look helplessly to my father, who is dressed as a clown. He goes into overdrive, doing circus tricks and preposterous pratfalls, but the kids shrink away from him. Jesus and Ramiro rock on their cowboy heels, flash white grins and snap at their kids to relax – until, finally, when the Piñata comes out, they all get into the spirit of the thing and whack the hell out of it. Candy falls out and we all scrabble around in the grass to get it first. My father smiles with clown relief. The party is a success: the children of the world are united by common greed…

And then they all blew away. I didn't make a single friend or catch a fly-by name. It didn't really feel like my party, because it wasn't. Little Tony from Oswald Street had stolen it away to use as an experiment in self-empowerment. He was from the same sad side of the tracks as these Mexican kids. He had invited them to this party – *his* party – at his beautiful house, only to discover in the process that he didn't like them much after all.

On 14 December 1975, *It's A Musical World* was presented at the Hollywood Palladium: a two-hour celebration of Bricusse and Newley. Many were the luminaries who contributed and performed the songs: Sammy Davis Jr, Burt Bacharach, Tony Bennett, Henry Mancini, Gene Kelly and Peter Sellers, among them. Even my mother was there to cue the hit parade orchestrated by Ian Fraser, who waved his wand in the orchestra pit as she gamely announced: 'Ladies and Gentleman, Bricusse and Newley!' At which point, Adam Bricusse and I, aged ten and twelve, bounded onstage dressed in matching tuxes. The audience went wild. We giggled and swung our arms to the wings to introduce our respective fathers, who strode onstage from opposite ends and bear-hugged us in the middle. I couldn't see the audience for the spotlights, but its rapturous energy was pure nectar. I left the stage reluctantly, looking back as my father stepped to the mic. 'Thank you, sweet friends, thank you for blessing me and Les with your presence tonight. I'd like to draw particular attention to the lovely speech made by Joan Collins. That's the first time she's opened for me in years...' Big laugh... not that I got it.

The one-off *It's a Musical World* was the last gasp of the Bricusse-Newley partnership. They would write only one more song together: the ballad 'Life is a Woman', which opened the second act of Sammy Davis Jr's version of *Stop the World*. Bricusse kept trying to resume the creative dialogue, but my father had tasted the life in Vegas, where he was headlining at Caesars Palace and making a fortune. He was also spending a fortune, but that didn't seem to bother him. He thought Vegas would go on giving forever and a day.

He still held out hope for a movie career and instructed his sceptical agent to keep an eye out for scripts. Unfortunately, one soon arrived – a low-budget comedy prophetically titled *It Seemed Like a Good Idea at the Time*. It would shoot in Canada to take advantage of the tax breaks there, and star Stefanie Powers, Lloyd Bochner, Isaac Hayes and the young Johnny Candy.

The upside for Tara and me was a three-week vacation in snowy Toronto with Daddy. Cathy bought us all-in-one snowsuits and Tara lost no time in using me as a human sled to zip down the long hill fronting Daddy's rented A-frame. As usual, he had spared no expense in making himself at home – even though he was getting a mere pittance for the movie. When we visited him on location, we found him brooding in his deckchair in a rumpled parka and filthy trousers. 'I'm playing an artist,' he explained. 'Artists have no money.' Then Stefanie Powers bounded over and entranced me with her sunflower energy. She was a strawberry-blonde beauty, light and playful; not the dark, troubled kind of femininity I was used to. I was rapidly falling in puppy love when a distant wailing drew our attention. I followed my father's gaze to his Winnebago, which was gently rocking from side-to-side. 'Jesus Christ,' he exclaimed, 'Tara!' We rushed over and stormed inside. Daddy yanked open the stuck door of the loo and she fell into his arms, knickers around her ankles, sobbing hysterically. She was a claustrophobe from then on.

The sticky door was a budget thing. The shoddy caravans provided for the actors had zero water pressure and were crawling with bugs. My father soldiered on with the movie, but his sense of humour was rapidly failing him. John Candy did his level best to keep everybody laughing, but *It Seemed Like a Good Idea at the Time* was dying of a thousand cuts and rewrites.

One particularly arctic day found me chomping on rubbery carrots from the crafts service table while the crew set up on a deserted, ice-bound plain. I guessed, from the shrivelled stumps pushing up the snow, that this was a cornfield in summer. The director barked, 'OK go!' and the camera panned across the wintry expanse to pick up Daddy, Stefanie and Isaac Hayes, shambling along a deserted road. No one had even told me what the movie was supposed to be about. I guessed it was something to do with adults getting into trouble and asking things of each other that were too much for them – and there'd be a lot of music played over the top to work it all through – though they'd all end up pretty much where they began, in a muddle. That, I was beginning to realize, was life. I noticed a Cadillac de Ville pulled up alongside the field; burnt orange, with a white leather top. There was a man inside, wearing a coat with a fur collar, sitting at the wheel smoking. He seemed bored. He threw out one butt and lit another. He had a large block-like head, and square steel-rim glasses. Something emanated from him that made the Cadillac seem more like a tank. Between takes, Stefanie rushed over and leaned in to kiss him. He came alive for a moment and whispered words to her, before she flapped back for the next take. I was insanely jealous.

It was William Holden.

I would grow up knowing men like this, fascinated by their aura. In later years I would paint their portraits.

On returning to the antiseptic whiteness of Chalette and its plastic walkway, Tara and I felt like we'd re-entered some experiment for lab rats. And in fact, Tara soon after bought herself a batch of white mice and we built them a plastic city of interconnecting tubes in her bedroom. They exploded in number and we sat for hours on end enthralled by our little mouse metropolis, the rodents' endless tube journeys, their manic attacks on the mouse-wheel. At Lloydcrest all this would have been unthinkable: Daddy would have frowned at the wrongness of their incarceration and laid on a free-the-mice ceremony in the flower garden. But at Chalette, Tara's mice thrived in captivity.

They also served to bring us together: I was on regular mouse duty in her room – formerly off-limits to me. Being at the same school helped, too; plus being ferried back and forth between Mummy's and Daddy's as a disorientated twosome. We were fellow vagabonds, and we needed each other.

When Tara bought *Venus and Mars* by Wings, we listened intently to the lyrics:

> Ebony and ivory
> Live together in perfect harmony
> Side-by-side on my piano
> So then, why can't we?

It was a great question, but one we didn't dare actually ask. The dissonance between the two houses persisted: Lloydcrest was a majestic, creaking galleon under wind power; Chalette a sleek powerboat, all ersatz speed and white vinyl that we feared would eventually run out of gas.

Tara was about to turn thirteen: a maudlin, inward-looking girl who had been born an extrovert, then forced by circumstances to scale back. On top of all the pressures at home, she was cowed, as I was, by the beauty and self-confidence of her Beverly Hills classmates. Even with braces and spots, they had a sense of entitlement and largesse that we English kids for some reason lacked. She developed mad crushes on oblivious, lolloping boys with names like Brad, Chad and Chuck, but was too shy to flick her feathered bangs in their direction. Her freckles had become her defining characteristic, festering around her button nose and arms and forcing her into long sleeves.

By contrast, four-year-old half-sister, Katy Kass, was fast becoming a bouncy little California kid totally in tune with her surroundings. Her hair was sun-dyed platinum and her cartoon giggle was irresistible. When she smiled mischievously, the little bulb of flesh that puckered over the bridge of her nose filled her parents with rapture. Ron was his daughter's slave, her puppy dog. She shared his sweet tooth, and they would indulge in orgies of fudge consumption together, cuddling and giggling as they chewed aloud.

There was no escaping the feeling that Mummy, Ron, and Katy formed a unit, while Tara and I did a lazy figure eight around the two houses. We were bifurcated, doomed to always see double. Sue was there to hold our two worlds together, but even she could only do so much. My father loathed her, to the point of dropping us off on the other side of the road from Chalette and accelerating away the second she opened the front door.

One morning without warning, Dr Rowan walked briskly into our classroom and immediately started shaking the tables. 'Earthquake! Earthquake!' he yelled, as we dived under our desks. He stalked about, chasing down the stragglers, until we were all well-stowed away, cowering. 'What if that had been real?' he demanded of us. We looked out meekly between our chair legs and had no answer.

Earthquake terror was everywhere. Los Angeles had been hit by a big one in 1972 and had barely recovered from it. At recess, I went out to the playground and warily inspected the cracks that snaked through the cement. In England, the most I had had to fear was that rain would ruin a picnic. Here the ground could literally open up and swallow me. There was a dragon underground with rancid breath and seething anger. It was only a matter of time before he roared again.

Then came *Earthquake*, the movie – with Charlton Heston and Ava Gardner heading the humungous Irwin Allen-produced cast. Sue took me to see it at the Cinerama Dome, where I looked with excited foreboding at the gigantic Sensurround speakers. This was to be the special effect to end all others. At the onset of the first tremor, we were not disappointed. Sue turned to me, gaping with delight, her popcorn and coke sticking up between her thighs. After several more increasingly catastrophic rumblers, the movie achieved its penultimate climax, with goggle-eyed survivors being ferried one-by-one from a decimated building. This was Heston's big moment to step forward and do the heroic honours, improvising a pulley system from a fire hose and a desk chair, sacrificing himself in the service of getting the women and children out first. The stock close-ups on the tearing hose jacked me up in my seat until I lost all self-possession and was one with them in that crumbling building. I looked to Chuck to save me, too – his straining, sweaty profile with the expertly-placed make-up gashes was all I knew of hope.

But our hero had to die, because this was a pessimistic seventies, not a pumped-up eighties, movie. Disaster was in – attuned to a national mood soured by Watergate, Vietnam and the Kent State massacre. So Chuck went down into the sewers to save his wretched, bitching wife, and the floodwaters overwhelmed them both. I cringed in my seat as they gasped, gurgled and went under. When the camera pulled out to show a final shot of Los Angeles in flaming ruins, there was no Old Glory to be seen slowly flapping in tattered defiance. That America was dead. We would all go down into the dragon's maw. Let planes crash, earthquakes pulverize; let tidal waves swallow and towering infernos consume those who were content with making small talk and toasting their good fortune. Wide-eyed, robo-feeding myself popcorn in the dark, I got the scary message: adults were *not* in charge; their beautifully laid plans could come undone at any moment.

In the opening sequence of the movie *The Devil Within Her* my mother lies in a hospital bed thrashing her head in birth-agony. The lurid accompaniment of Hendrix-like riffs tells us something is very wrong here. The doctor mops her brow as she convulses and finally delivers. The scream of a newborn rends the air: my mother regains her breath and smiles as the bundle is handed to her. Later, in the nursery, she bends over the crib and admires her blessed child. The sleep-mobile tinkles, goo-goo-ga-ga... then suddenly the baby's face intercuts with a deranged midget's, cackling at her. My mother backs away, mouth covered in horror. The baby is cooing again. Was the midget real or a nightmare? Then she remembers...

In flashback, we see her performing a burlesque number in a sequined bustier. Her sidekick is of course a midget. Attired in top hat and tails, he's getting all the laughs while she, attired in less than nothing, is supplying the T&A. He glances lustfully her way. She ignores him, concentrating on giving the audience its money's worth. Mummy and the midget bow to tepid applause and sweep backstage. She's wiping off her stage make-up when he creeps in. He proceeds to accost her, pressing his disgusting little button nose against her arching neck. She pushes him away and stalks out. She's halfway across the empty stage when he rips open the curtains behind her and points a quivering stubby finger: 'You will bear a child like me! He will take my shape and my form, and he will be... the DEVIL!!'

During the making of this movie, Sue had driven me out to Pinewood where I was being allowed to watch the filming of the climax. A prop guy breezed by me with a sloshing bucket of fake blood, then fitted a pump-action lid to it and squatted in readiness as if he were about to blow up a bridge. I followed with my widening eyes the long tube that fed from it all the way to my mother, where it disappeared under her nightie. She was wearing a harness around her signature cleavage with a pair of scissors sticking out. The director called for readiness and she braced herself against the door. 'Action!' he cried and she struggled against the intruder. I saw the midget's face in the crack of the door. He was cackling madly. Then he burst through and lunged at her. She turned to the camera, mouthing like a beached fish, as the prop guy frantically pumped and the crimson stain bloomed across her nightie. She fell heavily with a crash and the director yelled, 'Cut!' Everybody clapped; the midget smiled and shook hands all around. Another day in Make Believe Land.

Watching the movie in the dark of a proper cinema eighteen months later, my mother engrossed by my side, I was unsettled by the story and the scary music and the quick cuts made me flinch. In one scene, my mother sits by a roaring fire in her London house. She looks up as strange sounds come from the nursery. Her husband, a Latin-looking lunk with heavy sideburns and slow-burn eyes, goes to investigate. He finds the nursery deserted and destroyed. He shines his flashlight here and there and sees the open window and the fluttering curtains. Stepping out into the garden, he moves the search beam around and pulls his collar up against the cold. We hear a fetid giggling, a convulsed laughter... He looks up, but too late: a noose drops from the tree and ensnares his neck. He kicks in circles as he is lifted from the ground – until his legs go taut. Murder number one.

I know there are four kills to go before my mother gets the kitchen scissors through the sternum. Suddenly I can't take any more. I run from the theatre and hyperventilate in the hall. My mother finds me sliding down the wall into a sitting position, covering my head. 'I'm sorry, Darling,' she says. 'That was all a bit much, wasn't it.' I nod and breathe hard, watching the floor come at me with reassuring clarity.

But in the nights that follow, I can't sleep. The fiend is out there, stalking us, and it's only a matter of time before he gets me. Matters are not helped when Ron hangs a framed poster of the film in the den: an image of blood-soaked scissors gripped by a bulging forearm that morphs into a dangling pair of baby legs.

At bedtime, I make sure to secure the latch on the sliding glass doors to the pool. Shivering on the shores of sleep, I half see those splayed scissor-ends cutting back and forth in the pool like shark fins. And then, the inevitable cackling when the Devil himself moons up close to the glass, looking in at me. I can hear the blood bubbling in his brain as the flashing scissor blades come out from under his cassock. I spring up in bed. The heating element in my fish tank glows and fills the room with hellish orange. I run in panic across the dark house, skidding down the plastic walkway to Sue's room, my toes buckling and burning. I reach her door, burst inside, jibbering, 'The Midget! The Midget!'

'All right now, my love,' she says in her best Mary Poppins voice, 'Sue will protect you... Come on now, my little love...'

I lie down beside her, her vast bulk a bulwark against my murderous pursuer. A moment of silence – then she fidgets and suddenly grabs me by the throat: 'The Midget!' she screams, and I break down all over again. She laughs and tries to calm me, but the bad joke has sent me spinning off into the void.

*Jaws* awaited me there. Sue took me to the monstrous spectacle with Tara and drove us home afterwards in stunned silence, my nervous system tingling outside my body – a great, frazzled ganglion hung out to dry. But then when we got to Chalette, I did a perverse thing: I asked if I could go for a swim. Sue looked at me and smiled approvingly, then flicked on the pool lights.

'No.' I said. 'I want it dark. Like in the movie.'

Tara danced around excitedly as I stripped down to my underpants. Sue was at the patio doors ready to hit the lights if I freaked out. I let the ice-cold water envelop me, then took a few strokes out into the middle of the pool. The dark water seemed to go on forever. I imagined the open sea all around me and my heart throbbed. The pressure of chlorinated water made a dreamy screen of my eyes. Then my vision seemed to gather and pull together into a ghostly orb. The whiteness enlarged with sweeps of background shadow and became a solid face spreading its theatre of teeth. I backed up in the water. It was like wading through molasses. The beast was behind me, about to bite, as I splashed up and out, leaving my skin behind. I ran to my waiting towel and held it around me. Knock-kneed and trembling, I looked back at the empty, harmless pool. Tara was laughing hysterically; Sue was turning the lights on and off, mocking me in a girlish voice: 'Shark! Shark!'

What, I now ask myself, possessed me? The cleansing horror of facing things? Facing things in paint was what I would grow up to do. Back there, aged ten, I found a strange courage for such a timid, wishy-washy kid. And naturally I went ahead and chose sharks for my school science project. My deep research and careful presentation got me first prize. My father had the winner's blue ribbon framed, along with the bright-green certificate.

I was beginning to excel at school. The punitive policy employed at Hawthorne of having to get 'F' test papers signed and witnessed by your parents had caused me such mortification that I had resolved never again to get a failing grade. Maths was my weakest subject, so I got myself a set of multiplication flash cards and drilled obsessively until I was perfect – thrilling my mother with my 100 per cent recall.

My father received my straight 'A' report card on the road in Dallas where he was performing with Dionne Warwick.

April 14th 1977

My Dearest Son... I can't tell you how proud I am of your school grades. Your hunger for learning excites me so much because it will make your life so interesting. Ignorance may be bliss but the curious man, Sach, is the one who is really <u>alive!</u>

If I could drink I would stay drunk for this whole engagement... God knows what I'll do when I run out of my small stash of grass!!

He was back in time to see me break out and distinguish myself in the last match of our Rovers season. I scored a dramatic header – arriving for the cross in perfect time, my skull meeting and redirecting the ball with a resounding thud. Earlier, I had pulled off a spectacular run down the left sideline, finishing with a flawless cross to my centre forward, who easily knocked it in. And all with my father watching. There happened to be a talent scout watching, too – from the Junior California All Stars – and a few days later he came to Chalette Drive to recruit me.

My mother let him in and personally escorted him to my room. 'Sacha, this is Mister...'

I looked up from my homework.

'Richter,' he said with a German accent, 'Hawke Richter.' He offered his hand.

He and my mother sat down and we all discussed my future as a soccer star. He told me about the phenomenal tours the All Stars went on – how they played demonstration matches in all the great stadiums of America. 'Our first will be in Hawaii,' he said. 'We'll come on at half-time. Football is becoming very popular in America, or should I say soccer.' I could tell from the massive thighs straining under his grey pants that he had been a player himself. 'Training and try-outs begin in late May,' he went on. 'We tour and play matches all through the summer…'

I saw myself running in a bright yellow strip across the manicured green of the stadium, cheered on by crowds… But I was planning to spend the summer in France with the Bricusses. I couldn't let my best friend, Adam, down. The yellow strip, the green turf, paled in comparison.

Our stolid man from Stuttgart saw me hesitate. He laced his thick fingers and leaned in closer, his bald pate rippling with crescent light. 'You have definite skill,' he pleaded with keen upturned eyes. 'It would be such a shame not to develop it. No?'

I didn't know. On the one hand, there was the competition; the commitment; the exposure of myself to the judging crowds. On the other, a vacation in France – dinners with Leslie at the sun-drenched villa, drives in his mahogany speedboat…

'I-I don't think I can…' I stammered.

My mother looked at me. 'Are you *sure*, Sach?'

I nodded. The man smiled and leaned back in his chair, his hands flat on his thighs. 'I understand. A boy must have his little vacation.' He turned to my mother. 'If he changes his mind, here's my card.'

I went to France without passing go. There I was dominated by Adam as usual, treated like his plaything. I bounced along in his adrenalized wake, threw rocks on cue at Action Man figures, played with cap guns, but all the time my other self – the heralded, confident boy in the yellow strip – was tooling across the playing field in Hawaii. A fantasy I am chasing to this day.

# 10

# 1465 Carolyn Way

*Frail Portal*

I FOUND MY MOTHER SUNNING HERSELF BY THE POOL ONE weekend, and my eleven-year-old ego overcame me with a desire to show off.

'Watch me, Mummy,' I said, and dived in.

I swam twenty laps, checking at each turn to see if she was watching.

'That's wonderful, darling,' she said, after lap three and went back to her magazine.

I slowed in the water, hauled myself out and went over to her. She was reading in the shade of her large straw sun hat. Her body glistened with oil that had pooled in her belly button. The puckered flesh there was slightly baggy from three pregnancies. But she was still ravishing.

I pulled up a sunlounger and lay down beside her. The cypress trees across the pool pointed into a hot, cloudless sky. I was content just to be there, next to her on a soundless Sunday, hearing her pages turn. Then she put down her magazine and breathed heavily through her nose. 'Sacha,' she finally said, 'We're broke. I don't know what we're going to do.'

I went up on one elbow and shaded my eyes. She was staring blankly at the cypresses, her nostrils flaring, as if she was about to cry.

'Don't worry, Mummy,' I said. 'Everything will be all right.'

She looked at me and smiled quickly, tightly, then picked up her magazine.

The boxes arrived soon afterward. We were moving again.

Here there was no escape capsule under the stairs – I had to climb the wooded slopes by the tennis court, or hide away in the cobwebby alley behind the house, where I listened to the compressed wheezing of the pool-filtration system and where I thought of nothing, which was a good way to ride out the suspense.

Carolyn Way, our next stop, was only fifteen minutes from Chalette Drive, a winding feeder street at the bottom of Coldwater Canyon. The house was decidedly smaller than Chalette – one of those glass-and-steel boxes that cropped up everywhere in Los Angeles in the late fifties. It sat back from the road behind a slope of rat-infested ivy and felt damp and unloved inside. Wherever the glass panels met the steel-and-granite frame, long seams of rust festered. The ceiling was vaulted at one end and low at the other, giving the house an off-kilter feel. Its most exotic feature was an indoor waterway, covered in thick glass, that entered through a waterfall duct at one end of the living room, kinked artfully as it traversed the marble floor, and disappeared through an opening at the far end. I suppose the idea was to introduce fish or Chinese carp into this canal and give the house a Taoist twist of flowing chi. But there was no such enchantment during our time there. Pressing my nose to the floor-glass, I saw that the only denizens of the dark, flaking waterway were spiders and their ghostly webs.

There was enough profit from the sale of Chalette to make some modifications to the new house: a ten-by-twenty walk-in closet for my mother; a fibreglass Jacuzzi in the garden for Ron and a glass-enclosed walkway to connect the maid's room – a dank cell off the garage – to the main house. This was an acknowledgement that Sue was more important than a mere maid: now she would be inextricably linked to the house at all times.

I got the room I didn't want, naturally – the smallest and the one closest to the living room – which was painted cheddar to match the plastic-module furniture that dogged me from Chalette. Whenever my mother had a party (which was often), the little room thudded like a full-term uterus. I would flip back and forth on my hot pillow without rest. Sometimes I would go to the door and peek out, glimpsing a cigarette held rakishly, a flash of blonde hair, or white pants, or tanned skin… Five years on from South Street, the Joan Collins Express was still going strong, with an ever-changing cast of raffish characters.

I would close the door and pull focus to my tropical fish as they schooled back and forth in their illuminated ten-gallon tank. They'd grown big as silver dollars and could jump out of the tank if I left the lid off. The monthly tank clean had become a stressful affair: more than once I'd had to scoop a little jumper off the carpet and back into the drink, both of us hyperventilating like mad.

It was at Carolyn Way that my mother's presence dwindled away from me to random apparitions: a besequined phantasm that would appear at dinnertime, pilfer a French fry while protesting that she would so much rather stay home – and then disappear for the evening in a fallout cloud of perfume.

Yes, she was a struggling actress – that is, an actress still struggling after twenty years in the business – and had to get out there and 'be seen'. On one of those nights, she did manage to catch the eye of Aaron Spelling, who would later cast her as Cleopatra in an episode of *Fantasy Island* and, later still, remember her for *Dynasty*. But I was still a child and children are not equipped to take the long view. I simply saw what was there. Or rather, what wasn't: my mother.

Apart from weekends at Lloydcrest with Daddy and Cathy, the only person I saw was Sue. She fetched me from school and dropped me off; Sue woke me up and put me to bed. She doled out fish fingers and chips; and always, after dinner, there was Sue's room, and Sue's bed. The pattern had been in place for five years now and moving to another continent had not changed a thing.

When I woke to a shattering sound one night, I assumed it was Sue, as usual, slamming shut a drawer of cutlery. But then the alarm went off, hellishly loud. I jumped out of bed and rushed into the living room. Sue was already there, striding around in her caftan. There was a cement breezeblock lying on the carpet, surrounded by shards of glass. I looked and saw its entry point in the garden doors – a black, angry star.

'Where's Mummy?' I said.

'Out. Thank God,' replied Sue. 'Get back. I don't want you walking around in bare feet…'

The police arrived within minutes. Red lights strobed through the house, just like in the movies. I was reassured by their gravity and workmanlike demeanour. They squatted by the breezeblock and took measurements, their walkie-talkies squawking. I gave my report to an enormous guy, bristling with equipment: 'It was just a crashing noise, and then I heard the alarm go off… I didn't hear anything else…' He nodded and frowned, pencilling his clipboard. And he thanked me.

So what I'd imagined at Chalette had almost come to pass here. The intruder in the dark remained faceless, but I knew him. He'd pressed his midget's button nose against the glass and seen inside, and then his anger crashed against the house like a wave. He hated our fame and our wealth and had snatched our sparkling ornaments. Most of all, he hated the little boy who had taken refuge here.

The hole was taped over; and by the end of the week there was a replacement pane. But I knew I was no longer safe there. It was only a matter of time.

My mother landed a part in a sci-fi horror movie, *Empire of the Ants*, and was going to have to be away for five whole weeks on location in the Florida Everglades. She agreed that Tara and I could stay at Lloydcrest. We packed our bags and headed over to Daddy's for a good long stay.

Cathy lavished her best cooking on us, and Grandma came up from the Palisades to make her warm-hearted tarts and cakes. A stray dog had recently appeared on the premises and decided to stay. We named him Boomer – for boomerang – because no matter how many times my father ran him off the property, he always waggishly returned. Eventually my father conceded that Boom had been 'sent by the angels' and accepted him as a member of the family. After all, he was a stray like the rest of us.

One night Cathy said to Tara and me: 'You gotta hear this...' She put a record on the turntable and turned the volume up. I was working on a drawing of an Apollo rocket for science class, but the second I heard the thumping chords of the Bees Gees' 'Stayin' Alive', I forgot all about my drawing and took off for real. I *had* to find a way to dance to this. My body fidgeted and tried to work out its kinks. My Nike Waffles squeaked on the floor as I loosened up and found the groove-key. Cathy was clapping and yelping; Tara was breathless with laughter; Grandma entered from the kitchen, waving her soup ladle as a roused Boomer barked.

During our second week at Lloydcrest, an envelope arrived from my mother, containing a Polaroid. It was a self-portrait, showing her with a black eye she'd suffered when a car door slammed in her face on the Everglades set. It was a real doozy: the purple thundercloud spread angrily across her face from the squinched corona of her eye. Under the picture she had scrawled in red: 'This is what your mother has to do to earn a living.'

They had to shoot around her for three weeks, extending her stay in the snake-infested swamps and pushing her to the brink of a nervous breakdown. When she finally returned, Tara's face failed to light up – it did not say, 'Mummy, I'm so happy to see you.' She looked over at me and saw the same face as always: the little boy eager to please. When she asked Sue for an explanation of Tara's disaffection, she found herself on the receiving end of a barrage of criticism. Sue's lack of boundary control had long been a problem, but now my mother seized on her as the prime author of her children's alienation. Quite right, but the insight had come tragically late. When Sue left – without so much as a goodbye to us – our little world fell apart.

I wandered about the house like a lobotomy case, gravitating to Sue's empty room and weeping at the sight of the bleached squares where her pictures had hung, and the silly old TV we had watched so avidly together. It would never again come alive to her shouts and taunts of pleasure. We would never bounce around on this bed and wrestle each other unto death. She was gone, and it was like a death. Only worse, because she had gone on living.

My mother stalked the house in a self-righteous temper, trying hopelessly to take back control. Cooking for her kids, doing their school runs, entertaining them, just wasn't in Joan Collins's mission statement. She would bang about in the kitchen, fixing herself a tuna sandwich, while Tara morosely turned the pages of a fashion magazine.

'Can't you be quiet?' ventured the sullen teenager.

'When you wipe that sulky look off your face, sister,' said my mother.

'God, I can't wait to get back to Daddy's. At least Cathy talks to me, at least she listens… you're so busy putting on your make-up and your clothes and rushing out to all your fucking parties –'

'Don't talk to me like that! I'm your mother!'

'Then fucking act like one!'

…or words to that effect. The dialogue might have played out in a slightly different way, but I know I have the venom right. When Tara walked out of the house and down the front drive, it was without a backward glance. My mother may have stood in the doorway, wavering in cross-currents of emotion, but she was too proud to go trailing after her.

Tara turned on to Carolyn Way and broke down in hot tears – fists thrust into the pouch of her hoodie. She turned on to Coldwater Canyon and started the long walk up toward the park where she knew there was a pay phone. She had no money, but there would be nannies by the Jungle Jim, and she could beg a dime. The cars raced past her and there was no pavement, so she had to keep close to the gutters or climb up on to the grassy shoulders. But now she wasn't crying any more.

She achieved Coldwater Park, successfully begged the dime and put in an SOS to Lloydcrest. My father dropped everything and came rushing down to rescue her.

I was totally alone. No Tara. No Sue. No Nothing. I kept to my room and listened nonstop to Abba – but even the bubbly Swedes couldn't buoy me. I killed time by splicing together some of my mother's old location footage – her rehearsing with Tony Curtis in Spain on *The Persuaders!* (in real life, as I learned later, he'd just called her a 'cunt' which may have explained the sour look on her puss); her laughing and flirting with Gregory Peck as he taught her how to hold a gun in *The Bravados* – and, meanwhile, I was imagining a montage of the moments Tara must be enjoying at Lloydcrest:

fireside chats with Dee, walks in the butterfly garden, dinners with Dad and Grandma.

My mother could see that I was already elsewhere – that it was only a matter of time before I left, too. Ron barbecued thick steaks from our favourite deli, Nate 'N' Al, and laid on all the extras I relished – potato salad and coleslaw and chopped liver – but I had no appetite to speak of.

I went to bed early one night, only to wake from a fever dream to see a silver fish describe a long watery arc through space. I'd left the lid off the tank! Asshole! I leapt out of bed and tried to shift the heavy bureau. The fish had landed behind it and I could hear him fluttering in the airless cleft. But the edge of the bureau was dug into the carpet and wouldn't budge. I ran howling across the house and burst into my mother's room. She crawled out of bed and followed me across the living room, where I doubled up and retched all over the carpet. There it was for all to see: the ugly mess I'd been holding inside. My mother pulled me away and into my bedroom. She tried to shift the bureau, but it was too heavy even for her. My fish was still flapping against the wall, but only intermittently now. I walked in circles, pulling at my pyjamas and my hair: 'Where's Sue! Where's Sue! She could move it!' My mother ran off to wake Ron, but he was too stoned and fudged out. No one could help me, so I tried to reach the fish by myself again – angling so far behind the bureau I cut my cheek on its edge – but the fish was stiff in the desperate hooks of my fingers.

## II

# 9477 Lloydcrest

*Deeper*

I'M ELEVEN NOW AND I'M STILL MOURNING MY FISH. CATHY is showing me where my bathroom is and explaining that, even though this is only a maid's room, everything will be all right. I nod, sitting on the bed, while the washing machine and dryers whir in the adjacent laundry room. There had been no sentimental scene with my mother at the front door; no earnest discussion on her bed about my future, about what this step I was about to take might mean. She leaves me – or rather, I leave her – with nothing to hang a general understanding on, no support for a parable, no steadily accumulating sense of meaning. I simply find myself at Lloydcrest, in the maid's room by the washers and dryers.

Yet a miraculous thing happens: any night-time fear I have soon goes away. I adapt easily to my remoteness from the rest of the family, who are all upstairs. My room has a wallpaper of green fronds and plant life, not unlike my mother's room back at Carolyn, and is shaded by a great oak in a corner of the flower garden, making the window light brilliant green and yellow. When it's breezy out, dappled sunlight dithers and wheels about the walls and I feel happily adrift in my little bower of solitude. Fittingly, I first open *The Hobbit* there, and get mesmerically lost in Tolkien's leafy kingdom of Middle Earth. I decide I am like Bilbo Baggins, a sweet-tempered hermit content with reclusion.

Maybe I accept my situation because I *must*. Had my father been willing to share a bed with Cathy, things might have been very different. I might have been awarded her room on the top landing. But he had never gotten over his wartime experience of almost being smothered in the old lady's bed, and *had* to sleep alone. Cathy considered this psychological explanation an excuse – 'a crock of shit' – but the sensitive genius was adamant: he needed his space. This intransigence would ultimately mean that Lloydcrest was too small for all of us, and that we would have to move yet again.

My father was a natural obsessive. He had an extreme sensitivity to sound and an uncanny ability to detach and watch himself performing. Not to mention a deep need for unwavering order and structure. His daily preparations were particular and involved: the morning jog, the shower, the freshly cut bowl of fruit followed by fibre to 'really force things through.' Such delicacy and obstinacy drove Cathy to distraction. Theirs was a strange inversion of gender roles: he was the diva who took forever to 'get ready' and balked at the thought of repairing to a gas station; she was the one who was down early and took the cars for servicing.

He had taken up jogging as a way to stay fit for the demands of his sexual life, but it was also a good way to outpace his mortality. He was hooked on health food, vitamins, and self-help books. He refused to swallow meat. With strong, sucking jaws, he would juice a mouthful of blood and nutrients and then spit out the rest, calling it 'shoe leather, a major cause of colon cancer.' Dry pellets would accumulate along the edge of his plate – making for a disgusting, embarrassing display, especially at fancy restaurants.

'Don't hold things inside, Sachie,' he would always say. 'It leads to cancer.'

That was the real downer: it could get you just because you had the wrong thoughts. It wasn't only about what you ate or how much exercise you did, it could also be about how sick you were in your head. You could die from yourself. That was cancer.

And then, my father further cautioned, there were microbes and bacteria lurking everywhere. When I picked up a piece of food I'd dropped and put it in my mouth, my father went berserk. 'Do you have any idea,' he said, leaning toward me with rucked brows, 'how much bacteria climbed on to that morsel during its brief time on the floor?'

I looked hard at the floor, which only that morning had been scrubbed spotless by the maid. 'No, Dad.'

'Billions of 'em… literally billions. Promise me that you will never eat off the floor, Sachie.' I promised and sat watching him drink a long, cool glass of morning milk with closed eyes. He held the empty glass to his heart. I picked up my orange juice and did the same, closing my eyes and trying to imagine how Daddy would taste it and it was like orange sunshine cascading down my throat. The juice was too warm, so I asked for ice cubes; but Daddy cautioned me against putting frigid liquid into a body calibrated at 98.6 degrees – he said I could get pneumonia.

The washer and dryers whirred day and night at Lloydcrest in service of my father's hygiene habit. Our Mexican maid, Maria, was never to be seen without her huge hampers of clothes for ironing and folding. My father insisted on showering twice a day, morning and evening, and always used six fluffy terrycloth towels, one for each part of his body: armpits, groin, asshole, face and hair, legs, and torso. After each session, the used towels were heaped into a dirty pile and a fresh stack rotated into service. To dry oneself on more than one occasion with the same towel was anathema to him. Who's to say he wouldn't have mistakenly used the asshole towel on his face?

Shower pressure was, of course, all-important, and he rushed out to purchase the first of the flow-switchable showerheads that appeared in the seventies. I loved to watch his ablutions – I would lean in the doorway and listen to Vaughan Williams or Delius piped in through the bathroom speakers as he showered hot, then cold. The heat made his body go pink and the cold made him howl with penitential joy. He emerged semi-dry, as he had already begun towelling off inside, removing the excess moisture with a flannel. Then he would grab the top towel from the stack and dry down each leg, shooting a happy glance at me and asking about my day. Then he would lift a leg on to the toilet seat and dry himself between his ass cheeks. He'd take a tuft of toilet paper and stuff it up inside to get at the buried moisture. (This little tuft, protruding like a bunny tail, would stay in until the end of the procedure.) Next towel: over the shoulders and down the back in a zigzag motion. His whole body gyrated like he was doing the twist, like Baloo the bear, rubbing his backside on deliciously scratchy stones. Towel three: the armpits – two proud wipes in each. Then he worked down each arm to the fingertips, drying as he went, like a woman removing long gloves. Hair time now: tautening the hood of friction over his head until the 'fro stood up frightfully and he had to comb it back smooth, wincing from the snags. His hairbrushes, with their staunch, splayed bristles, penetrated deeply.

At length he wrapped himself about the waist in a towel adapted for the purpose, with a touch of Velcro to hold it in place. He observed the man in the mirror, frowned and fitted a hairnet over his damp head. In one movement, he withdrew the hairdryer from its holster and clicked it on. Low heat first, wagging over the head (the hairnet was used to expedite the process, holding the hair in shape as it dried) and then he whisked off the net to go for a strong blast of fluffing heat – the Conair Pro 2000 howling on maximum, threatening to defuse the whole house. He clicked off the dryer and the silence was sudden, tickled by Delius. He brushed through for final effect, using the free hand to follow and shape a great sculpt-ing quality about the face and head, until his leonine profile was crowned by air and bounce and proud feeling.

The shave. With two strong blasts of air into the shaver head to clear it of bristles, he turned it on. He was a quick worker. He had the heavy beard of a French peasant so a foam shave would have been too slow and tiresome twice a day. Sides first – the sideburns left low as was the fashion – and then the large top lip peeled down to splay the bristles, and the thorough driving of the shaver head right up into the furry caves of the nostrils to sheer them clean. His chin extruded and his neck lengthened as the shaver worked over the manly thrust of his jaw, the shaver burring and whining through the best growth. He was done. Two strong blasts to clear the shaver head, and then he was on to the particulars: drying the inside of the ears with Kleenex, sometimes probing them with Q-tips.

His bathroom cabinet held a surplus of everything: stacks of oatmeal soap, hairnets, and quivers full of Q-tips. His toothpaste was in powder form, which he tapped on to Kleenex and dabbed on to his brush. He didn't like the gooey composition of normal toothpaste, plus it contained sweetener. I tried his powder once myself and choked on a mouthful of astringent flour. He finished with floss and a toothpick, working the clefts of his back molars while he tried talking like Cagney. I took a pick myself and savoured the woodsy flavour. For the grand finale, he whipped off the Velcro towel, plucked out the toilet paper and powdered his genitals. The sweet talc exploded from his groin, making my nose itch, as his prick swayed over the stuffed bag of his balls.

Not long after the mass exodus of her children, my mother gave a party. It was the Queen's Silver Jubilee – a sterling excuse to have the Hollywood Brits over for a good-old knees-up. And they all came, in red, white and blue, posing histrionically for a group photo: Dudley Moore, Jackie Bisset, David Hemmings, Samantha Eggar, Auntie Jackie Collins…

I was imported to applaud and cheer them on. Tara scowled when I accepted the invitation and accused me of always 'sucking up' to Mummy. I had to go – I wanted to see my mother and to see her as I liked her best: shining amid a party of her own inspired devising.

It was strange to be back at Carolyn Way, as the life we had led there was being steadily erased. I looked into my old room, and found it a repository of cardboard boxes and Ron's office supplies. What I intuited in my deepening gloom was that this festive day was a lie, if one my mother was only too happy to indulge as an escape from her problems.

With no money and no real career prospects, she was soon to sell Carolyn Way and return to London, abandoning her American Dream for a second time. She was broke and drinking heavily. If the early seventies had been a time of security and happiness for her – Ron earning a fortune, the children seemingly happy – the latter part of the decade threw it into miserable relief. Her marriage was under threat as Ron's addictions and deceptions spiralled out of control. Charming to her in public, he bullied her in private, taking photographs of her drunk and threatening to hawk them to the tabloids if she ever dared to leave him.

Joan Collins was not only on the run, she was running out of options. She had no choice but to try to sell her reminiscences to the highest bidder. She had started sketching out the book between set-ups in the Florida swamps, but now work began in earnest. It wasn't easy (she would never be a desk-bound writer), but whenever and wherever she could – in make-up chairs, backstage, on flights to-and-fro – she hauled out the yellow pads and pushed the book forward with her hasty scrawl. When she got to the part about the break-up with my father, she was in no mood to be forgiving.

Although my mother could successfully rewrite her own history, she was powerless to reshape her image in the eyes of her children. And our defection had made the atmosphere between the two camps more toxic than ever. There was no direct contact between my parents: no phone calls, no quick visits – every communication was by telegram, letter or through secretaries and lawyers.

When, after two months away, my mother wired my father's secretary that she wanted to see me, Cathy sat me down and gave me my instructions: 'When your mother comes to pick you up today, do not – repeat, do not – go to her. I'll be waiting for you at the corner of the playground, in a car, with a detective. You come to me. OK?'

I said OK – all my mother-need had been refocused on her, and I couldn't disappoint.

When the school bell rang for dismissal that day, I filed out of the classroom and went to my locker. I heard my name called and looked up the hall. My mother was there, going down on one knee, throwing her arms wide.

'Sacha!' she called again.

I had my instructions – I knew what to do.

I turned on my heels and ran back into the classroom. I found an open window and climbed through it into the quad. I ran across the open space, through the upper school and out into the playground beyond. Cathy was waiting there, as she had promised, with a stern-looking man in a suit. She squealed with delight as I reached the car, hugged me tight, and we sped off in triumph.

Did my mother continue on to the classroom and peek inside? Did she gather the ice-cold truth from the open window, slump down in a desk chair and sob bitter tears? The child is tempted by this scenario, because he wishes to exalt his mother. But the adult writer knows better.

She had abandoned me to Sue and now I was prepared to abandon her back.

By fifth grade, the birthday parties of my Hawthorne classmates had graduated from clowns and bowling to dance floors and DJs and French kissing under the table.

I first went south with Betsy Assenheim, a pale girl with glasses and a forward personality. After our session of tortuous tongue-twisting, she pulled away and said in a gosh-wow drawl, 'That was an A plus!' at which point, ever the slave to good grades, I went at it again.

This interest from the opposite sex coincided with a growing self-awareness of *how I looked*. My father had pointed me in the right direction by insisting I blow-dry my hair at least once a day (I was that rare eleven-year-old who actually owned his own Conair Pro 2000) and I learned how to style it from watching him. I was soon experimenting with the flouncing fringe or 'quiff' – a modification that was not lost on the girl of my dreams, Dana Pepp. She actually glanced my way, breaching the fourth wall of my obsessive voyeurism. I *existed* for her.

I was too afraid to address my angel directly and would have continued that way had Cupid not arranged for us to sit next to each other in fifth-grade homeroom. I couldn't believe it: *there* was her nameplate on the desk right next to mine. When she entered the room, smiled and sat down beside me, I experienced a warp in reality, a vague feeling of comedy in the universe at large.

'Hi,' she said. 'I like your drawing.'

I couldn't speak. I looked down at the shark drawing I had just completed, its cutaway body graphically displaying the tightly packed internal organs to which I had helpfully attached descriptive arrows: *here is the gizzard, here is the gill slit, here is the long strand of microscopic canals that allows the shark to sense its struggling prey, even three miles distant...* Help me, fish, I prayed – help me to get Dana Pepp to go under the table with me.

She was talking, or rather her lips were moving, but courtly love had taught me not to expect speech from her, only a solemn look of annihilation. Then the words bled through: 'Sacha... would you like to come to Betsy's party with me?' I was paralysed by sudden access; cloven in two by the sound of one hand clapping. It didn't matter that I'd just won the Peaches & Herb album at Sally Shapiro's disco party, demonstrating my fatal zigzag manoeuvre, slowly working my way down Sally's gyrating body with my arms pointing this way and that – no, I was roadkill at heaven's gate.

'I'll take that as a "yes,"' Dana said mercifully.

And then we were there, almost... approaching the party through feathery ferns along a winding path of herringbone bricks. Dana had my hand and my head was bowed, like a penitent approaching judgement. The angel had brought me to paradise, but how would I ever unfurl my snakes in front of her pure gaze? The path led to a tented tennis court, pulsing with disco light. Inside, shame paralysed me and I couldn't dance. Dana was snapping her fingers and doing groovy things, but I just couldn't *get with it.* In despair, I closed my eyes and did a dervish whirl to another part of the dance floor. Betsy Assenheim was there, beckoning with a crooked finger and I went under the table with her, and when I came back, Dana Pepp was gone for good.

That summer, my father took me fishing in Washington state. It was the first holiday we'd ever had alone together, and I was happy to have him all to myself. He bought me an Instamatic camera for the trip and I snapped away haphazardly: our rental car pulled up outside the lakeside condo; the view across the water from the balcony; the marina and the smiling white-haired fisherman; Dad with a bending rod; me holding up a dogfish, my sweatshirt emblazoned with the number 12 – my age at the time – in vinyl Day-Glo colours.

My father was so impressed with the composition of my landscape photos that he had them blown up and bound in a leather album titled Port Ludlow, 1977. Going back through the album now, I can see with my own eyes how much I loved him. So many of the moments I captured celebrate the *beau idéal* of a father: Anthony Newley never looked more heroic than in these pictures taken by his twelve-year-old son. And when I finally appear myself, arms spread in Julie Andrews-like ecstasy, a mountain vista behind me, the delight on my little-boy face puts a smile on my middle-aged one.

Heading home, we overnighted in Seattle where we saw *Close Encounters of the Third Kind*. After the horrific purge of *Jaws*, Spielberg was evidently ready to believe again. But the love he longed for didn't come from this world. When Richard Dreyfuss approached the spaceship in his red silk spacesuit, intent on sailing away with the radiant, childlike others, I wanted to go, too. Perhaps 'they' could fix me up and return me to Earth a better boy.

Sensing I was ready for higher things, my father directed me to the stash of *Playboy* magazines under the window seat in his bedroom. I spent hours on end, flipping through the silky pages, mouth ajar, a twinkly feeling behind my fly. The soft, orange mood lighting; the enormous globes and glossy fur frosted with rim light: food I could not yet partake of, but for which my appetite was slowly erecting its tent. What was this new and burgeoning hunger? What were these images? 'Playmates'? But just how did one play with them?

By happy coincidence I turned on the TV and there was Eartha Kitt in *Batman* in a body-glove of black leather – the insinuating answer to my question. The way she mewled and purred as Catwoman, scratching the air and spitting her venomous lines, made me uneasy in a warm and buoyant way. I wanted to play with *her*. In the commercial break, I rushed to the bathroom for a pee, but was so eager to get back to Eartha that I caught my little man in my fly. My howling brought the house down. Tara and Cathy flanked the doorway, laughing hysterically, as my father came through in the pinch and performed the quasi-surgical deed, slowly unpicking the teeth from my penis.

Eartha was the annunciation, the first visiting angel of masturbation. I spread my father's *Playboys* out on the floor like homework requiring close study. As my groin warmed and throbbed, I started to understand. I scissored out the centrefolds and transferred them to my private hideout – a bamboo grove behind the flower garden – and pinioned them to the bristly poles. There I sat, surrounded by my slowly stirring wall of images – still, alas, monk-like, but cognizant of, and grateful for, the abundance. On the following day, it rained like hell and I visited my shrine only to find my playmates shrivelled on the vine, body parts all over the place.

But I was getting ready for business. When I saw Cathy playfully flash her breasts in one of my father's home movies, I was pleasantly disturbed by the after-image. I'd always felt conflicted in her company, but now it took on tangible form: I found myself wanting to hug and touch her. I sublimated this erotic tension on to her Cadillac Seville – cleaning it became my way of fondling her at one remove. I could polish her to my heart's content and feel her curves and lines without any risk. This transference was so seamless that I failed to see it for what it so transparently was. I just knew I *had* to clean that car; I had to make it as spotless and shiny as I could. I took out the mats and vacuumed around the pedals; I lay on my back and polished the silver of the running boards that curled under the car; I whiffled the tire spokes and flossed the grill. After this orgy of purification, I sat deliriously exhausted in the car, inhaling the sweet scent of new leather and faux mahogany.

When Cathy saw my gleaming masterpiece, she squealed with delight. Then she proposed a drive – an expedition fraught for the fantasist in me. Perhaps she would reach over and touch me. Perhaps her breasts would brush against me. Perhaps I would be able to taste her breath as she spoke directly into my face: 'You're such a good boy, Sach, you do so many great things for me…'

The car came alive at the turn of her key, tinkling politely to remind us to put on our seatbelts. After this initial rumble, it barely whispered. I closely observed how she lifted the lever on the steering column and found reverse, her polished nails clacking on the glossy wheel, ribbed for extra pleasure. As she reversed out of the garage into daylight, the shine I'd achieved on the hood almost blinded us. She slipped on her Jackie O shades and, in a wheeling vortex of sparkles and drifting diamond flares, we headed out the driveway. She took it slow on the downward gradient. At the turning for Coldwater Canyon she checked then pulled out with a fluid spurt of speed. The Seville gently kicked and found second gear. The wheels popped on the centre studs and she drifted right to stay in lane. How happy we were: she smiling and alive with privilege – Tony Newley's Chosen One, mother of one of his children, beneficiary of his glorious gifts, his magnetism, his proudly engorged Eros; and me, by her side – the little man with the little man, the perfect stepson she could mother at a distance, without all the mess of shared genes and demons.

For all that, she never once held or caressed me. She gave herself to me only through food. And I went on being able to pleasure her only with my droopy hose and my chamois cloth – standing there by her Seville in an unrequited lather – reduced to a sad sack of cold water and soap.

With Tara fast becoming a teenager and balking at having to share a room with her six-year-old stepsister, the problem of space allocation at Lloydcrest reared its head. For a while, a compromise was considered: building two rooms on top of the garage. This got so far as the planning phase, with actual architectural drawings spread out on the kitchen table. I was thrilled by these sketches of my new living space, with its wrap-around shelving, built-in desk and wall-mounted TV. But my father's accountant – another of those authority figures he couldn't resist listening to – convinced him that the renovations were not 'cost-effective'. We would have to go back to the drawing board, so to speak. The only solution was to find a bigger house. It was like losing Summit all over again.

My father took pains to make our last Lloydcrest Christmas extra special. As the days shortened and the nights turned damp and chilly, he charged me with the important duty of building natural fires in all the downstairs fireplaces. I made regular treks to the woodpile in the garage, and became adept at placing the logs just so, to ensure good airflow and a long burn. I liked nothing better than to dreamily watch the climbing tuft of flame overwhelm my design. Eventually the house became so hot that my father asked me to keep my pyrotechnics confined to the den.

In the big living room with its lemon and melon-pink velvet sofas, the Steinway was moved aside so that the Christmas tree could take its place in the corner. My father considered the usual Christmas balls and tinsel ersatz and tacky, so our tree was decorated with painted plaster facsimiles of lemons, apples, and pears, and festooned with old-world candle lights that he had found in some antique store. When I turned off the lights, the better to be transported by the firelit scene, I could imagine myself in a Dickensian Christmas Past.

The presents started piling up early in December and continued without a break until the lower branches were covered. Dee told my father to stop already, but he couldn't help himself: every time he left the house he saw something he was sure one of us would like to have. And his largesse didn't stop there – he continued inviting everyone he saw socially. As Christmas day approached, the guestlist grew, as it became clear that if you weren't going to Tony Newley's on 25 December, you weren't IN.

On Christmas morning, my father watched excitedly through his purring Bolex as I unwrapped an enormous pair of Dolby speakers, and an eight-track reel-to-reel with mixing deck and microphone. I didn't know what to say. 'You're going to be a regular Gerald McBoing-Boing, Sachie,' he clucked. On cue, I did a few quick improvs for him on the whooping speakers: my speeding car with Doppler effect; my whistling bomb and detonation; my phlegmy rocket take-off tailing out to a whisper – the complete repertoire. Next present unwrapped was a toy rocket driven by compressed water. My father helped me build the launching pad and peeled off the stickers while Cathy bagged the snowdrifts of paper. Jimmy Stewart's tearful gratitude in *It's a Wonderful Life* was playing on TV, and Grandma was busy airing the pastry in the kitchen. By late lunchtime, the house brimmed with a surfeit of food, treasure and thoroughly satisfied children. I tagged through the butterfly garden, brandishing my toy Chewbacca and my lightsabre.

After Roman feasting, hymns around the piano and hot toddies, my father excused himself. The adult guests looked at each other: the host was retiring so soon?

He had repaired upstairs to his dressing table to apply red paint to his nose and to glue on a snowy beard. I peaked in and saw Cathy help him into the padded suit. 'See you later, Santa,' she said, squeezing his crotch for good measure. His eyes twinkled: life was good.

Outside, Ramiro, our gardener, was leaning against the side of the house on a ladder, waiting. When Santa popped his hoary head out the window and gave the signal, the diminutive Mexican started madly drumming on the shingled roof. In the living room, there was no mistaking what was about to happen. 'Ho Prancer!

Ho Dancer! Ho Vixen and Blixen!…' Santa intoned, as he descended the stairs, giving the royal wave of greeting to the flocking children. They swarmed around him as he opened his bulging sack. At that moment I was so thrilled and proud to be Anthony Newley's son: only my father could do this; only *he* had the heart, the will, the *love*, to make Christmas this complete. He winked at me as he lumbered into the living room where the grown-ups were waiting. He greeted them, one and all, with the jovial yet weary air of an old man with much still to do. Hugs and kisses were exchanged – wives (and a few men) who had crushes on him held on to him a little too long – and then, with a salutary wave and a promise to return next Christmas, he climbed back up the stairs.

'Hey Santa! Take the chimney!' one of the kids yelled.

'With *this* waistline?' he quipped, and was gone.

Ramiro drummed again and we rushed outside to catch a glimpse of the departing sleigh, but all we saw were the twinkling lights of downtown.

After a frenzied round of house-hunting during which they saw, warmed to, and then went cold on a number of options, my father and Cathy settled on what they felt was a marked improvement on Lloydcrest: 946 Bristol Avenue, in the westerly suburb of Brentwood. Cathy informed us that the house had once belonged to Joan Crawford and, as such, was the unsavoury setting for the incidents detailed in *Mommie Dearest*. With its Olympic-sized swimming pool and impressive square footage, it spoke to my father's sense of himself.

To me, the house was not a patch on Lloydcrest with its fabulous views and mystery, but Cathy assured us that 'it just needs a lot of work' and seemed excited by the prospect. She ticked off the improvements to come: chop down the courtyard tree and brick it over; extend the west wing into an atrium; convert the pool house to a viewing theatre; and so on, and so forth… ad (dollars) infinitum.

Why this money could not have been better spent accommodating Lloydcrest for us, I don't know. I have to conclude that my father must have *wanted* to leave the hallowed house on the hill. Perhaps the aura of Tink still lingered and he wanted to move on and give Cathy the foursquare life she wanted. Or perhaps he was just afflicted with 'gypsy blood' like my mother.

The contract was signed, and we moved into a transitional home to await the completion of renovations. Lloydcrest meanwhile had been snapped up by Christine McVie of Fleetwood Mac. As renovations dragged on, our time in the 'rental' stretched to more than a year and became a weighty chapter in itself.

## 12

# 3261 Stone Canyon

*Head of the Artist's Father*

IF HE IS STILL ALIVE, I WOULD LIKE TO HAVE A WORD, AND then some, with my father's accountant from the seventies. Better yet, I would like the opportunity to sample whatever substance was in his glove compartment at the time. Not only did he encourage his hapless celebrity client to renovate a house at enormous and unfathomable cost, he sanctioned my father's undertaking the ruinous $10,000-a-week cost of the transitional rental.

The Stone Canyon house was a salmon-pink McMansion in the luxurious enclave of Bel Air. (In comparison to this fabled grove of truly great houses – the preserve of Hollywood royalty – Beverly Hills counts as drab suburbia.) It came complete with a tennis court, a huge pool, a four-car garage, a fruit orchard and acres of landscaped garden. There was one small problem – no proper room for me. Once again, I was relegated to the maid's quarters, off the kitchen. If the rest of the family had seemed a bit removed at Lloydcrest, here in this cavernous palace they weren't even within shouting distance.

I settled in without complaint and didn't question the perverse injustice. I had to believe that my father and Cathy knew what they were doing. I even agreed with Tara that it was cool to have my own corner of the house where I could get up to things unmonitored.

Oscar Night, 1977. I lie on my father's bed watching the broadcast. Vanessa Redgrave has just won Best Supporting Actress for *Julia* and toughed out the extraordinary booing that greeted her speech against 'Zionism' (not a good idea in a room groaning with Jews). Next up is Paddy Chayefsky (best screenplay for *Network* the year before), who is to announce the winner in the writing category. But before he does, he says, he must clear his conscience about something, 'or I'm going to kick myself in the morning. I'm fed up with people using this occasion to spout their political views.'

A roar of approval goes up. I, too – little me – am thrilled by his candour. I don't even know what 'Zionism' means, I don't really understand why he's upset, but I *do* know that he's just said *exactly what he wanted to on national television*, with little thought for the consequences.

I go down to the maid's quarters and try it myself. I stare at my reflection in the bathroom mirror and point an accusatory finger: 'I'm gonna kick myself in the morning if I don't say this – so get ready! I'm sick and tired of being put in fucking maids' rooms!' I pause for rapturous applause – but none comes. I see my face fall and soften. I'm not Paddy and I'm not Vanessa. I'm going to have to shut up and continue to be a good boy.

Soon after we moved to Bel Air, my father began his long trips on the road. He was having to work practically nonstop to cover the steep costs associated with the two houses. Cathy was being assisted in her planning and execution of the renovations by a pair of dotty girlfriends who had decided to develop second careers, but whose taste turned out to be up their collective asses.

To maximize our time together on the precious occasions that he was home, my father often took me to work with him. This meant the Hollywood talk-show circuit, on which he'd become a favourite. I would habitually sit in the green room lapping up his segment on the monitor. Often he would sing first – a standard or a new song he wanted to promote. If it was a musical-variety show, like *Sonny and Cher*, he'd work in with them and do a number.

I was in his dressing room before *The Tonight Show* taped. Carson looked in, said 'Hi Tony,' and, when introduced to me, gave a quick, dry handshake, crackling with electricity. The other guest that night was Charo, the Hispanic bombshell, whose machine gun delivery and bulging cleavage also left me staticky.

There were game shows, too, like *Hollywood Squares* with its standing, tic-tac-toe set of celebrities. My father usually sat top left, sniping at Paul Lynde's centre square. Lynde wore eye-splittingly loud shirts, holding court with his outré one-liners and queenly innuendoes.

Question: 'What brings tears to a monkey's eyes?'

Paul: (Pause for effect) 'Learning that Tarzan swings both ways…'

And there were embarrassing appearances on *Celebrity Bowling* and *Celebrity Charades* which brought no money, but might yield a set of golf clubs or a weekend in Cabo San Lucas, while *Tattletales* offered the fun of pairing Dad up with his and Cathy's old friends

Dolly and Dick Martin (of *Laugh In* fame) to expose to a voyeuristic national audience the intimate secret knowledge, or lack thereof, between celebrity husbands and their wives.

Question: 'Tony, do you hold Cathy after lovemaking?'

Tony: 'Well Burt... on the whole... and, of course, off the hole... I would have to admit that... while I'm sure Dolly gets enough Dick, *I* might be guilty of the odd... hit and run.' (Cathy is shown on the monitor, wearing earmuffs – oblivious – while Dick lies on the floor holding his gut.)

Throughout these game-show larks, my father kept his tongue firmly in cheek, adopting the insouciant air of a roué. He was sending himself up, if only to maintain some sort of purchase on reality. Not to mention the purchase of the Brentwood house-cum-renovations.

It was in the more intimate setting of the talk shows, as he contended with the earnest questions and the admiring regard of his peers, that this mask would sometimes slip and he'd find himself saying the first thing that came into his head. Hosts like Mike Douglas and Merv Griffin were often stumped by his curt delivery, his occasional air of baffled disgruntlement at being there, in front of a studio audience. He once remarked to Bob Newhart, who was sitting in for Carson, that he'd 'just come from pleasuring my wife...' and was 'only there for the $380 and free kitchen range.' Adding insult to injury, he confessed that he 'didn't really like performing' and sang 'only for himself.' Afterward, Newhart gently chided him, saying that people didn't really want to hear that sort of thing from a star – they wanted to believe he was really enjoying himself up there.

The months of waiting to get into our new house dragged to more than a year. Cathy would take Tara and me to see the work in progress at 946 Bristol Avenue. We made goo-goo eyes at the bubblegum-pink entrance hall with the green Chinese dragons in shiny porcelain and did handspring landings at the sight of the cheddar dining room with its shiny black wainscoting, plushly upholstered dining chairs in primary colours and flashy zebra-pattern rug. Scoping out the house was like exploring the interior of a migraine while whistling a happy tune. I was shown prospective swatches for my room and, to the cooing delight of the ladies with the taste in their asses, got with the programme and opted for an upbeat palette of ultramarine blue, sunshine yellow, and high-alert orange – with a matching armchair in a Mondrian-like hash of all of the above colours. The cherry on my chromatic hellhole was a wall-mounted Zenith TV in a crimson box, boasting seventy-nine channels.

Tara didn't want colours – she wanted blank, to match her expression. Her honeymoon with Cathy was long over. She was fast becoming an adolescent, and developing the bullshit monitor to go with it. Cathy tried to stay in sync, but Tara wasn't buying it.

When Cathy walked in on Tara one day to find her bed strewn with an impressive array of bongs and pot-smoking paraphernalia brought over by a friend, she defaulted to evil stepmother. She grounded Tara for an entire week and forbade her to see her pot pal. Their dialogue dwindled to angry spats of needling inquiry and sullen one-line retorts. It was akin to what had happened at Carolyn Way between my mother and Tara. I was once again the nominal favourite, living on the greener side of the desert island; which didn't help matters between Tara and me.

I started sixth grade at Hawthorne by making some nice new friends: the Shapiro twins. My greater bond was with Alvy, who was slightly shorter and a lot funnier than Elliot, the high-strung golden-boy tennis star. They adopted me as their brother and we became a social tripod, able to bear a shitload of rejection. Just why we weren't better liked is unclear: perhaps it was because we were blonde and self-confident and sufficient unto ourselves. At least *they* were. I got a contact high from their strong Jewish home life. Their father was the balding, virile type; ran his own real estate firm and had a rabbinical sense of humour. Their mother doted on them, while taking care to reserve the best cuts of meat for their miniature schnauzer, Palmsley.

Every recess, the Hawthorne handball courts became a pitched battleground between 'them' and 'us', them being the jocks Robbie Rosen, Richie Mirisch and their slavish droogs. Always outnumbered, we three Shapiroteers managed some herculean feats of court coverage and gutsy defiance. The trick was to set up your fellow teammate with an easy shot to return, which he could then slice low to the wall, calling out a name from the opposing team to return *before* the double bounce. Elliot was the best slicer of the three of us, so we were always saving and setting up the ball for him. Robbie was the opposing ace, usually calling out *my* name – SASQUACH! – in anger as he flamed the ball low, causing me to stumble after it and slam into the sidewall. The big pink ball became silky-smooth from all the abrasion. We would return to class with blackened hands – prima facie evidence of our struggle to survive, and win.

Elliot could best Alvy and me on the tennis court, even when we played two against one. As a result, my tennis improved through trial humiliation. On a good day I could look very much like an under-fifteen ace, with hard, beautifully placed serves on a curving trajectory and a double-handed backhand that went low and deep. My topspin forehand lifted me off the ground; and when I was really feeling my game, the ball seemed to balloon and slow down, so I could take my time and meet it with maximum topspin.

My father was delighted with my tennis prowess and was always its willing victim. He would come on court at Stone Canyon in his baggy shorts, swatting the air pre-emptively with his oversize Prince racket. I would then proceed to demolish him with my serve-and-volley game, observing, with pangs of affection, his staggeringly awkward court coverage; his airy, lofted strokes and gasps of surprise as he saved one of my penetrating corner shots. I felt like the young firebrand to his lolloping old lady. Tennis was the one place I could outshine him and lay claim to my birthright as the son he unquestioningly admired.

I would have enjoyed our games even more had not my squawking perfectionism been perched on my shoulder, pecking at me and holding up my game. A first serve into the net would stab me with disappointment; if the ball regularly overshot the baseline and I couldn't steady my gyroscope, I would melt down into a McEnroe-like parody of racket smashing and foul language. 'Calm down, Sachie,' my father would say, 'don't take it all so seriously. You're doing beautifully…' But the point was I couldn't be perfect – therefore I was defective, and could be abandoned. Sue's voice still echoed in my mind as the overburdening enforcer. Whenever I spilled my shit on the clean white cloth of her expectations, all hell had broken loose. I would have to be mastered all over again: suffocated, shut down, controlled. My worry started there and spread to everything. If I performed poorly on a school test, I came home and moped around the garden for hours, hooking my fingers into the tennis court fence and dry-retching with worry.

Cannabis helped me unlock the valves of pressure. I first smoked it on a scruffy hillside of dry growth and eucalyptus near Alvy's house. We found a cleft in the garden shrubbery – probably made by deer fording through to graze on the sweet garden grass – and followed it out to a covered ridge, where charred remains and broken bottles betokened bacchanals. We smoked the humble weed from a small silver pipe, coughing and spluttering through our first hits, until the air went heavily soft and our smiles smeared around our faces. The trees made an intricate weave overhead and I saw my childhood snakes in happy macramé, holding the sky in place. Across the valley, the Hollywood sign undulated like a centipede, and when I looked down at Palmsley who was sitting patiently at my feet, I saw all the complexities of a human soul in his deep, dark canine eyes. I tried to share this revelation with Alvy, but he just started laughing: 'Sarch, Dude, you are so fucking *stoned…*' Then I started dissolving too in a fit of giggles.

We stumbled back to the house, overcome by hunger, and found some Campbell's vegetable soup in the kitchen cupboard. After more convulsive giggling, we managed to heat it up, staring goggled-eyed at the blue petals of gas flame. We carried the steaming bowls to the table and took our first, trembling mouthfuls of ambrosia. The taste centres fire-crackered in my brain. My tongue worked like an urgent slug, fat with savour. The lowly soup was transformed into an ultimate bouillabaisse of tints and flavours. I couldn't believe my tongue. Where had it been all these years – wrapped in cellophane? *This was real*; not the dull, generic soup I'd tasted so many times; that was the soup of the world, of common sense and sobriety – *this* was the soup of desire, the soup of infinite mercy – proof of the divine indwelling in all things. I gasped in recognition and took another spoonful, aswoon with pleasure as the rich tumble of coated vegetables melted in my mouth and slipped down my throat. 'Holy shit, Sarch,' said Alvy, 'this soup is good…'

It was only natural that the craze enveloping southern California in pot smoke – and filling emergency rooms with ankle sprains and breaks – would co-opt us, too. Every self-respecting kid was on a skateboard that summer frantically trying to master the principles of cool. Playground discussions went deep into the arcana and lore of the culture, evolving a new vernacular of superlatives – radicool, totally awesome, killer, gnarly – to encompass the world of feeling that came to you on a board. The relative strengths and weaknesses of skateboard 'trucks' and wheels were hotly debated, and new tricks and stunts were always being invented by those with 'No Fear'. It was the dawning of the Just Do It culture; and we were all desperate to talk and dress like surfers. Ocean Pacific (OP, we called it) was the big surf label of the time, with all the right associations: pictures of guys shredding enormous waves and skateboarders upside down in space, suspended over a curling ramp. If you didn't have one of these posters on your wall you were a *dick-smoker*, the lowest form of adolescent life. These guys were the heroes of zero gravity and they were beckoning YOU to wear the uniform of transcendence: the cut-off corduroy shorts with the swept pockets; the light cotton shirts in a dizzy-making variety of colour patterns designed to seduce the stoner. *Dude, like your OP's...* was a good way to start the day as you swept into the playground wearing your electric-blue shorts with the frizzy, stonewashed hems, riding your Sims Pure Juice board with the aerial grab-ons...

The Three Shapiroteers moved operations – pot smoking and skateboard manufacture inc. – to an improvised hut inside the Shapiro garage. As visionary denizens of the great tarmac waves of the Trousdale Estates, we wanted to invent boards that could ride the mountainous steeps of our neighbourhood. With concerted industry we evolved and developed prototypes: The Monster Load (extra-wide board); The Wave Crusher (extra-thick board); The Cum and Swallow (board with tail feathers). I did the painting and the cursive lettering down the middle, Alvy did the measuring and the sawing and Elliot drove the screwdriver.

I romanticize our sense of innovation – what we were really doing was taking the wheels and trucks from our short boards and screwing them on to long wooden planks to make custom hill riders with little or no turning radius. The problem was that, at a certain point, these stretch limos would belly in the middle and break under the bouncing pressure of a boy. The art and the science of it became a search for maximum stretch without undue strain. Eventually we settled on The Sweet Spot, a marvel of form and balance: in fact, a wooden plank sawn off to about four feet, with a primitively sharpened nose and strips of texture tape laid all down it for traction. We'd had several 'totally awesome' hill trials on the curving driveway outside their house when Alvy almost turned into raspberry jam in the grill of his father's homeward-returning

Mercedes. We were all grounded for that, and spent the rest of the afternoon sulking in our hut.

One day when Cathy came to pick me up, I noticed something wrong. She was unnaturally flirty with Mr Shapiro and I wondered if she'd been drinking. I certainly wasn't happy getting into the car with her. As we coasted down the driveway and on to the main road, she seemed like a teenager letting loose. Her hands were literally slithering over the wheel. She became engrossed in getting the right rock 'n' roll station on the radio. I glanced at Chelsea in the back seat, and she stared back blankly – I guessed she'd gotten used to it on the way over. Having found her station, Cathy drummed the wheel and lap-danced. The centre-studs popped and the wheels let out plaintive screams as she weaved around in lane. She shot excited glances at me, like we were sharing a ride at the funfair. I was so terrified I sat on my hands and prepared for impact. As we ran the stop signs and picked up speed toward the bottom of the hill, she suddenly said, 'Let's try this!' and wrenched the car into the pull-out lane. It lurched and dug into gravel and I fell helplessly forward and back, stunned and breathless. Cathy flung open the door and fell out. Chelsea looked terrified and I didn't know what to do. I struggled against my door, but we were buried. I finally managed to kick it open, and made my way scrunching around the back of the car. Where the hell was Cathy? Then I saw her, and immediately wished I hadn't: squatting over the double yellow lines in the middle of the road. She dropped her panties, broke wind, and then let out a generous stream of urine… laughing hysterically as the rich foam followed the yellow brick road.

I couldn't believe what I was seeing, and I sure as hell wasn't going to wait around for the bowel movement. I marched up the hill, feeling not a little guilty about leaving Chelsea behind. After half an hour of sweaty, panic-driven walking, I arrived back at the Shapiros' and breathlessly reported that Cathy had 'gone weird.' My father was summoned and showed up stony-faced at the wheel of his Vette. Nothing was said in the car until the gates swung open at Stone Canyon. 'Cathy's very sorry about what happened,' he said. 'She had something that didn't agree with her up at Howie Greenfield's house. She's feeling better now. Sleeping.' I just nodded and went off to my room.

For some children it comes early, but eventually it comes for all children: the sick-making feeling that adults don't really know what they're doing and are making it up as they go along.

After the initial panic that this knowledge engenders comes the slow, sad withdrawal of trust. Most children can't hide it, but a child sensitive to the narcissistic demands of his parents may be able to successfully mask the withdrawal. God knows, I still tried to smile for the family photo-ops – to be the happy little boy who pleased everybody – but in some deep part of myself I knew that Daddy was not going to be able to save us. There was something very wrong with Cathy, and there was something no less wrong with Daddy for choosing her.

The man on TV wore a caftan embroidered with flowers. He had long hair, a greying beard and spoke with an upper-class English accent. Butterflies alighted on him and, with his twinkling eyes, he seemed to expect nothing less.

'Is he a magician?' I asked.

'Of sorts...' my father replied. 'That's Alan Watts, one of the most brilliant men on the planet.'

I liked the name: its Oriental simplicity and sense of voltage. I couldn't fathom what he was saying – something about the universe and nothingness – but I was drawn in by his aura of mastery and serenity. One of his books, *The Joyous Cosmology*, was on my father's bedside and I studied the starburst cover. Inside, there was stuff about LSD, the big drug for hippies and grown-ups. I didn't think Dad had ever taken it – even though he'd told us that drugs were good for you, they 'opened you up' and showed you what was really there; they didn't *impose* the experience – what they did was *reveal* how beautiful the experience was. I'd had that feeling with the soup, so I knew it was true.

There was a lot of pot around the house. Dad had big Plexiglas bongs in his bathroom and Alvy and I had found his bag of Thai Stick in the refrigerator. Dad smoked it with his friends Dick and Dolly whenever they came over. Dick was a TV comedian who was even funnier off-screen and Dolly was his equally funny wife. Dad would close the living room doors and they'd have a session. Sometimes I eavesdropped at the door. Cathy's high-pitched laughter and Dad's spanking laugh announced the onset of their respective highs. Dad was a hilarious stoner. The two girls laughed at and with him non-stop. Then he'd reach his peak and go silent: he was 'mulching' – not funny any more, not anything really, just seeing things deeply and 'understanding so much.' That's when Dick would rib him: 'The master has gone to the temple...' Then Cathy would spirit him off to bed.

Sometimes we went to Dick and Dolly's in Malibu for the weekends. She baked hash brownies, not always successfully. On one occasion, the warped tray she used meant the hash liquefied and all ran to a corner brownie. We deduced afterwards that poor, unsuspecting Dad scoffed it – washing it down with a glass of milk, closing his eyes and savouring like he always did – because on the walk they went on afterward, he started seeing things: the seaweed clumps were quivering and the tide was hissing, spitting like a radio. They got as far as Danny DeVito's house, where Dad turned in the driveway. Cathy found him upstairs on his hands and knees, tipping forward and begging someone or something not to let him fall into the abyss.

I ran out when I saw them dragging him back, his useless legs trailing and making zigzags in the sand. When I asked what was wrong, they just looked guilty. Dad walked over to me unsteadily, like a grizzly holding out his paw. I took it and looked up into his pale, awestruck face. There was a palm tree over us, swaying in the wind, and he swayed, too, saying, 'It's... so... beautiful...'

I knew what he meant.

Back at the hut, Alvy and I were sick of skateboards. We had another idea, and Elliot, on tennis tour, wasn't there to vote us down. Mr Shapiro had just installed a new sprinkler system and the garden was strewn with bits of spare piping and curved joiners. We gathered these up on the sly and, back in our hut, fitted them together into elaborate Dr Seuss-like bongs – the bigger, the better – until our spidery invention fell apart, haemorrhaging smoke. Then, of course, we'd have to start all over. Our experiments synthesized down to a Swiss horn-like monster we christened Dear John, which produced an even draw, complete with clouds of immaculately cooled smoke, for our spongy little lungs.

When we repaired to the head shop in Westwood for more pipe screens, the sales guy stared us down, over the counter. 'You know pot stunts your growth, guys.' We just nodded, fully aware that we were both pretty short for our age. Back home, we lost no time fitting the new screens into Dear John – we couldn't wait to take more growth-stunting high dives.

Cathy subsequently discovered one of my aborted bongs in the kitchen trash – a small one I'd made out of a glue bottle, tinfoil and a straw. I don't know why I'd been so careless as to throw it in there – probably self-sabotage. Dad politely knocked, then entered my bedroom holding the bong between thumb and forefinger like a dead rat. He had a sour look on his face. I was innocently reading *Mad Magazine* and Alvy was on the floor flipping through *Car and Driver*.

'What's this, Sach?'

'I don't know.'

Alvy cracked up and looked quickly away.

Dad sat down on my bed and held the thing aloft like Exhibit A.

'It looks to me like a homemade device for smoking marijuana in.'

I glanced at it. 'Yes, that's what it looks like, Dad.'

Alvy hid his head, the giggles squeezing out.

'Is it yours?'

'No.'

'Don't lie to me, Sachie.'

'It's not mine.'

'Is that the truth? Look at me, son.'

I couldn't – my eyes were tearing up. 'It's not mine, I swear...'

'And what have *you* got to say about this, Alvy?'

Alvy peered through a chink in his arms: 'Nothing, Mr Newley.'

He breathed deeply. 'OK, Sachie, I want to see you when Alvy leaves, which I suggest is soon. Gottit?'

I found him alone in the den, biding his time. He was sitting on the brown corduroy sofa, his arm stretched out along the back.

'Sit down.'

I listened to the clock ticking. My guts boiled.

'Well, was it yours?'

'Yes, Dad.'

He nodded and said, 'Thank you.' He leaned forward and massaged my shoulder. 'I understand why you had to tell that fib – because Alvy was there. But I always want you to tell me the truth – no matter what – OK?'

'Yes, Dad...'

'I'm not angry you smoked a little grass. I'm just disappointed that you had that first incredible experience without me.'

I looked at him.

'I keep feeling we've missed so much of each other, Sachie. I want to be there with you at every important point. Don't cut me out of anything, OK? Never feel you have to hide anything from me.'

'I won't,' I said. 'I promise.'

He kissed the top of my head, and we rocked together on the brown corduroy sofa.

But he never shared the Thai Stick.

# 13

# Harvard Prep

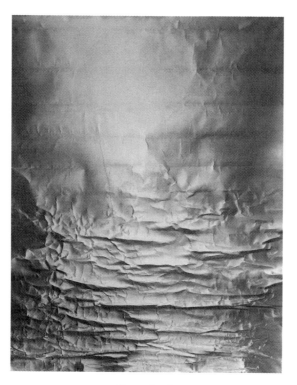

*First Crush*

AS MY THIRTEENTH BIRTHDAY APPROACHED, I CHANGED schools again. The new one was pretty far away – in the San Fernando Valley – and getting there and back was going to be a drag, but it had a good record of getting its boys into Ivy League schools; at the level of aspiration, at least, it was entitled to call itself Harvard Prep. It would also serve to keep me away from Alvy, whom my father considered a bad influence. One look at the football field emblazoned in the centre with the school crest; at the

Romanesque pillars of the old library thrusting into the blue sky, convinced me that I wanted to go there.

A week before the exams I was having to take to get in, the rains came. I'd lived through my share of sodden English winters, but this was something else: a tropical deluge that turned the Bel Air canyon roads into torrents of brown water. The morning of the test, I woke to the rain's incessant drumming. I breakfasted with my father on oatmeal, my belly a gas-bulb of anxiety. Ahead of me lay the thirty-page multiple-choice monster known as the SAT. I preferred written tests where I could embellish and qualify. But here there was no escape: my answers would be graded by a computer.

'Ready?' said my father with an encouraging smile.

'Ready.'

We got into the Vette and backed out into the inimical elements. The gates swung open on the swollen river that was our road and we eased the car into the flow. At first I thought it would stall. Then Dad pressed the gas and we seemed to roll along with the current, making a wake that rolled out and bilged over the pavement. The rain hammered the roof and made my nerves flood over. I closed my eyes and started talking to myself: *If I don't get into Harvard Prep, it's not the end of the world. I'll stay at Hawthorne and go to Beverly Hills High with Alvy. That's not so bad...* But when I opened them, the panic was still there, drumming on the windscreen. The wipers couldn't stop it; even the great storm drains of Sunset Boulevard couldn't gulp it down fast enough. As we turned on to the main thoroughfare, I made out the clogged traffic through the whacking wipers, and hoped we wouldn't make it to the test in time. I looked at my father in profile, his black sideburns bracing him with male strength. He felt my eyes on him and turned to me with a warming smile. 'We'll make it, Sachie, don't worry.'

An hour later, we were winding down Mulholland Drive into the San Fernando Valley. I was manically changing radio stations, looking for something upbeat, when I came across some soft rock.

Dad said, 'Oh, I love this song. I wish I'd written it.' So we pulled up to the line of cars outside Harvard Prep to the elegiac tones of Billy Joel's 'Just the Way You Are.'

Maybe it was the melancholy tone of the song – or perhaps the steam-press of anxiety I was under – but the music found a deep place of listening in me. It was achy and blue, like poor little me, but redeemed by the dappled gold of a pure piano melody. How far, I wondered, hunkered down in the car's gloomy interior, could I follow this thread of hope? All the way to success in the Harvard Prep exams? When the saxophone took over and lifted the melody skyward, I imagined a dolphin spiralling from the dark depths into sunlight. Could *I* reach the surface, too, and breathe free?

After parking in the jammed lot, we joined the dark, umbrella-burdened crowd of nervous boys and their parents climbing the auditorium steps. The examination hall loomed above. The other boys were turning in circles outside, talking to themselves or crouched with books, cramming like mad.

'You're going to do brilliantly, Sach,' my father tried to reassure me. 'Just go with your gut. The first answer that pops into your head is usually the right one. Remember that.'

A warning bell rang. My father hugged me tight, then we walked together toward the open doors. The acre of empty desks was filling up fast. My father kissed me, squeezed my hand and let me go like a balloon. I walked forward, rising... the room was topsy-turvy under me, then I put out a hand and miraculously found a desk. I sat down and felt steady in the airy space. Before me was a paper booklet face down, and four sharpened pencils. I swivelled around to see if I could see my father, but he was gone – sealed out, like the rest of the parents.

'Eyes front, please.'

I turned and saw a neat lady up front, standing with clasped hands. She recited the rules that pertained to cheating, looked at the clock behind her, and said, 'You can start now.'

*You can start now.* The prod went in my guts and I turned the booklet over. *If a farmer goes to market with fourteen sacks of potatoes and sells one every third hour...* It wanted to know from me how many potatoes the farmer would have left if he sold so many and lost so many and so on. The answer was just a number, after all, but I couldn't figure it out. *Three sacks* said the brain; *come back to it when you're feeling less tense*, said the gut, and I went with that. I skipped a lot of questions and just nailed the easy ones, then doubled back to the sticky ones. It was torture. Time was hot, and if I lingered too long over any one question, it actually burned. Boys all around me were finishing up and getting ready to leave and I was still gnawing on my pencil, still hung up on that first question, the potato sacks. Then the finishing bell rang.

'I'm not sure how well I did, Dad...' We were driving home. The clouds had cleared away and the silvery sky promised sun.

'You're always too hard on yourself, Sachie. I'm sure you did better than you think.'

But the results confirmed my direst fears: sixty-seven per cent – barely a C grade. The infallible computer had deemed me unsatisfactory. I would never spiral up to the light. I moped about the garden, listlessly tearing tangerines from the trees and hurling them at the wall to watch them fruitlessly explode. My father found me and put an angry stop to the fruit carnage. This was his orchard, after all.

'You're just not good under time constraint,' he reasoned. 'You don't have that sort of mind. Or nervous system. You're creative. You're much better at posing questions than answering them...'

I nodded and took his merciful hand. I was glad to be like him – creative.

Then one day a letter came from Harvard Prep requesting an interview. The dolphin turned. Cathy took me on the appointed day because Dad was away. It was sunny and I felt buoyant. We walked through the bright colonnades of the upper school to the vice principal's office. Mr Amato had a small head of tight black curls, was muscular, and throbbed with health. He smiled at the pretty woman and her attentive charge. When he asked me questions, I somehow knew just how to answer. This wasn't a series of multiple-choice bubbles; this was a live person who was telegraphing his expectations clearly to me. I could see the answers written already in his face and readily told him what he clearly wanted to hear. When he asked, 'Who are the two Americans, living or dead, you would most like to meet?' I easily answered, 'Thomas Jefferson and Marilyn Monroe.' I knew he'd like that: it showed a confident grasp of high and low culture, with a winning sense of mischief casually thrown in.

A few weeks later I was hanging in the orchard with Alvy, hacking at a fruit tree with the claw end of a hammer, when Cathy opened the window and shook a heaven-sent letter at me: 'Congratulations, Sach – you're in!'

I found the Harvard boys different – more grown-up than the kids at school that I was used to. They already had opinions and attitudes. I felt adrift by comparison, and gravitated to a French kid, Jean-Pierre, who seemed even more tentative and lost than I. A bully briefly presented himself in the deceptively puny person of Colin O'Neal, a hyperactive Irish kid with lank red hair and freckles, who managed to turn the English drawl of my name into a venomous: SAAWSHA NEWLAAY... I didn't rise to the baiting. I practised Zen-like resistance and he soon went trolling elsewhere for victims. Meanwhile Jean-Pierre and I found a couple of like-minded friends: Robbie, a brilliant mathematician carpet-bombed by acne; and Larry, a dark-skinned, soft-faced Jewish boy with the astute delivery of a trial lawyer.

There were no girls to interfere with our budding brain-promise and redirect it to our trousers. This was pure, transcendental boy-hood – the Greco-Roman ideal transported to seventies Los Angeles. It was at Harvard Prep that I had the supposedly formative masculine experiences of hitting a softball out of the park, rounding the bases and being carried on the shoulders of my cheering teammates; wrestling and pinning a bigger boy to the mat; feeling a riptide of strength as I caught a 'long bomb' and dived into the end-zone. I was mentally exercised to the same degree: drilling myself in Russian diphthongs (Russian was considered a good thing to know in those days, the way Chinese is now) or lingering appreciatively over William Golding's *Lord of the Flies*.

We learned about business and economics, became acquainted with Keynes and Marx, and studied the flow charts of capital and trade. Percentages made their first appearance; and with them a sense of a world sundered into fractions, which had to be somehow marshalled into the 'big picture'. Only 'business' could do this – a manly call to arms to which I was only briefly tempted, before my inborn dreaminess interfered.

The school video lab was outfitted with the latest three-colour projector. It was there that I watched the classic movie version of *Lord of the Flies*. The scene of the island-abandoned boys dressed as primitives, tearing with avid mouths at the roasted carcass of a wild boar worked on me like porn, leaving me both embarrassed and a little turned-on. After Golding, we moved on to Arthur Conan Doyle. Our hushed, cerebral English master, with his soft shoes and paranoid stare, assigned us *The Red-Headed League* to 'analyse and digest'. After we had immersed ourselves in its beguiling matrix of criminal motive and Holmesian diagnosis, we were asked to write a play in the manner of Conan Doyle. I sat at my desk in Stone Canyon and tried to reproduce the old man's cursive script and the unsurpassably polished brilliance of his Edwardian English. The boyish pantomime of hauteur that resulted was wince inducing. But at least I was there, there in that moment of trying. Harvard Prep had lofted me there.

The manicured playing field was ringed by an Olympic-standard track, and here we ran the distances: 100-metre sprint, 200 hurdles, single-lap 400, heart-battering 1,500... We were supervised by Coach, a squat bull of a man with a droopy stoner moustache, Apache parting, and, of all things, a thick Brooklyn accent.

I'd been mortified by my mediocre showings in the 100, and was determined, as the 400 approached, to win it outright. I lined up along the starting line, kicking my legs to keep them loose. Coach fired his pistol, and I took off sprinting, like I was running the 100. My astonished competitors quickly receded. I had no plan, no strategy – just anxiety shooting up my body and setting the impossible pace. As I rounded the first bend I was cycling the air, my feet barely tapping the track as I actually felt myself exceeding my limits. My body was light, filled with joy. The lactic acid was still in abeyance and I glanced back to see the fastest boy far behind, head bowed, straining to keep up.

But then the shadows caught me and the creeping vines found my legs. I began to tire, to lag. Now when I glanced back, I saw the boy, larger, gaining. His breath was audible, angry and determined, but there was no answer in my body when I called for one. My feet were digging a grave. I wanted to fall in at that point; my flailing arms and rubber legs longed to embrace death. I heard the boy pounding behind, his breath sharp and keen at my ear. Three… 'Keep going, kid, you got it, keep going…' Coach was there, jogging alongside me, urging me on. I had to prove I could go the distance. Momentum carried me now, as I went collapsing and stumbling forward – the boy practically at my shoulder as the tape came cresting to meet me… a white band of grace that I broke as in a dream.

Then I was walking in circles and gulping air. I was hot with exhaustion and achievement and felt like puking. The other boys kept away; they didn't want to catch my winning disease. Coach came over and slapped me on the back: 'Newley, you took off like a gazelle there.'

I watched through waves of nausea as he walked away.

*'Like a gazelle…'*

It was the most beautiful thing anyone had ever said to me.

In the changing rooms I retched into a toilet. I heard the others coming in and pulling open their lockers and getting undressed. Then the showers began hissing. The laughter and the rough-housing began in earnest. I hated all this: the nakedness of boys; the cold, dungeon-like whiteness; the windows, high and barred. It was appalling. My classmates had already started puberty: they had proper dongs and bristling pubic hair while my balls were high and tight like my voice. When would *I* receive the syringe of prized hormone that would start the monstrous change? I was a little boy among semi-men. There were others like me, glancing furtively around before dropping their shorts, facing the lockers, and pulling up their jockstraps quickly. This was why I never showered.

Next period, in drama class, I propped my aching head as the teacher paced before us explaining improvisation. He had a manic, Robin Williams-like energy, and a darkly shining scarab toupee. On one occasion, he overhead us giggling about the wig and actually flipped it up, like a cap in greeting. The class blanched in unison. We respected him after that.

He noticed me dozing, and called me up for improv. 'Just listen to the other guy and riff off what he says. Jean-Pierre, can you come up here please?'

My friend appeared before me, equally terror-struck.

'Just start a conversation,' said the teacher, putting his hands on our shoulders. 'Imagine you're two characters in a situation and just go with it...'

I saw calculation in Jean-Pierre's eyes; then two zeroes appeared. *Over to you,* said his rabbit stare.

I flinched and changed posture. A little puff of inspiration gave me a dude voice, a laid-back attitude, and shoot-from-the-hip mannerisms that really impressed the teacher. Jean-Pierre did his best to ape the dude, but came off sounding like Jimmy Cagney gone gay. I couldn't figure out what exactly the class was laughing at, but at least they *were* laughing – a lot – and the teacher too. He applauded at the end and I felt the thespian gene tingling. When, soon after this, a casting agent contacted the school asking for boys to audition with Michael Caine in Peter Benchley's *The Island*, the drama teacher put me forward. But once again, as with my soccer opportunity, I passed – in the name of some stupid family vacation we were about to go on.

That summer, the occupants of 3261 Stone Canyon decamped to Gloucester, Massachusetts, for a stay at the shore with Cathy's mother and stepfather. I arrived as the golden boy of Harvard Prep. In the best traditions of Hemingway, my sense of purpose and power was soon spurred on by sports fishing. The annual bluefin tuna tournament was in full swing, and we all went out with Cathy's stepfather to catch our leviathan.

I first espied a school of them on a ream of sonar paper: a cloud of nervously sketched atoms at fifty fathoms. 'That's a mess of 'em,' said the boat captain, pointing a crooked finger. We were about ten miles out, trolling the edge of the great coastal shelf that falls suddenly to the Atlantic abyss. Here the fish massed in season to feast on the rich overspill of food from warmer waters.

I went astern to watch the first mate shovel out a mixture of fish guts and blood into the gently bubbling wake. The oily swill trailed out like a slick between the skyward-pointing rods holstered on either side of the back deck. The fat, phallic poles were strung with a 130-pound test line and barbed with huge hooks. Last year's tournament had been won by a 1,750-pounder that took five hours and a burly veteran sportsman to land.

Cathy was hell-bent on fighting the fish that day if one hooked up – and she seemed perfectly unfazed by the prospect, casually sipping her Chardonnay and turning the pages of *People* magazine. I looked with casual awe at the sports-fishing chair with its mahogany armrests and white upholstery, bolted to the deck like some throne of defiance. This was nothing like the dilapidated chair on Quint's boat in *Jaws*. Nor, happily, were the bluefins anything like man-eating sharks. They were gentle giants – like whales or elephants – that swam together and protected their young.

The boat murmured along, rocking queasily. My father munched on a sandwich and daydreamed. Cathy smoked a menthol and flicked the ash into the water. I went up on top deck to scan the horizon. There was a fleet of boats similar to ours, all chumming along and hoping to hook the Big One. I was dozing off when the cry went out. I jumped up and ran astern to see the first mate seize the whizzing rod and crank it tight. The boat tumbled into action. Cathy took her chair and hastily got into harness. The mate helped her lock the rod between her thighs and brace back against the running fish.

I couldn't help ogling my stepmother as she panted, yanking on her appended phallus. Her belts and straps looked like an erotic contraption. I experienced the consummate thrill as the fish, in taking off, lifted her denim bum from the seat. The mate poured seawater on the smoking reel and swivelled Cathy's chair around to keep her in line with the turbo fish. She strained and cranked and won line from the avatar of marine life that was furiously resisting her. The boat backed up and ate the distance between them, but the motor must have scared it, because the fish plunged and made a dull weight that wouldn't ease up. Cathy groaned and came forward. I imagined the creature going deeper, turning and flashing as it soldiered into depth, the line a scalding filament in its side. The first mate called the depth: 'two hundred... two fifty... two sixty-five... three hundred...' Cathy sat back and breathlessly complained, 'Son of a bitch.' My father stood by her – an anxious husband in the delivery room.

Then the rod bounced. 'He's up,' said the mate, as it whiplashed skyward. My heart lurched: *He's gone*, I thought – then a deadening weight pulled the tip down into an elemental trembling, a last timpani in the sea's depth, the fish reaching for the farthest expanse of silence. We waited. My father stood by his woman. The men seemed lost in thought. Then the rod relaxed.

'He's turning,' said the mate. We backed away as one, sensing the fish surging toward us. Cathy couldn't crank the line fast enough. The slack threatened to snarl in the winding machine, so the mate helped her, explaining that the fish could escape this way, running at the boat and goofing off the flaccid line.

I went up top to see him surface. I took binoculars and followed the line down to where it trembled and plucked near the water, throwing off drops. Then, in the green depths just beyond, I spied an enlarging moon, wobbling to fullness. It exploded in spray and I looked up. Forty feet off, the fish broke water in a mess of quivering blades and flashing swales of silver. Cathy screamed and pulled harder. My father speed-crouched by her, goading, 'Good Babe, good!' I couldn't imagine her victory – but the writhing fish was clearly within our tractor beam, coming closer, sickening me to pity and exciting me by turns. The two mates stationed themselves astern with harpoons. The captain looked over his shoulder and reversed the burbling boat. The men were lusty for contact; their hooks hankered after the proximate fish. It rolled and thrashed in their slithering purchase, venting blood from the gills. One hook got him, then two, and then they yanked him close to behave and die. He slapped the boat with his withering strength, but they soon had a dirty rope around his tail, and dragged him backward, reversing the flow of water through his gills, until he simply suffocated.

I went down on deck to see him hoisted aboard. The sudden reveal of his total gleaming mass made me back off in awe. Drained, he bled a waterfall that still reached and spattered my pants. I went close and ventured a hand over the glistening silver of his belly that modulated into the blue-blackness of his back. The fins were sickle-sharp; the mouth death-astonished; the huge black eye a glossy ball of starless space.

We headed in under a cloud-torn sky. The others lifted drinks inside while Dad and I sat by the fish, funereal and silent. Dad cupped and drank from his hand, laughing fatuously and mocking those inside. I understood the wonderful contrast that he was making me see: we were mourning at the cold tomb of beauty while they danced in infernal pride.

Back at the marina, we posed for photographs. Cathy brandished her rod like a staff of vengeance and the fish caught the flashbulbs beautifully. It weighed 750 pounds and placed third. Beyond our party lay the dark cannery where it would be turned into so many tins.

Dad and I broke away for a quiet walk along the shore, collecting driftwood and interesting beach junk. Back at the house, we got busy with glue and paint. Dad made an abstract arrangement of sticks, sea sponge, and coloured glass on a dark ground, to which he added pieces of red brick sucked lozenge-smooth by the tide. The finishing touch was a gangrenous Florida driver's license that he had found netted in some seaweed and positioned in the centre of the composition – I could just make out the smiling, moustached driver from Tallahassee. My effort was more representational: a sitting sea bird, beak agape, against a sketchy blue sky. For its webbed feet I used two spade handles. Dad held it at arm's length and pronounced it 'brilliant'. I liked to think he was a little jealous.

From Boston, I flew out on the second leg of my summer vacation, to the fabled South of France, where my mother and Ron Kass had rented a villa, hoping to recapture the joys of summers past. Ron's boys turned up, heavier and more melancholy than ever. After a few awkward days, we all piled in and tried to make a family of it for the duration. *Grease* had just come out, and we basically went crazy for that. It played incessantly on the tape player until the machine couldn't stand it any more and ate Olivia Newton John in the middle of 'Summer Nights'.

It was a sad summer for the most part. My mother had enjoyed some recent successes in England, but she seemed tense and distracted – and things were not helped by Ron, who seemed even more peripheral and insubstantial than ever. We had two English sisters taking care of us, but they had serious boyfriend issues and were often sullen and withdrawn. Sue was not there to make it all work: to suffer and understand the vanities of the adults, to keep the kids entertained and in check.

The standout event of the summer was my accident. I broke my wrist in a game of tag and was rushed to the hospital in Nice with my mother and a visiting Roger Moore bickering over the cab fare. The global star power of James Bond notwithstanding, I was kept on a gurney for hours and fed morphine. The doctors puffed on Gauloises and flip-flopped by, while my mother went ever hotter with impatience and Roger stormed off and returned to the villa for cocktail hour. Eventually, I was wheeled in for corrective surgery. The doctor took one look at my wrist bones and remarked: 'thiz is goeen to uurt…' Without the benefit of anaesthetic, I howled the place down as he pried apart my bones and realigned them. I spent the rest of the summer with my arm plastered and wrapped in plastic, awkwardly hiked up on a life preserver as I abjectly paddled back and forth in the pool.

I boarded the plane home with relief. Toward the end of the flight, about an hour out from Los Angeles, the plane banked steeply over Martian wastes and I saw a deep gash in the earth's surface, a planetary wound hardened by age. I heard my fatherly brain voice exhorting me to look closely and pressed my nose against the ever-so-gently yielding plastic of the window. The bleeding inside the wound below had dwindled to a rusty thread. I knew from my geography books that it had once been a torrent: a mighty, corrosive water-blade sawing its way down into the crust. Now the wounded edges loomed high around it and made the grandest of canyons.

After I transferred to Harvard Prep, I didn't see Alvy much. And since my new friends were mostly valley dwellers and lived too far away for dropping by, I was alone at home a lot. I spent hours poring over the marine biology encyclopaedia that Dad had bought me after our trip to Gloucester. At one point I was even thinking of going and becoming a marine biologist someday. The classifications and all the orderly presentation spoke to my nature and were a big anxiety balm. I regularly turned to the section on bluefins. The mighty fish was so beautifully drawn and described, its Latin name – *Thunnus thynnus* – a woolly texture in my mouth, an unlikely merging of tonnage and grace. On my wall I had the trophy tail from Cathy's catch. Mounted on a piece of faux driftwood, it had languished in a corner of the den, gathering dust, until she concluded she had nowhere to hang it and let me have it. It served as a petrifying reminder of what could happen if she caught *me*, too. Somehow, I would have to throw the hook and break my connection to her.

That autumn, my father commissioned a cake for my thirteenth birthday. It was made to look like a big book open in the middle. The top of the right-hand page was turned down and said 'Manhood' in bold baby-blue letters. That was the next chapter, for which I wasn't sure I was ready. I'd seen manhood to spare in the showers at Harvard Prep and painfully knew it wasn't on the immediate cards. Matters were made worse by Alvy confiding in me at my party that the puberty fairy had smiled kindly on him and that his 'cock is getting huge!'

There was definitely something different about him. I watched in envy and disbelief as he actually started hitting on one of the tasty mums at my party. He was only five-three, but he oh-so-casually touched her arm and complimented her on her looks. She just smiled, crossed her arms over her bosom, and rocked one heel forward, considering the little squirt.

'What was that all about?' I said, as he came back over. He glanced back with a connoisseur's eye.

'She's hot. Don't you think?'

'She's old enough to be your mother!'

I'd lost my friend. He'd gone on ahead into the next chapter. I was still namby-pambying around in pre-puberty, reading about sharks in my encyclopaedia, playing with my cars and trucks. One day I was pushing my toy car along the back of the brown corduroy sofa when I found myself looking at the car and at my hand holding it and listening to myself making a stupid car noise with my dumb mouth.

I quickly upgraded myself to radio control. Here the toy was tethered to me by a signal. My interest switched from the car to the control box. And this severance from the object, this evolution from actual play to play mediated through a device – a *joystick* – was, for me, the beginning of masturbation.

The first time I ejaculated – aged thirteen-and-a-half – my radio-controlled car was on a charge right next to me. The sudden, shuddering spurting of hot fluid was electric. I was soon chronically engaged in engendering this new sensation and worked on my joint until it was chocolate-chipped with scabs.

In the hut, Alvy and I took manly drags on Dear John and talked nonstop about sex. Or rather; Alvy talked and I took mental notes. One afternoon while we were watching cartoons, he pulled out his semi-erect cock to show me, and I was sufficiently intimidated. I swallowed hard and tucked my pitiful plonker back into my briefs. He'd already had his first blowjob – from a girl in eighth grade, he said – and lost his cherry to the beautiful blonde daughter of a famous Hollywood writer. Or so he crowed. He was now a rabid masturbator, creeping into the bathroom at all hours to lie on the tiled floor on a towel and milk himself of lust while his twin, Elliot, snored away in their shared bedroom, dreaming indubitably of Wimbledon.

One night he stayed late at Stone Canyon and we got to talking about the new nanny down the hall. Debbie was a nice Jewish girl with a heavy fringe of dark hair and a twinkly grin that hinted at an interesting shadow side to her personality. She bore more than a passing resemblance to Dawn, my first muse and teacher at King Alfred's, so I was subliminally on the lookout for intimacy and transcendence. We had a couple of awkward, late-night talk sessions during which I tried to impress her with my depth and cool. She was just twenty, from Seattle. I was sure she wouldn't last long in Cathy's employ – she was too good, too fine, for that – but I was thankful for her presence.

'Does she get high?' asked Alvy.

'I don't think so.'

'Let's ask...'

'No, no,' I caught him at the door. 'Let's *not*.'

'Don't be a pussy, Sarch.' He pushed past me and down the hall. We grappled outside her door – his knocking hand quivering like a weapon between us, until it slipped my grasp and whammed her portal.

Instantly it opened and she was there. 'Oh. Hi. You guys OK?'

Standing and smoothing and doing our hair: 'Yeah, fine... Debbie, this is my friend, Alvy. Alvy – Debbie.'

'Hello there,' said Alvy.

'Hi,' she replied, holding her greeting hand high and close.

Alvy took it, cupped it, and brought it to his heart. 'It's a pleasure to meet you finally,' he said.

Her head went slightly sideways, moving, it seemed, to the power of his charm-ray, but then something seemed to irritate her left nostril, and she snapped out of it. 'OK – yeah – well – great – you guys wanna come in?'

'Awesome...' said Alvy, pushing inside.

I watched him mooch around her dark, sparsely furnished room. Billy Joel's *The Stranger* was on the turntable, and a scented candle guttered.

'You guys wanna sit a minute?' she asked.

Alvy made himself right at home on her bed and I took the floor by the door. Debbie returned to her place at the top of the bed, where she'd been sitting before we startled her. She crossed her legs in a meditative posture and leaned back against the wall. The rest was silence.

'Debbie,' said Alvy, 'do you ever get high?'

Her grin almost ate the room. She jumped up and went to the closet, her ass swaying like a bell. 'This stuff is from Oregon,' she said as she took a baggie down from the top shelf. 'These guys grow it in inflatable pools on top of their building. Stuff's out-of-control strong.' She shook the bag for emphasis. 'You sure this is OK? I mean, Sacha, if your stepmom finds out, I'm done for.'

I smiled and held up my hand à la *noblesse oblige*. Alvy was already moving toward her, drying his sweaty palms on his shorts: 'Want me to roll it?'

'I'm good...' She performed the task expertly, unconsciously licking her lips before she supplied the sealing film along the joint's tightly-packed length. She lit up, took a hit and passed it to Alvy. He puffed, kissed the air, and tugged the toke into the back of his head, held it there, then sighed: 'Holyshitthisstuffisgood...'

'Yeah, you don't need a lot.' She closed her eyes and let her neck roll to the music.

My turn. I observed the damp, smoking tail end of the reefer. I commended it to my lips and took a long, slow sip of sulphurous wine. It was skunk-pure, burnt plantation rubber corking my lungs. I suddenly choked and splattered: KAK – RACK – RACKA – HACKO...SHIT! I rolled on my side and held the joint aloft for someone to take. Alvy obliged and went monster on the squib. I thought his eyes would leak out of his face. I was a long time shuddering and wheezing out my epilepsy until I finally lay there exhausted and floating. I could hear Alvy and Debbie talking, but the sense was less important than the sound, the rhythm, the feeling that they were laughing and really grooving on each other. All

I wanted to do was roll over on the tufty brown carpet and cuddle my good vibrations. But first I would have to take my eyes off the ceiling lamp. And that was difficult, because they were glued there. The cupped radiance was like a beating heart. The lid of the fixture melted away and the two bulbs came toward me naked. I could almost taste a piquancy of rosy breast flesh, of scintillating nipple. I was sucking the air when Debbie mooned over me. 'You all right, Sach?' I nodded and licked my lips. Alvy was at the periphery of my vision, a small, sinking sun, grinning red.

Debbie drew back to him. They both seemed so far away, as if they were at the other end of a long coalmine. Then a miner's light flashed and Billy Joel came by on a conveyer belt, tickling the keys and whistling a beautiful tune. I tried to sing along, but sounded croaky and old.

'He's done,' said Debbie – meaning me.

Suddenly Alvy's face was over me. 'Sarch, Dude, you OK?'

'Yeah I'm great, I'm great, I'm great…'

Muddled as I was, I could clearly see that he cared only because *she* seemed to. He was happily suffocated by the thought of her vagina on his face like a sea slug. I felt envy rise, and other dragons, but waved them aside. I tried to get up and the room pitched. Somehow I managed to turn out the doorway and pinball down the hall. My bedroom door yawned open, my outstretched arm seemed to reach for a distant, star-shaped hand – falling on my bed took a good long time. I landed in cloud. A sigh of forlorn pleasure escaped me. *Let your eyes close*, said the nebulae, *I will take care of you…*

At some point the door banged open. The lights came on, and I went up on one elbow. Alvy was in the doorway, giggling, looking like a cartoon mouse that was carrying an enormous payload of cheese. 'Shall I show Debbie my dick?' he said, indicating his crotch with the repeated, mechanical gesture of a freak-show mannequin. I saw that he had a rhino-horn erection, straining for recognition and relief in the little white shorts.

'Don't!' I pleaded.

'Dude…' he said, coming over, '*Look* at this thing. It wants to fuck Debbie!'

'Don't!' I repeated, 'Just don't,' and rolled over to face the wall.

He went on tittering and wheezing behind me, then found a place on the floor and curled up like a dog and went to sleep.

# 14

# Vegas

IN 1977, AT THE SIXTH ANNUAL LAS VEGAS AWARDS CEREMONY, his fellow performers voted my father Male Musical Star of the Year, over Sinatra, Tom Jones and Don Rickles. He was both a performers' performer and a public favourite, drawing huge crowds at Caesars Palace. He couldn't have been riding higher; but he was ambivalent about it all. In Vegas, he knew he was the hook: a dancing marionette designed to draw the suckers to the slots and keep them there until the late show. He was on the payroll of thugs and mobsters, and, among other things, this scared the shit out of him.

He was performing with Alan King one night when he offhandedly and unaccountably remarked, 'I'd like to thank the Mafia for the room hire…' This didn't go down too well with the boys upstairs. He was made to eat crow onstage the following night. 'Last night I made a disparaging remark about the management,' he said, positively white-faced with fear, 'I'd like to take this opportunity to publicly apologize for my lack of judgement and good grace. They're a wonderful bunch of people.'

My poor father needed the financial protection that Vegas offered. As the seventies drew to a close, the world outside the sequined bubble of cabaret was looking dark. The venues and opportunities for his sort of talent were steadily closing down. He was becoming an anachronism, a middle-of-the-road crooner of elevator music. At forty-five, he was moving out of his alignment with popular culture and indeed, and alas, would never recapture it in his lifetime.

He was bitterly aware that the kids were no longer listening to him. With rock bands like Kiss, The Eagles and Styx eating up radio airtime, he couldn't get a foot – or a vocal cord – back in. Nor could his album sales compete with Sammy Davis's and Sinatra's. They were content to mine the riches of the classic American Songbook, whereas my father, being not only a performer but a composer/ lyricist, felt always compelled to create new material for himself – material that was increasingly out of sync with his audience.

Newley was leading a double life: by night, he was one of the highest paid and sought-after cabaret performers on the circuit; by day, he was the poet sitting stymied before a blank page, with his earmuffs on to screen out interference as he struggled to make sense of a changing society and his place in it. The songs he composed for himself in the late seventies and early eighties read like the hermetic utterances of a man creating defiantly for his muse, but with one pleading eye on the audience. Perhaps he should have just written a slender volume of verse to cleanse his repertoire of high-mindedness. But he was never confident enough as a writer. He had to sauce his poetry with generous helpings of musical accompaniment; and, of course, sing it in that inimitable voice of his – bodied forth onstage by the nonpareil vaudevillian and story-teller that he was, right up to his dying day.

His cabaret act was heavily weighted in favour of the Bricusse-Newley standards – 'Fool', 'Who Can I Turn To?', 'The Candy Man' – but more and more he began to introduce his new creations into the mix. 'Gay Girl', his panegyric against lesbianism, mercifully never made it into his act:

> Your eyes have the look
> Of a woman with a hook inside your heart
> And danger hangs around you, like perfume…
> You must understand wearing pants
> Don't mean you get to play the part
> You're trying much too hard to be someone
> You're trying not to hate…

It's no wonder he never reached the youth movement – in the way that, say, Dylan, Neil Young and Leonard Cohen did. His view of women was hopelessly outdated, formed in the age of Sinatra and Dean Martin. Despite all his sixties libertarianism, he still viewed women as 'broads' and 'dames' and 'dykes' not to be taken too seriously, unless they were coming after you with a lawyer. A 'butch' lesbian was his worst nightmare: a woman who dared proclaim her sexual self-sufficiency. Because where did that leave him?

One of his new songs, 'Teach The Children', was inspired, in part, by Tara's and my returning to live with him. It was that downer of downers: a message song:

> The children of the world are doomed
> Before they reach a school
> By parents who are unprepared and helpless
> As long as procreation
> Is a paradise for fools
> The world will be the victim of its parents…

Can you hear Darin or Sinatra or Bennett breezing through *that*? Onstage, he spoke most of it, with a lilting musical accompaniment that built to a triumphant, let-freedom-ring chorus, complete with banging tambourines:

> Teach the children of the world
> Teach them now before it gets too late
> Teach them how to be the parents of tomorrow
> Or they'll become the parents of today
> And pass on all our hate and madness
> To a whole new generation
> And so it goes ad infinitum
> Ad nauseam, Amen…

The man onstage shimmied around in a tuxedo, with an oversize carnation in his lapel and velvet embroidered slippers, but he might as well have been lecturing at some north-eastern university. Then, inevitably, he would have to open his eyes, look out and see the Vegas crowd staring unresponsively back at him – the avaricious, blue-rinsed ladies and the shady male types with their polyester suits and bad comb-overs...

*Who are they to judge me?* he would not very helpfully ask himself. And then he'd have to remember that this was just a way to pay the rent and the school fees and forestall the next quarterly wave of bad news from his accountant, from Cathy, and from the out-of-control decorators at 946 Bristol Avenue. He would get his head together for the next number: a sensational disco version of 'Who Can I Turn To?' that featured two black girls and him in a pimp hat and sequined gloves.

He was all over the place, in other words. He was trying to slip his real thoughts and feelings under the audience's radar, while, on the surface, he was fulfilling his contract and giving them what they wanted: 'Candy Man' – he had a basket of sweets hung over his arm as he skipped along the edge of the stage throwing butterscotches at outstretched arms – and his special medley of 'wish-I-had-written-them' songs – 'Send in The Clowns', 'There's No Business Like Show Business', 'My Favourite Things'.

He always ended with 'What Kind of Fool Am I?': the one unassailable classic that he and Bricusse really did write. 'If you're listening, Sammy,' he would always say, addressing his dear dead friend who had sung it show-stoppingly but perhaps not with quite the exquisite regret born of personal experience, 'this is how it *should* be sung...'

That always gave me gooseflesh – his total ownership of that song – as if it were a beautiful woman he would never allow to leave him, whom only *he* understood. To the haunting diminuendo of Ian Fraser's opening scales, he would swoon into that first moment of self-questioning, his exalted equivalent of 'To be or not to be' – except that this wasn't a simple on-off question, this was an interrogation of the 'why' of his entire existence.

I never got tired of watching him. No matter how many times I saw the show throughout my childhood and early manhood, the spell never broke. His every gesture resonated in me; his deep vibrato channelled up my own byways and passageways. Was that why, as a little boy, I had felt so truncated – cut short? Because Daddy was always completing me onstage?

Vegas was a cesspool of temptation, but Heironymus Merkin, now happily *en famille* with a new woman and child, was doing his best to straighten up and fly right – even when a real-life version of Good Time Eddie Filth presented itself in the form of a diminutive Australian comic by the name of Berry Lee.

Berry had his own show at the Thunderbird, essentially a T&A place, where he'd come on before and after the girls and fire off a few smutty jokes. He worshipped my father and became something of a lapdog and lucky charm, following him around. He was constantly testing my father's abstinence with his tales of how he gorged himself at the all-you-can-eat-bar of sex that his show provided. 'She comes in… full-length mink, drops it to the floor, fucking naked. She saunters over, goes down on one knee, starts blowing me…'

My father gritted his teeth and raked the table with one hand. 'Oh God, stop it Berry…'

I got my own thirteen-year-old eyeful one night when the naughty Aussie took me on a private tour backstage. In the filthy alley behind the gleaming facade, he pulled open a rusty door. His firm hand on my shoulder steered me down a dark, flaking corridor that reeked of cheap perfume. I heard the flood coming before I saw it: a twitter and clack of heels, a building maelstrom of giggly chatter… Berry squeezed my shoulder as the girls smashed into view around a turn, speeding toward me in a foaming cataract of fur and flesh, sequins and pink feathers, flashing smiles and emerald eyes.

'It gets even better,' Berry smiled.

We continued on toward the sound of music – a kind of burlesque rumba and regimental clatter of feet. A few stray girls whiffled past, sweaty from performing, as we came to the edge of the stage. Through a cleft in the darkness I glimpsed the performance: a swirling lava, a hot-pink mass of splitting atoms and lurid fire. The girls were burning there like fallen angels, smiling through the flames. Berry beckoned, and we made our way behind the coloured scrim. Wheeling shapes flew around me and I cowered, feeling the press of audience attention. We reached the far side – safety – and continued on through the backstage maze, passing a fire hydrant and then a bulletin board – torn appeals for 'apt. shares', missing cats and meditation lessons 'super cheap'. Finally we came to a heavy door, cracked open on an intense light. Hairdryers and hysterical shouts came from within. Berry looked down at me: this was the mother lode. With splayed fingers he pushed it open…

The room was long and flanked by mirrors, doubling the number of bodies inside. Which were all naked. And attached to heads that were swivelling in my direction.

'Girls,' said Berry, 'I'd like you to meet my friend, Sacha Newley. Tony's son.'

A moment of suspenseful contemplation on their part, then a thunderclap of pleasure as they descended upon me, clucking like hens: 'Oh he's so cute – *look* how cute – how old are you, baby? – come to see the show? – Oh I love him…' They couldn't keep their hands off me: I was frisked and trussed and salved by silken arms, legs and breasts until I went Popeye-rigid. At that moment a bell rang and they scattered in panic to their various tasks: fitting a final eyelash, adjusting a nipple tassel, applying a slow vowel of glossy lipstick, perfecting a smile or a hunted look – before flapping past me with hoots and curses. Berry got a crotch rub and a French kiss for his pains, and the final girl, the muse of my imagination, turned to me and said, 'Bye, lover,' blew me a kiss, then showed me the retreating spectacle of her perfect, bobbling behind.

Berry and I were silent, abandoned and bereft in a world without women.

'Like that?' he said, looking down at me. I nodded and he laughed, 'You're just like your dad.'

Berry had a houseboat on Lake Mead, only thirty minutes from the Strip, and one Sunday he invited Dad and me to go for a cruise. While they shopped for provisions, I lay pillowed on my stomach in the living room of Berry's little house in Vegas, discharging a .22 calibre rifle at a target across the yard. His stripper girlfriend, wearing only a shirt, was bustling around in the kitchen and asked what I wanted for breakfast. 'French toast,' I said, squeezing off another shot.

Berry and Dad came by to pick me up and we headed out to the lake. I couldn't believe there was actually water in the middle of this barren place. Berry explained that the lake was man-made and provided all the water for Vegas. Dad insisted it couldn't last forever, that Vegas was a 'growing monster' that would lap it up, drink it dry. But then from a high loop of the road, we caught sight of it: a burnished piece of silver fitting its puzzle-extremities into the nooks and crannies of the rusty hills. Water!

I was disappointed by how small Berry's boat was when I saw it. It was a fibreglass one-piece, flat-bottomed and yellowed with age. He put on his sailor cap, cocked it at a rakish angle, and masterfully gave the order, 'Put off the ropes, lad.' We sputtered out into the blue expanse and cut the engine, letting ourselves drift. Dad was breathing deep and taking in the distances.

He and I sat on the shaded side of the boat, holding hands. 'Sometimes it all just seems so perfect, doesn't it, Sachie?' he said.

'Every little wave on the water perfectly formed, every cloud perfect. There's nothing, really... to complain about... is there?'

I nodded my head and laid it against him. Our hands were crabbed tight. I felt his chest rise and fall with his deep draughts of pleasure. There was a lake inside him, too. And a desert. And a dark city. He hated Vegas; he didn't like drawing the suckers to the slots. He thought he was better than that. I knew he was.

On the way back, we stopped at an open-air firing range. Solitary men stood by their cars wearing shades and earmuffs, discharging firearms at distant body silhouettes ranged along a cliffside. The barrage was deafening.

'What are they shooting at?' my father asked, laughing.

'You name it,' said Berry, 'the wife, the boss, the whole stupid, goddam, fucked-up world.' He gave my father a Glock pistol. 'Go for it, Tone!'

'Who should I kill?' Dad steadied himself to aim.

'My agent,' said Berry.

'No. My accountant...' He pulled the trigger. The gun kicked hard and he staggered back laughing... 'Je-zus... that felt good.' He emptied the clip in a cloud of smoke and flung shells, and handed the heat to me. 'Want to try, Sachie?'

'No,' said Berry, 'give him this...' He unwrapped an old silver-plated Confederate war pistol. 'It's a .45 millimetre barrel. Feeling lucky?'

My father looked concerned. 'Are you sure, Ber?'

'He can handle it. Can't you, lad?'

I nodded and took the gun. It dropped my arm and I had to heft it up, trembling, to the target. I couldn't steady my aim, even with both arms locked.

Berry stepped forward and cocked it for me. 'Breathe easy, Sach. *Squeeze* the trigger...'

The explosion ripped my arms up and over my head. Berry and Dad jumped back.

'That one went to Mars,' Berry laughed. I was still trembling, and about to go again, when a 4x4 truck screeched up beside us. It had smoked windows and silver running pipes. A skinhead marine got out and zip-loaded a machine gun.

'Must be the wife,' said Dad; and we skidooed out of there to the blat-blatting of his rage.

Back at the Desert Inn, my father's name in lights outside as he slogged through another matinee, I killed time by wandering unaccompanied, unsupervised, through the casino. It was an addictive atmosphere, and everybody felt it: from the old ladies working ten machines with their Dixie cups full of dimes, to the hellish pit bosses with their bloodless stares who kept the draughts of want and desperation circulating through the place. Drinking here made you thirstier. I couldn't fathom the trick, I only knew that it worked. The great tumblers of the Million Dollar Jackpot machines turned day and night without paying up. Dad said the losers liked it that way.

The guards kept me away from the tables, but even from a respectable distance I could sense the hunched despair and concentration. The drunken, spirited gamblers whom blind fortune had favoured were shamelessly enjoying their brief moment of resurrection. Hookers were hanging off them like sucker fish around a feeding shark. Occasional cries of triumph could intermittently be heard over the din of inhaled cash... But on the overwhelming whole, the people were losing to mute, constipated machines.

But the greatest gamble was soon to come. 'EVEL KNIEVEL TO JUMP THE GRAND CANYON' read the headline in the *Vegas Sun*. I begged the paper off my father so I could study the picture of the man of the impending hour, standing by the canyon in his white spacesuit with the star-spangled stripes, a helmet under his arm. To me, the vehicle beside him looked less like a motorbike than a rocket tube.

I'd seen his previous jumps on TV: the endless build-up; the short squirt of adrenalin and out-breath of suspended disbelief as he sailed over cars and buses, landing with a near-fatal concussion of the bike. He would skid to a halt, take off his helmet and wave. The romance of it was so thrillingly American. And of course I had the toy: the Evel Knievel motorbike and action figure that you could crank up and release into a wheelie. I knew by heart the legend of his broken bones and destroyed body and that he never quit.

After my father's show that night, I went backstage as always to watch him clean off the flesh-tone make-up. 'Did you enjoy the show?' he asked.

'Yes, you were really on tonight.'

'I'll tell you a little secret,' he said, carefully ungluing a contact lens. 'I'm finally learning to relax. Before I go on, I remind myself that all these people have come here to see me shine, not to judge me. It makes such a difference.'

I waited in the adjoining room while he showered. Baskets of fruit and flowers were everywhere. I cracked open a Brazil nut with a pair of crackers shaped like spread-eagled female legs (a gift from Sinatra) and chomped on the buttery kernel.

When Dad finally walked in, wearing a burgundy velour track-suit, he was smiling indulgently. 'I've got a surprise for you.' He opened the door a crack, whispered to somebody outside, then opened it wide. In limped a tall white-haired man in a cape, followed by a squat guy who looked like a bodyguard. The tall man had a tanned, rugged face and was leaning slightly on a gold cane.

'You must be Sacha,' he said in a cowboy accent, offering a hand covered in chunky rings.

'Yes,' I said.

'Nice to meetcha.' He motioned over his shoulder to the squat guy, who produced a large white box, tied with a ribbon. The guy opened it and pulled out a white mountain bike, emblazoned with stars and stripes.

'A little present from Evel Knievel,' said the caped man.

My mouth dropped open.

'Promise me one thing,' said Evel, coming closer, his electric-blue irises tautening to a point. 'Promise me you'll never ride this bike on the street. There's a lot of crazy people out there tryin' to be daredevils, and they don't know what they're doin'. Promise?'

'Yes, Mister Knievel.'

He gave a brief nod and laboriously straightened up.

'Thank you, Evel,' said my father, vigorously pumping his hand and seeing him out. 'And break a leg next Tuesday.'

There was another daredevil in Vegas at the time – also sporting a white suit emblazoned with stars and stripes. Elvis was doing his final run of shows at the Sands and there was a crush to get in and see him. My father pulled some strings, and Cathy, a huge Elvis fan, took Tara and me for an audience with the King.

Crazy as it must sound now, I didn't really get Elvis. I'd seen the footage of him gyrating and wowing the kids and had caught fifteen minutes of his Vegas movie – his black coil of oily hair; his curled lip and smashing smile as he sang in that jiggy baritone – but this had nothing to do with the man who now appeared onstage. His white, all-in-one spacesuit bulged to encompass him. Black hair dye ran in rivulets down his pasty white face, and he looked all played-out – and pissed off.

I squirmed for him, imagining the fetid embrace of that white leather, the stiff, high collar, festooned with earlobe-chafing chains. As he assumed the pose of heroic determination to send his notes skyward – the arm lifted to point at the infinite, the leg propped on an imaginary mountain ridge – a trio of backing singers seamlessly took over his out-breath, stretching it to an unearthly roar. This caused a quiver of female arms to go up all around me and bodies to sway in delirium. Here was the beaten old man's cue to stumble downstage and strip himself of the numerous coloured scarves draped around his shoulders. They went flying out into the audience, soaked in his precious sweat, to be snatched up by the hungry, in-fighting worms. It was all kinds of sick-making. I kept having to check my reactions against Cathy's to make sure I was having a good time.

I watched Evel's Grand Canyon jump from Stone Canyon. The rocket ignited and propelled him off the ramp at bullet speed. My heart lifted, missed a beat and then another... as, halfway across, the torpedo's nose dipped prematurely – and I realized with a chill that he wasn't going to make it. The parachutes exploded, filled with air and ignominiously stalled him. Whereupon he drifted into the canyon depths, taking however many millions of stricken hearts with him.

Still, I kept my Evel bike off the road as he'd instructed. Until Alvy came over and took it out and broke the great man's spell.

## 15

# 946 Bristol Avenue

*Self-Portrait on Broken Mirror*

AFTER A YEAR-LONG RENOVATION THAT COST TWO MILLION fucking dollars, Bristol Avenue was finished. Wholesale (and retail) confusion had wrought a masterpiece. Cathy and my father seemed delighted. Tara, inspired by the decor, died her hair purple and started wearing puke-green. Then she took to her room and basically never came out. I settled into my palatial bedroom with the wall-mounted Zenith TV, the black bearskin coverlet, and the potted palms – the lair of a mini pornographer – and felt fatally happy. I was finally in my rightful place: directly across the landing from my father.

Unfortunately, Cathy grabbed the bedroom between us – the third door leading off the great landing – that had once been Joan Crawford's 2,000-square-foot boudoir. Here Cathy had pushed kitsch beyond even Liberace's comfort zone. Her bed with its humungous seashell headboard was displayed on a raised dais of pink shag between Parthenon columns. No edge in the room had gone untasselled, no seam or join uncorniced. From her marbleized Jacuzzi/bath with the gold-plated dolphin taps she could watch her wall-mounted TV and push a panic button if she stubbed her toe. Her walk-in closet was bigger than my mother's, and that was saying something. From the command centre of her bed, she presided, splayed out in jeans and T-shirt, smoking menthols, and reading magazines – a Midwest flight attendant impersonating a Hollywood goddess.

Her satisfaction was short-lived. Something was wrong with our dream house; she sensed it. About two months in, she went to my father to confess extreme psychic discomfort: there were 'very bad vibes' in the house and we should leave immediately. My father was understandably gobsmacked. He had practically killed himself to reconfigure and stock this wonder palace and now he was being told that all his slaving on the road had been for naught. Swallowing his bile-green anger, he took Cathy by the hand and begged her to give the house a chance to grow around us.

But she wasn't having any of it. From being the house's champion and apologist, she had turned on a dime to become its worst enemy. It was a good way to explain away what was happening to our family – just blame it on the 'bad house'. Tara's punk rebellion was intensifying – her descent into adolescent hell and consequent estrangement from everybody resulted in her being perpetually absent at mealtimes. My father would return from the road (yes, he was still slaving away to pay off back taxes and expenses on the house) and be commandeered by Cathy to hold a closed-door meeting to discuss Tara's 'bad attitude'. Then he would wearily cross the vast house to his miscreant daughter's room, all athump with the Sex Pistols, and knock reluctantly on the door. She would turn down the music and let him in. At some point her defensive shell would crack and she'd cave-in to sobbing; and then she would have her cradling time with Daddy, rocking gently in his arms. Her complaining about Cathy, impossible homework and her unpopularity at school always boiled down to one, accusatory question: 'Daddy, why do you have to be away all the time?'

Naturally, he would turn away from her pleading gaze. How could he explain that he, too, felt lost – confused and betrayed by a life that made less and less sense to him? They held each other tight, clinging together after the shipwrecks of Summit and Lloydcrest, after so many promises broken. And then, inevitably, he would have to go, leaving her to the page of insoluble equations and Johnny Rotten's spitting complaint.

It didn't help that her half-sister was eight now and beyond-adorable with her Natalie Wood eyes and her little tinkling bells voice. Whenever Dad was home, he made space in his schedule for 'Chelsea Time'. They'd cuddle up on his four-poster and read, draw, or simply chat away about this or that. These scenes of them together were so touching and warm and true and good they could have been framed in Pre-Raphaelite gold and hung in a gallery.

All this lavished attention meant that Chelsea was bubble-wrapped against bad vibes, while Tara was awash in them. They had rooms across the back landing from each other, but enjoyed no sisterhood to speak of. Tara had dug down for safety and security, turning a rump of cold earth to the enemy. To her friends and sometimes to me she could reveal a tender, beautiful side – but otherwise she was the alien attractor drawing to herself all the badness of the house. It had to go somewhere after all.

With my habitual shield of good cheer, I cleverly bounced it from my door. Mind you, I was no less in shadow than Tara, but being a passable little actor, and desperate to maintain Cathy's approval, I made an effort to remain the personable, presentable boy I'd always been. I even developed a routine to cope with the haunted house. I'd come home from school and go straight to the kitchen to make myself a glass of chocolate milk. Then up to my room to watch an hour of cartoons on my big sixty-nine-channel Zenith TV. Then homework on my bed, covered in the black faux-mink coverlet. Then forty minutes of weight-lifting, with the attendant posing and flexing in front of the mirror. Then masturbation and a shower and blow-dry before dinner.

Sitting quietly with Cathy and Chelsea in the breakfast room (the dining room was almost never used) while punk music pounded overhead, I surmised that Tara was once again not coming down. Cathy would shake her head and put Tara's plate in the warmer. She'd slump down on the acid-yellow sofa with the floral pattern, light a cigarette, and melodramatically hide her face. 'I don't know what I'm going to do about your sister, Sacha...'

I knew just what to say – I'd already said it to my anxious mother facing bankruptcy, and now I would say it to my stepmother: 'Don't worry, Cath, everything will be all right...' My magical thinking had always worked. If I could convince the major women in my life – Cathy, my mother, Sue – that I would not go postal and follow Tara into the precincts of righteous anger and indignation, all would be well. I was the family linchpin; the little diplomat. I flattered myself that I made it all OK.

My father's final solution to the Cathy-Tara problem was characteristically evasive: he threw money at it – money he didn't really have – hiring an expensive Mexican couple to live in and relieve the domestic pressure on Cathy, who was then free to do her own disappearing act. So I passed into the care of two smiling, white-uniformed twits from Guadalajara: Lupo, with his slicked-back hair and gangster baby-voice, and his docile accomplice of a wife who lived in perpetual fear of him. He had a record as long as your arm – including indecent exposure – but my father had hired him anyway. The couple cooked, cleaned, bustled about and – surprise,

surprise – things started going missing here and there: a gold watch, a necklace, a camera. Putting two and two together, Cathy called in her detective friend to investigate. After a few pointed questions, Lupo confessed. He penitently led the detective to the garage, where the missing booty was discovered stored in a cardboard box. He was cuffed and led away.

The house felt empty again; doubly so, because our beloved Boomer had also mysteriously disappeared. Was it the Mexicans? Or just the bad vibes?

That summer, shortly before my fourteenth birthday, my father took me on a fishing trip to Alaska. This was a reprise of our boys-only holiday in Washington state, and an expiation of the guilt he always felt about not spending enough time with me. Alaska was farther north and much more daunting than Washington – wild, mostly uncharted territory – and we were going in there, deep into the northern tundra, for the 'really big salmon'.

In Anchorage we boarded a small seaplane. There were others in the cramped cabin: a hearty old woman with her grandson; a struggling actor grabbing some air after a divorce. My father joked with him as we picked up speed and bounced on the waves: 'Does she still get alimony if you die?' The plane lurched upward and banked steeply over the water; then we levelled off and flew toward a vast horizon of wilderness.

About an hour into the flight, the pilot shouted, gesturing down: 'Sockeye salmon!' What I saw was a huge river snaking through the terrain – half of it black, as if oil had spilled down its bank. Then with a thrill I realized it was the massed backs of the running salmon. I followed the serpentine stain as far as my eye could see, until it dissolved in pale blue distance over the curving earth.

When we landed, it was with a crash of cymbals and a pleasing deceleration. Low in the water, we idled to shore and the pilot tied the seaplane to a sturdy poplar. The phenomenon could now be seen up-close and personal, in the darkness beyond the sky-bleached shallows: a wall of fish – a green traffic jam of shimmering scales. We practically fell over each other to start casting. Our hooks snagged them everywhere – in the belly, the dorsal fin, the tail; we caught and landed and caught them again without pause, like Geppetto in the belly of the monstrous whale. My father worked beside me, laughing madly and gasping as we hoarded silver. It was like a Vegas hit on the big machines. We almost felt guilty.

When we'd filled one whole float of the seaplane with salmon, the pilot called time on our orgy and built a fire. He gutted and sectioned several of the fish, wrapping each fillet in baking foil and adding onions and a knob of butter. These he laid on the embers, flipped quickly, and ceremoniously served. I pried open the foil on a feast of smoking fish savour. Salmon still swam strongly by us as we wolfed down their baked brethren. I tasted motion – struggle – in the hot flesh still; electric vestiges of pink, abundant life. I looked over and saw my father close his eyes in rapture as he worked his jaw in circles. 'Can you believe this, Sachie! It makes me want to sing...'

We took off and flew north again, landing on a forest lake by twilight. The salmon hoard was unloaded at the lodge and taken to the smokehouse for storing. The lodge master – a white-haired bear of a man called Joe – was thrilled to have a celebrity like my father to stay. He showed us to the cabin we were sharing, which we settled quickly into, falling into an oxygen-rich sleep.

We woke to alpine silence, an awesome box of air around our smoggy heads. We made an early start in perfect light; the mountains, pines, and the lake all diamond-clear. A jet boat spirited us up one of the tributaries, in pursuit of rainbow trout. Leaning over the side, I saw the pebbly riverbed rip by in a blur, just two feet below us. The boat had no prop, or we'd never have cheated the shallows. Joe stood in the stern, hair blown flat, patiently tying a fly as we skimmed the gravel beds. He told me how he'd once hit a shoal at high speed and gone caterwauling out of the boat, landing some twenty feet upriver. He smiled at the memory and went on tying.

In a widening stretch of marsh grass we slowed and found a dark pothole teeming with rainbows. I cast my lure and was the first to hook one. It tail-danced around the boat, then jumped clear over it. That was the 'Alaska in'm,' said Joe – that 'extra fight.' The fish flexed and convulsed against my line, flashing rainbows. I got it on board and Joe pried out the hook. He showed me the gasping prize, spotted black and hued with ghostly colour, then gently reimmersed it. For an anxious moment I thought it had died; then Joe stroked it until the life jolted back and it was gone.

There was a cry then, a heaven-piercing cry, and we all looked up. A bald eagle wheeled above us, its wing tips splayed like fingers. I watched it fly to its nest atop a distant rock that was stuck like a spearhead in the lake – a 'worthy peak' for it, Dad said. Joe took out a bill and a coin to show me that this was the bird of our heritage, the avian embodiment of our freedom.

On the following day we flew to a misty plateau cratered with lakes, landing in a perfect bowl of meltwater. The landscape was spooky, the silence absolutely lunar. Joe bid goodbye to the pilot and informed us that we would be hiking back to the lodge from here. As the plane took off, we looked at one another, wondering if perhaps we'd bitten off too much. It was blustery and the air whipped us with mist. We walked the spongy, featureless tundra for hours. Dad thought up names for us to lighten the mood. He dubbed the actor Rainbow Barry and me Sockeye Sacha, but he couldn't think of anything for himself. We finally made it to the edge of the tundra, which was like a drooping blanket, falling down over huge steps of black stone. We descended them slowly, tacking back and forth, until we came to the northern edge of the lake. We could see the lodge in the distance. 'A good four miles,' said Joe. Then came a far-away mooing – full-bellied, gruff.

'Is that a bear?' the old lady asked.

'It is,' said Joe, 'but don't be scared. They're more frightened of us than we are of them. And I have *this*.' He held up his trusty rifle.

As we negotiated the slippery lakeside rocks, Joe held forth with his arsenal of bear lore – how they not only rifled trash but ate laundry; how the best thing to do was face them down if they charged you. I pictured a *High Noon* moment: the bear charging at me, then stalling as it sensed the strong North Pole of my determination, the two magnets repelling each other to a respectful distance: the boy, at last, a man. Dream on!

It was twilight when we got bogged down in a swampy patch near the lodge. Suddenly, out of the clear bandwidth of evening, an angry static rose: mosquitoes in their thousands. This was a dangerous hoard, a cloud of angry pins that got in our mouths and nostrils, filming our faces with sucking sutures. Dad grabbed me and held me close. We swaddled our heads and stumbled on through the roiling cloud. My exposed hands puffed up and burned, so I pulled down my sleeves and balled my fists in cloth. We got through the infestation like this, saying nothing. The old lady hugged her whimpering grandson; gradually the bog hardened and dried out to higher ground. The cloud of bugs receded to the point where we felt it was safe to unwrap our mummified heads and chance a breath.

'Sorry folks,' said Joe, 'we usually make it home before the mozzies come out. I wish I had a gun for *those* little devils…'

They had Alaska in'm, no doubt.

Toward the end of our week-long stay, we flew two hours further north by seaplane to a meadow of scrub and wild flower. The river here was wide and deep, and sounded faintly musical as it laved the edge of a seemingly worldwide silence. Dragonflies droned and zigzagged across it, birds needled it with notes of colour and the silence seemed more profound for all these small designs.

I unlocked my reel, casting my lure far into the middled strength of the river. We were going for king salmon, the 'granddaddy' of all freshwater fish. And here we would find them – a swale of silver tonnage heading north to the river's highest reaches to spawn. I'd seen their pilgrimage in a Jacques Cousteau film: they leapt and tail-fanned the air in slow motion, trying to gain advantage over the falls. But still they fell, and concussed against the rocks, though some leapt far enough to spawn and die in the higher pools of glacial purity. Their hot-pink eggs wafted and collected in cold clarity as clouds of sperm drifted to encompass them. This was sex outside the bodies, the generative moment entrusted to nature and all her mishaps, chief among them being the bears that liked to lap up the delicious slobber and pinion the flailing progenitors.

I looked down the bank and saw my father, hunched over and birdlike, waiting for the big strike. I loved this tension we all shared. It seemed to rid me of my own nerves.

My lure came back and I recast. The sun was high. I took off my sweater, glancing down the bank at my father who was talking to Rainbow – probably giving him more divorce advice. That made me think about my mother. She was probably in London. I wondered if she'd like Alaska and how she would take to my father's moniker for me: Sockeye Sacha. Personally, I liked the name King Sacha even better, and aspired to live up to it.

I cast again. The lure plopped sweetly in a boiling stretch of water. I let it sink down, then started winding in, willing it to turn and flash its tinselled wares. The strike came like lightning. My rod quivered, binding me and my catch on one frequency. I felt life in the line: jolting and flatlining and jolting again. The gears of my mouth ground as I wound the reel in spasms. My fish was running, pulling out the ticking drag, but I gained line on all his lapses and saw his quivering form break water. It tore desperately left and right underwater, slashing the surface, the water-beaded line flinging off liquid sparks. I held it with mental wire and locked hips. It felt as big as me: a single, sculpted muscle, electrocuted by the current. Then there was a give, and then a swooning, a soft capitulation and it came my way… I was almost sorry. I'd felt the weight of it, but now I saw the size: a three-footer at least, tire-thick around the middle. It came closer, head cocked above water, my line disappearing down the dark 'O' of its mouth that was daintily lined with transparent teeth. It swerved and chucked itself on to the rocks and was suddenly all there for the taking: a mammoth slab of densely-scaled, crushed-ice silver, prismatic with emerald blues and greens. Time to act. Holding the rod in one hand, I dipped the net and scooped it up. Its body was so heavy I could barely pivot it on to the bank. I lay it deep in the long grass and delicately unpeeled the netting. It was so beautiful and rare, gasping for breath and speechlessly dying. With trembling, tender fingers I hooked it in the flaring gill slits and lifted it. Twenty pounds at least; I had to support it by the tail and hold it aloft like a headline for my father to see. 'DAD!!' I shouted. He whipped around. His whole body heaved as he saw the writhing miracle. He ran over to take the full measure of my prize.

We flew back to the lodge in triumph – my king was the biggest catch of the day. Joe was waiting for us with a grave expression. He took my father aside. I saw them speak and my father's head fell. His damnable father was dead.

The following day we flew back to Los Angeles.

The lucky sod had died in his sleep, at home. The sweetish stink of death lingered in the room where my father was going through his things. He found an old shoebox full of newspaper clippings; among them, an interview he'd given shortly after meeting his father, in which he confessed that he had found him to be a 'disappointment'. The old man had clipped it and kept it in his memory box. My father sat back, inhaling the odour of reproach that seemed to emanate from that box. The circle of blame was now complete.

Meanwhile King Sacha's salmon was doing time in the freezer and being slowly consumed. I enjoyed every ounce I ate of the sacrificial beast. Its death was my life. Over time, the life-tang faded from its feathery flesh and was replaced by the metallic aftertaste of refrigeration. At my suggestion, Cathy turned what was left of it into mousse and made my school sandwiches with it.

# 16

# Brentwood High

OUR MOVE WESTWARD A FEW MILES TO BRENTWOOD HAD PUT Harvard Prep that much further away. A Libyan car-pool driver by the name of Hadi was employed to pick me up in his white Impala – along with several other sullen, sleepy boys – and drive us the seemingly interminable distance to school and back. The morning traffic moved like sludge, and the car's red vinyl interior had a sickeningly gassy smell. Hadi, for his part, drove with the peaceful expression of a man who had transcended road rage – or just given up, I could never decide which – but his passivity made me boil all the more. After an accident we had one day – the door was smashed in on my side and the drive console fell into my lap – my father decided it was high time to put me in Brentwood High where Tara was already enrolled.

Academically, it was on a par with Harvard Prep and it had the added bonus of girls. Any qualms I might have had about leaving Harvard were laid immediately to rest when I saw the full breasts and feathered hair of Brentwood's distaff student body.

So once again I was the new kid, but this time I was hell-bent on making good and being well-liked. The quickest way to acceptance was to get befriended by the popular boys – and, if need be, the bullies. Lacking physical heft, I had to resort to my native charms to achieve this – sitting in the back row and making smart-ass comments and token gestures of naughtiness in order to be perceived as cool. My grades dipped a bit, my report cards were no longer stellar, but at least I was settling in and establishing a presence. (This was the beginning of the social mask I wear to this day – a concoction

245

of badinage and good cheer designed to hide the antisocial me beneath – Eliot's face prepared 'to meet the faces that you meet.' In late adolescence, I would experience Prufrock's horror that the mask would not come off; that, like some parasite, it had merged with my flesh and *become* me. But as a relentlessly displaced child, I needed to survive, no matter what the psychological cost.)

The boys I glommed on to were second-string. The golden ones or jocks, who at fourteen already had deep voices and necks thicker than their heads, were beyond me. Nor was there enough going on between their ears for me to be able to capture their interest with wit and charm. My friends – Drew, Chad and Chris – were not like *them* – they were the sort of boys who'd grow up to become actors and start-up entrepreneurs: slightly subversive, good enough looking, risk-friendly. They seduced through strategy and connivance rather than sculpted body mass and could, in their turn, be seduced by an accomplished bullshitter like myself.

Drew was the tallest, with a mop of blonde hair combed sideways in surfer fashion. Chad, a handsome southern boy with a winning vulnerability, had the same surfer 'do' in brunette. Chris was a nervous, compact Canadian – flaxen-haired, bright, quick to a joke: the perfect spark-man to my innuendoes. Drew got the point of me first. He seemed to understand the careful rebellion of my collarless shirts and faux surfer-laid-backness. My vestigial English accent was cool, too – and my foreigner's take on things made him think and smile – while I also passed as a Californian kid who liked 'chicks and boards'.

Together we staked our territorial claim in the last row of class, leaning perilously far back in our seats as we cruised through the data-smog of pedagogical instruction. Maths was 'a real butt-fucker', but geology was exciting, with its plate tectonics and erupting volcanoes. And we actually liked the awkward, perspiring teacher with his one wall eye and awful Hawaiian shirts, and were able to rib him with impunity, because the guy had a tin ear for our playful insults. We cursed around the cross-country course every morning in physical education, bemoaning the stupidity of the exercise and longing for break time when we could ogle girls in their abbreviated summer dresses.

They were already taller than us and biologically able to bear children. Chad was banging a lank-haired blonde with a slutty stare, while Drew had his eye trained on a giant brunette whose wobbly breasts and spreading acne promised the 'juiciest snatch in eighth grade.' I just looked – I wasn't ready to take on girls like these. I still had the voice of a choirboy and only a few pitiful wisps of pubic hair, and barely topped five feet three inches. The horrors of locker-room life at Harvard Prep had not abated here. I was surrounded by changelings and morphoids: minotaurs with boy-heads and shaggy bodies. They walked from the showers with pendulous members that took my breath away. Envy shaded into shame, I would turn abjectly away, facing the locker and dressing my unwashed body in silence. Walking out into the outside air felt like a deliverance from hell. Sex was rearing its frightening, spiky towers all around me. Why wouldn't my body weigh in? Why wouldn't it open its pimply pod and spit me out of boyhood?

One day Drew slapped me on the back and flopped down next to me. 'Hey, check out Gwen, she's *toootally* hot for you, man, it's sooo obvious.'

I looked her way. She was busily braiding a friend's hair by the volleyball courts. She was tall, blonde, and beautiful.

'Let the bitch wait,' I said.

'Right on, man,' he said, sucking on a sprig of grass, 'you wanna take your time.'

Over at Chad's house, we snuck a six-pack from his father's cooler up to his rec room over the garage. It was dark and messy and smelt of boy. Girls, too, were in the air – the subject was 'how to fuck them'. Drew boasted he'd gotten a blowjob from a college freshman who'd peeled off his shorts at a pool party and exclaimed:

'My, you've got a nice head on your shoulders!' We guffawed incredulously, at which point, he pulled down his shorts and exposed his vaunted 'six-and-a-half-inch' scimitar, synching his ass muscles to make it bounce up and down on his flat belly. Then Chad got into the act, dropping the bedclothes to lord his prominent spear of gristle over us.

'Whoooa!' said Drew with a gravelly, genuinely admiring roar.

Now Chris was fiddling with his fly and pulling out his passable pud – at which point all eyes swivelled and fixed on *me*.

'You guys are a bunch of fucking faggots!' I said.

They all rocked back and forth, proclaiming my pussyhood to the heavens, but there was no way at this point that I could afford to play along.

Like many puny, hung-up, miserably hung boys before me, I got myself a weights set and started pumping iron and listening to the perfect soundtrack of adolescent angst: Bruce Springsteen's *Darkness on the Edge of Town*. I practised the scowling, dissipated look that the Boss wore on the album cover – it had all the angry maleness I was looking for – but couldn't keep the mask from sliding off whenever I saw a sunset, or a beautiful girl's rosebud face. Then I heard The Police, and fell hard for Sting's extravagant siren song. 'Roxanne' was a plaintive appeal to the girl of my dreams to come home to me. Surely she would hear me if I could sing like this? I would go to Tower Records to buy every Police album as it came out. Then Neil Young walked into my room like an old friend, took out his guitar and sang of the poet's pain later in life. With time and patience, the prize could be won. Through him, I found my way to the great James Taylor; these were all natural poets and from them I learned about life's sweetness and sourness, about forgiveness and necessary forgetting.

Then I turned a corner. I was passing Tara's door when I heard the first jagged chords of The Clash's 'London Calling' and stopped in my tracks. What was this insatiable angst, this devouring rage that tripped some deep wire? I went inside and sat punked out with my sister while the music ate my head and sucked me into a cult: it was now OK – it was actually cool – to accept the worst and rejoice in it. That meant you were a man at last. When the band came to L.A., I pogoed in front of their wall of sound. Joe Strummer emoted at fever pitch, his words buzzing in formation like a fleet of bombers blitzing London. I could see the city burning in furious black and white, and I yearned to get over there and sample the fire.

Then Alvy slouched back into my life. The beach had bleached his brain. He talked slowly, littering his conversation with 'fur sures', 'awesomes' and 'totally tubulars'. He'd graduated from skating the streets to carving and subduing the ocean waves. I noticed a change in his posture. His legs went ahead of him as he walked and he seemed to hang back in the carriage of his pelvis, born along by a gentle swell.

The old garage hut in which we had dreamed up boards and bongs was gone. We sat in his room instead while he talked interminably on the phone to his girlfriends. He seemed to be an expert at arranging things – movie dates, beach weekends, blowjobs – the nature of the activity depending on how serious he was about the chick in question. He would walk back and forth across the shag carpet, puffing on a joint, heavy-lidded, gamely mumbling: 'Sure, Babe, whatever you want; we can meet there, or at the bowling alley, whatever…[long suck on a joint] awesome, whatever you want, Babe – wait, gotta go, someone's on the other line…' Then he would be on to the next one…

Alvy's ride back and forth to the surfing beach was Chaz Ramirez, his new best friend. Chaz was in his early twenties and half-Mexican, with a pronounced Adam's apple and a stringy body. He wore glasses that freakishly magnified his eyes, and had the lank brown hair and listless moustache of a guy who liked Valley Radio. They'd met when Chaz started cleaning the Shapiro pool, and soon found that they shared a gargantuan pot habit and a love of staring, stoned,

into sunlit water. Alvy had begun accompanying Chaz on his neighbourhood pool route so he could earn a little pocket money on the
side. They'd show up at a job so high that the precision necessary
to measure and pour the chlorine went straight to hell and the pool
became a sulphuric vat that fried the eyes. They lost several jobs
that way, but not each other: they stayed 'best buds'.

When Chaz wasn't driving his derelict Toyota pickup, he was
night-riding in his second-hand maroon Corvette – the purchase that
had swallowed all his savings. He used it to cruise for 'low-hanging
fruit' and he occasionally got lucky. I saw him burn rings in the Vette
one lurid sunset by the sea; but for surfing trips, he always lurched
up in the old Toyota, which smelled of ash, gasoline, and junk food.
As we trundled toward the beach, Chaz regaled us with stories of
his friend Pat who had 'a ten-inch dick', of how he liked to have
girls blowing him as he cruised down Van Nuys Boulevard. What
he liked even more than that was to have a cop tailing him during
fellatio and to cum without 'weaving in the lane' – a feat not always
pulled off. It was inevitable, I suppose, that the stories would end
with Chaz showing us his own pecker, straining purple and erect
from the sleeve of his shorts and extending, he boasted, to 'seven-
and-a-half inches'. My heart thumped in shock, fear, admiration, envy.

Chaz did, however, initiate me into other sacred mysteries.
When I complained that the motorized go-kart my father had
recently bought me was too slow, he found the inhibitor bolt on the
accelerator wire and promptly removed it. I was now free to floor
the accelerator pedal and literally take off – the engine climbing
to unheard-of revs. Here was that trove of male power that Sue
had snatched from me – the glorious vision of me that my father
had entertained: the boy in his chariot crossing the sun! My eyes
bugged like Wile Coyote; my tongue unravelled from my mouth
as I gained on the Road Runner.

Unfortunately, *my* chariot had brakes that were next to useless
at these newsreel speeds. I had near-miss collisions as I hurtled past

stop signs and hidden driveways, and probably would have been killed if not for the kindly old couple who knocked on our front door one day to complain to my father about the insane menace terrorizing the neighbourhood.

I was three or four streets away at the time, drag racing with Alvy. He sped past and I clicked the stopwatch – fifty-two seconds. He was still beating me by a hair. *Must do better*, I told myself, as I noted down the time and took a bite of a hash brownie.

'DUDE! You're up!' said Alvy, vacating the go-kart.

I revved the engine and pulled up level with his raised stopwatch.

'GO!' he barked – but only my beanstalk eyes obeyed, coiling up the road ahead and sticking themselves to the swaying asses of two girls.

'SARCH, GO!' Alvy repeated several times, before he saw what my bionic vision had appraised and jumped on the kart side-saddle to ride with me. We pulled up level with the girls, and Alvy let loose in his best surfer drawl: 'Hey ladies… how ya' doin'?'

They giggled and looked away. One was blonde, the other brunette, both about fifteen, bursting with vernal juice.

'Wanna ride?' he pursued.

'In *that*?' said the brunette, with the tube top, perky breasts and terrycloth short shorts.

'It's a go-kart,' said Alvy, 'Way cool. Super fast. Wanna ride?'

'OK,' she said, and we vacated the kart and she got in, giggling and jiggling and spreading her legs wide to reach the pedals. Standing in front, I caught a glimpse of shocking fur. Her beaver seemed to scuffle up her leg, leap space and mouth-wump me. I gag-inhaled and jumped out of the way as she sped past, leaving an acrid smell of perfume and gas.

My father was waiting in the middle of the road when I approached home. He waved his arms for attention but I just sped past, in no mood to knuckle down. 'Dad! Watch this!' I called as I dropped Alvy at the top of the street. My father had his arms folded, in anger and impatience. He moved aside as I bore down. My unlimited engine climbed to wicked revs. Jet air crammed my ears; my gonads popped; I was going to execute a perfect, 360-degree skid-turn in front of my gaping dad. As I drew level, I jerked the wheel around and went into a perfect skid… Grace incarnate… until my wheels bit, whiplashed me around, and flipped me over. I landed upside-down with an unwholesome crunch. Gasoline dripped into my face; the wheel spun until the engine choked off. I viewed my father's worried face through a tangle of pipes as he tried to pull the kart off me.

'You all right, Sachie, you all right?'

'Yeah I'm fine.'

Alvy ran up, and my father turned to him in a rage. 'Leave my son alone you little fuck. I'm buggered if I'm letting you around here again. Now FUCK OFF!'

Had a surveillance team done a heat scan of 946 Bristol Avenue, they might have concluded that only the servants were home. The resident warm dots skirted around the main living spaces and went to their peripheral compartments. Living room, great room, dining room were seldom, if ever, visited, let alone tenanted. The grey drawing room with its taffeta drapes, pearlescent sofas and stiff cushions, was as forbidding as it was decoratively impeccable. I seldom went in there, just leaned in the doorway to observe its icy perfection – another Silver Room that ruled out my dirt.

If I had suffered the bad joke of my fate while living in the maid's room at Stone Canyon, Bristol Avenue now revealed the wholly rotten punchline: I was back at Chalette Drive, but with no Lloydcrest to run to. In fact, Chalette was better than this mausoleum. At least there we'd had parties – my mother's life-force filling the place with ebullience. Here, there were no late-night gatherings around the Steinway Grand, my father singing standards and dropping fabulous one-liners to an enthralled coterie.

I sat myself down at the immaculate, untouched Steinway and tapped out the melody from *Close Encounters*: five little notes that seemed to sum up my unanswered quest for a home. The reverb travelled out into the empty mansion and vanished. I closed the bright lid over the keys and went back up to my room. There I could let the universe expand. My astronomy book showed a diagram of concentric circles rippling out from the Big Bang. The echoes would go on for billions of years before dying out to nothing. That's where we were all headed. Dark Matter was driving everything further and further apart. I felt it in the house: a repellent force; a pressure between the seconds, between the atoms of the air that opened everything up to misconception and misalliance. I saw its slow-creeping blade move across the wall of my bedroom – a cold blue shadow sundering my room from the strings of day, from hope and all buoyancy.

I had to turn on the TV to regain my boyish sanguinity. The shadows hid behind me and became my eyes, two little tunnels of darkness to my brain. My hands held the remote – warm with electricity and the promise of escape. I could go anywhere with this thing. And I did, snapping its buttons in a searching frenzy. But its magic held the curse of unlimited possibilities. On this channel they are eating pancakes and syrup. On the next, they are watching their weight. Here they are driving fast along a mountain road; there they are going to hospital to 'lick the Big C'. All these signals were mixing me up, while the universe just kept expanding with more and more channels.

I mooched about the house. My father had bought me a powerful reflecting telescope and I would sit on my balcony late into the night and inspect the spherical tomb of the moon. The dereliction of the place captivated me. Asleep, I dreamt of a hike across those grey dunes in pressing deathly silence and buoyant zero-gravity as I approached a crater rim. Then a sudden miracle: the crater was a burgeoning green valley, full of plants and animals; I'd stumbled on a lunar paradise… then woke up.

Summer term was ending, the long holidays lay ahead. I should have felt expansive as I sat alone on the bleachers and watched the cheerleading squad drill for the forthcoming football season. They were all astoundingly bright and bouncy. As they spelled out B-R-E-N-T-W-O-O-D in breathless delight, they sent their shimmering pom-poms into outer space. Which was not far from how *I* was feeling... My head was hot, my stomach was roiling. By late afternoon, itchy red spots had appeared all over my body and I was sent home. Cathy took my temperature and glibly confirmed: 'Yep. Chickenpox, it's going around...' I stumbled woozily to my bed. By evening, the itching points had joined together and stampeded across my face in a multiplying spawn. *Mustn't scratch*, I told myself through gritted teeth, lying on my hands, my body aflame with tickles. *Think of the scars*, I told myself, as myriad little devils tenderized me with their pitchforks. Lotions gave some relief, but nights were warped and time-twisted with fever.

In the middle of my two-week malarial ordeal, I woke at 3 a.m. to the room pitching. I thought I had heard a faint noise at the far end of the house – a vague scuffling that seemed to travel through the walls and reach me telekinetically. *Must go and investigate*, I told myself, stumbling out of bed and reaching for my machete knife. As I swayed along the polished downstairs hallway, feet karate-keen, machete raised and flashing, I realized that the noise was coming from the kitchen. I saw myself springing inside, disembowelling the intruder with a banshee yell and wiping the bloodstained hot steel on my pyjama pants. Fixed and dilated, breathing heavy, I moved inside... Empty. But from the pantry came a sound like a huge rat foraging. *All right now... Strike ready...* I saw the blade coming down, saw red, saw blood... then saw my father looking bemusedly over his shoulder: 'What the *hell* are you doing?'

I looked at the blade poised above me and deflated.

'I heard sounds, I thought you must be an intruder.'

'Jesus Christ, Sachie, put that thing away.'

'Sorry Dad, I...'

'It's all right, you were dreaming; you're matted with sweat.' He kissed the top of my head and patted my bottom, 'Go back to bed.'

I walked dejectedly back down the hallway, trailing my blade behind me, mission unaccomplished – the bad-vibes house having wanted me to kill him.

The pox kept me home from school for two weeks, a hiatus that nicely coincided with the 1980 Winter Olympics, broadcast live from Lake Placid, New York. The American speed skater, Eric Heiden, was a national darling with a manner that was unassuming, for all his gold medals. I can say that I literally sweated out his progressions to each and every golden peak. By the final lap of his fifth medal win, I was bouncing on my bed as he carved and scissored his way to victory over the glass. When he passed the finish line and hoisted his arms, mine went up too. It was like he'd won for me. The stupid time trial of life. He'd proven something against my own lethargy and lameness. Could I, in my own way, slip on the golden body sock and do something winning, too?

I flipped the channel to the figure skaters and dreamt my way into the skin-tight clefts of their lycra costumes. I hated it when they fell; and the strained, mask-like smiles they wore when they got up and kept going. This was Show Business, too, but I felt their heavy shame. When they waited for the judges' numbers, buttressed by stern-faced coaches and doting mothers, I cringed behind my pillow.

I returned to school spotless and chickenpox-less, and was confronted by a mountain of homework to make up. I carried the books home with forklift arms and dumped them on my bed. It was way too much. I could never do it all. I could never make the grade and be an Eric Heiden, climbing the mountain to gold and freedom. I fell back on my bed, pounding the pillows in inanition and frustration. For one so well-schooled in accommodation and denial, this was a tipping point. The homework was only part of it. I was lonely as well as impossibly challenged. Who, in the enormous no-love house, could I turn to?

As if on cue, there was a knock on the door and in walked the giantess. Sue. Laughing her manly laugh. I froze in place.

'Hello, Kiddo,' she said, coming closer and ruffling my hair. 'What's up?'

I hadn't seen her in years. Without warning, some vengeful god had spliced her back into the movie of my life. Well, why not – the life was full of holes, into which people fell willy-nilly and from which they emerged without sense or explanation.

She sat down on my bed and babbled away. I learned to my astonishment that she and Cathy had been in continuous correspondence ever since Lloydcrest. My mother's firing Sue had succeeded in cementing her and Cathy's common grievance against Cruella. Sue said that Cathy had even lent her sums of money when she needed them. Now, after several jobs, she was back with us and ready to pitch in. It was clear that she had heard all about Tara's worsening rebellion and my questionable friends. Worst of all, it was clear that Cathy had called in Good Ole Sue to bring us into line.

I looked at her, my face dry-tracked with tears.

'What's wrong?' she finally said.

'Nothing...'

'Too much homework from the looks of it.'

'Yeah...'

'You'll manage. You always do.' She sat me up and massaged my shoulders. 'Wow, you're tighter than a spring.'

'I'm fine.'

'Sue knows when her boy's not happy. You *are* my boy, remember?'

I nodded vaguely.

She turned me around and stroked the hair from my face, fixing me with that look of hers. 'You need a change. And you're going to get it – you're going back to England to live.'

'With Mummy?'

'Not necessarily. You could go to boarding school…'

I shook my head. 'I don't want to go to boarding school.'

After she left the room, I put on my record of *London Calling* and let the spirit move me. I looked at the unliftable pile of textbooks strewn across the bed and entertained a revolutionary thought: *what if I didn't even need to open them?* I felt a blossoming sense of freedom and relief. I could call time on Bristol Avenue and the whole big mess of things in L.A. The mere mention of England had given me air to breathe and I realized I'd been suffocating all this time.

I picked up the phone and called my mother in London. She was quickly swept up in my desire to come home. Did I know what I was doing? She just wanted to make sure. Was boarding school really what I wanted? Yes, I said. Yes, yes.

Glossy brochures started arriving from Bedales, Stowe, Westminster and a host of other toplofty schools. By the time my father and Cathy realized that I wasn't just making a teenage scene, I had already decided on Oakham, a liberal co-ed school in the Midlands – it had the prettiest girls (I had mooned over enough photographs of them swatting hockey balls) and the boys were all on the short side, like me. I sensed I would belong.

As I look coolly back, it seems a mature decision for a fourteen-year-old to have made: asking – actually demanding – to be sent away to boarding school, a threat usually reserved by the parents of uncontrollable children. It was *I* who had decisively requested the punishment; because it was the least of three evils. The thought of living in London with my mother was impossible (I had been there, done that), I had been *here*, at Bristol Avenue, and done *that*. Now I wanted to go someplace new – *a place without parents*.

I never questioned Sue's motivation for putting the idea in my mind. I mean, was Cathy behind it? Was some hostility toward my father involved? Or was it Sue, the Sue of old, just trying to control me and manipulate my desires? She knew *she* couldn't have me again – my father had always found her unbearable and wouldn't allow her to settle back in. Her grasp on me was tenuous – though her hold was not – and was at the mercy of Cathy's good graces. If she had to lose me again, at least she would have been pivotal in the decision that lost me to all concerned – or rather, to all not so concerned. But perhaps it was spontaneous and generous on her part. Perhaps she sensed my deep need to stand up and become my own man.

Shortly before I left, Cathy announced that she was pregnant – with a boy. I took the news in my stride: at least I wasn't going to be there to suffer the competition. I went for a skate down Bristol Avenue and came off my board and landed heavily, breaking my wrist again. I packed for London with my arm in a sling. It was perfect: I was returning home wounded. Tara leaned in the doorway – her hair had been dyed back to its normal colour by a hairdresser hired by my father.

'You're so fucking lucky to be leaving this shithole.'

I just nodded, trying to fold a sweatshirt with my good arm.

'I'll do it…' She came over, folded it, and put it in my case. 'I'm going to miss you, Bro.'

'Me, too.'

We hugged and she jerked with sobs: 'What am I gonna do without you?'

'You'll be OK here.'

But I didn't believe it even as I said it. And in fact, it was only a matter of time before she abandoned Bristol herself and followed me to England, reversing the trend we'd set five years before, when I ran away after her.

I said goodbye to Cathy in the breakfast room. She dragged on her menthol and smugly remarked, 'You'll be back.' But I knew I wouldn't be, if it was the last thing I ever did.

My father drove me to the airport in silence. His mood was heavy in the car. The atmosphere was like the morning of the Harvard

Prep exam – except that now it was *he* who was facing the difficult questions, even if he had to ask them of himself. We waited for the 747 to refuel for its long polar flight and then I hugged him goodbye. Yes, I was leaving him behind. He had taught me next to nothing in the last couple of years and I felt no gratitude or allegiance toward him – only a great and helpless love.

I walked down the jet bridge to the plane, no longer the unaccompanied minor. I was being accompanied for the first time by a heady and forthright sense of self.

The doors closed, the metal bird taxied to the runway, and we flew away.

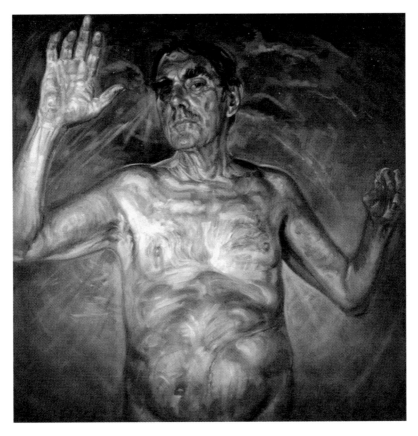

*Farewell to Prospero*

# ACKNOWLEDGEMENTS

To Steven Aronson, whose tough love and brilliance helped make a vineyard of my sometimes weedy and wild manuscript; to Jeffrey Archer and Jonathan Lloyd, who retrieved my prospects from an unholy publishing mess; to Basia Briggs, whose angelic assistance brought my work to the rare and wonderful attention of Naim Attallah; and to my editor, James Pulford, and all the other staff at Quartet Books – printers, proofers, typesetters – who helped bring my book to publication –

A sincere and heartfelt thank you.

And finally, my profoundest thanks to Sheela Raman; who, with unfailing love and guidance, has sought to accompany me to a better life.

# LIST OF ILLUSTRATIONS